Off the Record

A People's History
of
Keele

Author's collection

The Sneyd Arms

Compiled by

Angela Drakakis-Smith

CHURNET VALLEY BOOKS
01538 399033

© Angela Drakakis-Smith and Churnet Valley Books 1998
ISBN 1 897949 21 9

Dedication

I would like to dedicate this volume to my dear children, Chloe and Emmanuel, who spent their formative years at Keele and had such a happy time in the process.

Acknowledgements

I would like to thank the following people for their invaluable help in compiling this oral history of Keele:

For the friendliness, sometimes frankness, cups of tea and cake, and lots of fun, I would like to thank:
Doris Bates, William Bedson, Meg and Professor Broome, Mollie Casselton,
Professor Wolverson Cope, Mairwen Evans, Joe Glover,
Dorothy and John Hodgkinson, Rodney Hampson, Harold and Margaret Hayley,
Jason Hill, Freda Jones, Harry Jones, Horace Lafford, Margaret Millar, Bert Moss, Alfred Robbins,
Ethel Spragg, Jean Springall, Janet and Brian Stokes, Sir Bruce Williams
and all those who asked not to be identified.

I would also like to thank those who loaned photographs and other memorabilia, Dr Robin Studd for casting an eye over the rough draft, Dr Chris Harrison for checking the historical content of the introduction, Dr Brian Turton for giving it a thorough check and for encouraging me to publish it, Martin Phillips and Helen Burton for allowing me to dig and delve in the University Library's Special Collection and Karen Gunther who assisted with some of the early interviews.

My greatest regret is that there are those who contributed who did not live to see their stories in print.

I am grateful to the Stanley Beaver Memorial Trust for providing the capital for the illustrative material and to *The Sentinel* and *The Express and Star* (Wolverhampton) for permission to use their photographs.

CONTENTS

Part One: THE GOOD

Part Two: THE GREAT

Keele, the home at that time of William Sneyd Esq, as produced in Plot's *Natural History of Staffordshire 1686*

Keele University Library Archives

Keele Hall during its rebuilding in 1857

INTRODUCTION: KEELE PARISH - A PERSONAL VIEWPOINT

Keele owed its existence first to the Knights Templar, then to the Sneyd family who established a workers' commune there outside the restraining walls; and ultimately, when the estate was finally sold, to the University which usurped the role of powerful landlord. It is now, possibly, thanks to Keele University that the village of Keele retains its place 'on the map'.

Living on the campus and being a member of the Keele Parish Council, I was privileged to have a foot in both camps. It was whilst I was a member of the Parish Council that I became aware that the older Parish Councillors, who had long inhabited Keele, had histories and tales to tell which were important as well as interesting. It was to this end that the interviews were begun. Unfortunately some of the respondents died before their tapes and the project was completed. However, it is hoped that through the tapes and this volume, their memories will survive them.

The project fell naturally into two parts: the respondents who were deeply rooted in Keele, and those who had come later from close by who had developed an affinity with Keele. All had contributed in some way to Keele's development - both socially and economically. They are encountered in the first part - 'The Good'. The second part follows the histories of the respondents who became the tenants of the Keele estate, the university employees and their wives, who helped the university to flourish - 'The Great'.

The interviews were structured around certain themes; beginnings, the world of work, health care and diet, and other categories which emerge, depending on the contribution made by the individuals concerned. The information is arranged under such headings for easy cross/reference. The idea was not to collect facts so much as memories and impressions. As with any multi-sourced account, variation of detail occurs. It is hoped that the researched pieces interspersed with the 'dialogue' of those who were close to the epicentre of any event, will enable the readers to decide the 'truth' of the matter for themselves. The researched pieces have been taken from newspaper cuttings (national and local), log books, minute books, etc. I have also dipped into Chris Harrison's 'The History of Keele' and Sir J.Mountford who wrote on the early years of Keele University. It is hoped that this volume will add a little humanity to the above mentioned works! This is not 'high history.', but a record (not even complete) of the minutiae of the lives of people often forgotten, who assisted and enabled the great to forge the history which is all too often remembered.

Keele is a unique parish. It was regarded as 'a challenge' by the Knights Templars who first recognised its potential in the 12th century, and it remained such to its subsequent landlords, the Knights Hospitallers, the Sneyds and latterly, Keele University.

Robin Studd (1986:8-9) in The History of Keele claims that when the Knights Templars, a privileged order, first purchased land in the area, they needed a resident workforce 'to clear, colonize and work the lands' (ibid:10) because 'the Templar Brethren could not possibly do this work themselves'. Unfortunately, we are not told the reasons why. Incentives were therefore offered to attract settlers to this wind-swept promontory 600-650 feet above sea level. Feng Shui experts and local commonsense might have proclaimed the area to be too much out of kilter to be auspicious for a permanent hearth and home. But for those whose wealth outstripped their wisdom, it was regarded as an investment and clearly worth the risk. Given this somewhat infirm foundation, it was not surprising, that the Keele estate history has been one of boom and near bust.

The Knights Templars, the first landlords, to their credit and with the aid of a local labour force, 'made a success of the estate' to the extent that it was eventually removed from their portfolio of real estate and handed to the Knights Hospitallers in 1324 (ibid:12). In the hands of the Hospitallers it was regularly leased as a useful source of income (ibid:32) until 1540 when it was usurped by the Crown and auctioned off. It appears to have come into Sneyd hands in 1544 when it was purchased for the sum of £334 (ibid:32). Although the estate remained in the hands of the Sneyds for the longest period of its history (1544-1949), the Sneyds were taken to the edge of bankruptcy on several occasions during this period. One could comment that the newest owners - Keele University (1949 onwards) labour under similar financial burdens of low peaks and deep troughs.

Despite the fiscal uncertainties of the Keele estate at various points in its history, and the social and political upheavals which were taking place elsewhere in the country, the local labour force, resident within the parish, appear to have been kept fairly well insulated. Indeed, they had a home - albeit tied to the estate - and employment which put food on their table. Basic needs were being met so that rebellion, possibly, was not uppermost in their minds. The absence of any recorded insurgency tends to lead us to believe this. It might have been, however, that the mutterings of the dissatisfied were disregarded or they were simply sacked. Fear of removal could well have kept the more socially aware, silent. Thus Studd informs us that the Peasants Revolt of 1381 in England passed Keele by. Future historians searching local records could discover that the first 'local revolt' at Keele occurred in the mid 1980s when the then Lord of the Manor - Keele University - attempted to secure planning permission to convert the Villa, in the centre of the village, into a conference centre/hotel. Spearheaded by the Keele Parish Council, the planning application was taken to a public enquiry and the locals were defeated - not an unpredictable outcome. The conference hotel was duly completed and apart from traffic/parking complaints, the two now co-exist fairly peaceably.

The amicable relations engendered appear, then, to have been based on a symbiotic relationship between worker and landlord. The Sneyds created a village infrastructure of school, church, hostelry, workers' cottages and the workhouse. Land was leased to the more upwardly mobile farmers in the same way that largesse was bestowed on the barons to keep them sweet and on-side, no doubt. The school educated the local children to labour on the estate - on the land, in the Hall or down the mine. The church kept everyone in moral check and attendance was compulsory, with the vicar acting as the landlord's 'eyes and ears'. Local tradesmen were patronised and employment was generated beyond the parish. The workers reciprocated by being 'flexible'. When major reorganisations within the village took place in the mid 1800s, cottages were pulled down and rebuilt and the tenants were redistributed like pawns on a chess board. Phillips, in The History of Keele (1986:107-108) notes that when the major reconstruction of the village took place between 1846 and 1869, a reduction of 14 per cent of the buildings occurred and 'house total numbers decreased by 19 per cent from 1841-1871'. It is unclear whether this was an engineered down-sizing of the workforce or whether the work force had become depleted by natural causes. Unfortunately we are not told. The workhouse, already in existence by 1869, might have been the receiving establishment for those who had been made redundant and therefore homeless.

The Hall and grounds came in for regular reconstruction and refurbishment. As fashions changed so did the the outward appearance of the estate. Phillips claims that any 'random distribution of properties, function and social groups evident in the village in 1828-1830 had been subjected to careful reconstruction by 1869' (ibid:109), and much of this 'without consulting anyone except his agent and architect as to the best mode of doing it' (ibid:119). With the assistance of a good estate agent, the Sneyd plans for Estate and Village came to fruition, at a cost. Phillips believes that the village became 'firmly closed' (ibid:121) and 'totally under estate control by 1870'. With 'complete ownership' accomplished the Sneyds appeared to begin to lose interest.

In 1901 the Hall and grounds were rented to the Grand Duke Michael who, having had much experience in Russia, appeared to relish being 'Master' of an English village. It appears that he participated fully, in a regal way, in village rule. He utilised the entertainment value and employment potential of the school children. When VIPs visited, the villagers were invited onto the estate to perform for his guests. In return he gave garden parties and 'treats'. When the countess needed more hired help, the Master of the school was called upon to advise on the suitability of certain of his pupils. Nevertheless, he did as much as any paternal landlord would have done, if not more and it would appear that the parish 'enjoyed' the Russian largesse which was bestowed upon it. When, after ten years, the Duke and his family removed to London, every child was presented with a silver medal to remind them of his visit. After this interlude of activity within the Hall, the estate became closed once more to outsiders, and Keele became no doubt a quieter place.

The war years, 1939-1945, brought prisoners of war and the military to Keele. Much damage was done to the Hall and grounds in the name of the 'Commonweal'. This could have been the estate's lowest ebb. Some of the Aubusson tapestries in Keele Hall were smoke damaged in one of the many fires and whilst the fabric of the building might have undergone extensive renovation, the tapestries were destined never to be cleaned or restored to their former glory. The finely carved banisters on the stairs were said to have been 'recarved' and removed by those soldiers who wanted a souvenir of their stay at Keele Hall.

During this period the village was somewhat enlivened. A certain amount of social intercourse took place between the military and the parishioners. This came in the form of dances, the setting up of kitchens, and villagers' homes being shared with the families of some of those billetted at the Hall or in the village. Some prisoners of war worked on the local farms and there were, of course, the inevitable romances and marriages.

When the military marched away at the end of the war the future of the estate was far from promising. Whilst various uses were suggested from time to time, each one was rejected as being unsuitable. It is possible that the coming of the University College of North Staffordshire in 1949, was, in fact, a blessing in disguise. When the remainder of the estate was finally sold, parishioners were, at last, able to purchase their homes and maintain, for the first time, an independence from the Hall.

From this point it would appear that the 'estate' and the village began to move apart. The composition of the village began to change. The existence of the University College, later to become Keele University, had a similar effect as the Sneyds had had on the public perception of Keele, that the village was 'desirable'. University personnel and other professionals began to move in as local people moved away or died. House prices increased and the parish was left with a dilemma in that parishioners found it difficult to buy into their home patch. When the Keele by-pass was finally constructed in 1992, the Parish Council saw the possibilty of a low-cost housing scheme to reverse this trend.

Meanwhile once the University College gained possession of the estate, attempts were made to restore the Hall and grounds. The Hall was returned to a quasi-gentleman's residence in that the upper storey was converted into staff dormitory accommodation, the Salvin Room, Old Library, Great Hall and morning room were by turns used as lecture theatre, library and as part of the Senior Common Room. Ceilings, walls and floors in the Salvin room were returned, almost, to their former splendour. Only the tapestries appeared to be overlooked. The grounds, dotted with nissen huts, took a little longer to control. New building for departments and staff and student residences began almost immediately and the process continues in fits and starts. Initially there was a certain tension between those who saw their role as the new Estate stake-holders. They held to the view that the 'estateness' should be preserved at all costs. This was at variance with those who wanted the estate as a working campus. As market forces were introduced into the University sector, the latter course was eventually taken, although the campus appeared to retain (and still does) the elements of an estate.

Whilst the University came to take on the role, initially, of landlord, in that it provided employment for the locality and did succeed in keeping Keele 'on the map', it took a long while for local Councils, the University itself, and Keele parish, to realise how big a stimulus for the economy a university could be. In the meantime all three tended to remain aloof with collaboration taking place only when it was thought to be expedient. People from the campus did join in village events, such as the Parish Council and the WI, and villagers worked or took recreation on the campus in terms of walks in the grounds or attendance at public events such as lectures and concerts, etc.

As the campus was extended from 150 acres to 650 acres, another village within the parish slowly emerged amongst the nissen huts, which were duly converted into temporary student and staff accommodation, a chapel, a bank, the shop, student refectory, lecture hall and sports centre. Indeed some of the sturdier huts remain and the last of the plasterboard variety was only demolished in the mid 1980s as more permanent structures were built. Not all of the new buildings were considered to be aesthetically pleasing, however, and at one point the University was called to task for not having a coherent building plan. Currently, the campus is a mixture of 1960s concrete, utilitarian brick, new-age Tudor and Victorian ostentation, relieved by the odd architectural gem. There is much dispute as to which buildings fall into the latter category. Nikolaus Pevsner (1974:16), for example, claims the Students' Union as 'the best building so far', whilst the Chapel, designed by G G Pace, he describes as 'lumpish 'of sombre engineering bricks'. Poor Larchwood is given short shrift when he deems it 'rather comical, just semi-detached like on any council estate, arranged around three sides of an oblong lawn' (ibid:162). However, bricks and mortar alone do not always a successful building make, and whilst Larchwood was indeed reminiscent of a social housing estate, in human and social terms it was an ideal community setting for families and the rearing of chidren - elements which the architects and the University, who financed the construction, might not have held as major considerations at the time.

Both Village and University continue to develop under the watchful eye of the local Councils. The University continues to make inroads into the Village - the current development is a series of maisonettes adjacent to the Sneyd Arms, along Quarry Bank Road - and to develop its land on campus into something more financially tangible than pasture or woodland. As the University grows, the village school now educates only a small proportion of village children. Parishioners are growing old. A curious osmosis is taking place, which should not only intrigue, but also keep anthropologists, sociologists and historians interested for decades to come.

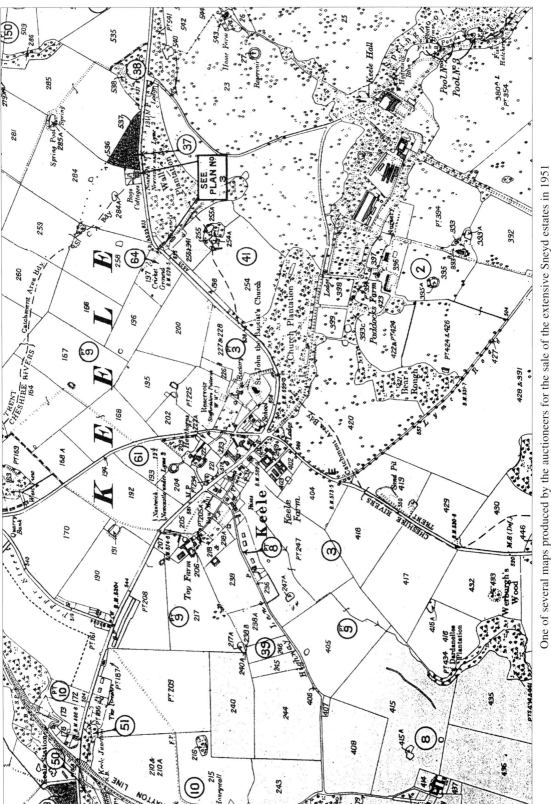

One of several maps produced by the auctioneers for the sale of the extensive Sneyd estates in 1951

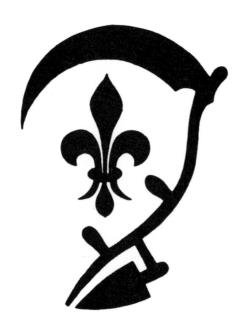

**The Coat of Arms
of the Sneyds of Keele**

Part One: THE GOOD

CHAPTER ONE
WORKING THE LAND

BEGINNINGS

I was ten when I came to Keele and 14 when I started work. Before that I used to go hand milking for Mr Raif Bloor of a morning. When I left school on Thursday, April Fool's Day, lunchtime, I went up with my mate Askey. I didn't get any work for the first week. On the following Saturday I was Cowman, £2. The farmer came to me and says, 'Pigman, Shepherd, 2/6d! Bloody dear as salt on me taters!' I've always been proud to say that I've done a job whether it be ploughing, mowing, reaping, ridging, sowing, stacking, thatching, draining, digging. I did it!

My father came from Madeley for work. He was living in a rented cottage in Madeley and there come a job, at Top Farm for a cowman, with a tied cottage. He was the highest paid man in Keele - £2 for 72 hours a week. When we come, everybody in a tied cottage had to do as they were told or you were out. Then, there was two-and-a-half to three million unemployed. There was no dole and everyone was after jobs.

We had no bathroom or bath, so we bathed in the horse trough - get a pair of trousers, cut off here and get in the horse trough. For a shower we'd get under the downspout when there was a thunderstorm on - soft water, hard carbolic soap and have a good wash. I've been in the yard and my mother's had the scrubbing brush on me.

We had nothing; neither food or money. The wages were terrible. My father for a head cowman had £2 a week. What was that to keep eight of you? There was £2 harvest money, £1 for the hay, £1 for the corn harvest. And they made sure you did some hours! Single men got nothing. The clothes you went out in were the same clothes you went to work in. With hand milking you got more muck and milk on your trousers, no rain 'ld ever get in. I had a pair of gloves, a pair of shorts and a jersey. Nothing else. Couldn't afford nothing else. I never knew what it was to have a Christmas Box. I used to have a orange and apple and nowt else.

We'd got a table, rocking chair, armchair and two little chairs. We regularly had our meals with the King and Queen because we had newspaper on the table. The jam never went off, the bread never went off - it was always upside down on the table. The margarine was in the paper and the sugar would come straight from the packet. They never come off the table. When the newspaper was all mucked up they'd light the fire with the 'tablecloth'.

To eat, in the daytime, you'd have a round of bread and jam for your breakfast. At dinner time you'd have mashed potatoes and bread and at night you'd have boiled cabbage, a round of bread, or anything you could catch hold of. On a Sunday morning you'd have one egg between three and a round of bread apiece. And we had rice pudding on a Sunday. For tea on a Sunday you'd have jelly, bread and butter and a piece of cake on a Sunday night.

When I was going to school on a Saturday morning, I used to have pram wheels with a board on and I used to go from Keele to Madeley Heath to fetch a hundredweight of coal for anyone as wanted it and push it back to Keele for a shilling - 11d a hundredweight and I had the penny. Some did two journeys in a morning. Then, tuppence 'ld buy you 20 Woodbines. I never smoked. I gave the tuppence to my mother and dad because we'd got nowt to live on. I used to go out milking night and morning when I was still at school.

THE WORLD OF WORK

I was taught all jobs on the farm; how to truss hay, how to strip and stack, turn it up and tie it up

Courtesy H. Lafford

Using the thrashing machine

Courtesy H. Lafford

Making hay

Courtesy H. Lafford

Downes farm

Courtesy H. Lafford

Working the land

and take it to Hanley. It was all loose you see. You used to have your hay knife and cut it off at certain lengths, truss it with two strings and load it on the wagon and take it to Hanley.

You were expected to cut an acre of corn with a scythe. It would take you a day and you'd be paid by the acre. They used to have £2 in summer for harvest - harvest money for hay and corn. That was overtime. One year they worked it out and it came to a farthing an hour. If you wanted extra money you had to go on piece work; halfpenny for a score of turnips, turnip pulling; potato lifting, a shilling a rue - fifty yards up a drill, pick 'em, sort 'em, bring 'em home and hog 'em in clamps ready for sorting. You had to do it all for this one price. Hedgecutting was threepence a chain - that's 22 yards - cut it all, rake it up and burn it. You weren't allowed to take a stick out of the hedge for your fire. Men had the sack for taking dead hawthorn out of the hedge.

For sheep shearing it was 5d a sheep - tuppence halfpenny for the man that was turning out and tuppence halfpenny for you. You had to wrap up the wool and load it. I used to go sheep shearing at night. The turn out was the machinery on your shoulder, the head, the oil and the blades. We'd walk a mile, shear sheep until 10.00 pm, cart everything back and start work next morning. You had to get the sheep in, sheer 'em, grab your wool and put it in a bag ready for off. I could do about 12 in an hour depending on how dirty they were.

When you lived in you had a good meal - breakfast, dinner and tea, but no money. The single lads got nothing for harvesting except food. Them as was living out got their tea. Those from Betley used to ride to Keele for work. They got to be there by 5.00 am. We ate our tea in the farmhouse - a great big wooden table in the kitchen. If you worked in the fields with the horses you had on board what they called a 'ploughman's lunch' - two rounds of dried bread, a nuggin of cheese and a bottle of cold tea with no sugar or milk. I used to have buttermilk. You got one pint of milk a day. If you got your meal in a tin you were all right, if not the mice would have had it! Then you used to go home about half an hour before milking for dinner. We had meat, taters - everything grown at Top Farm. They'd have these big shooting parties up on Keele estate. We used to do the washing up so we'd get the scrag ends of the party - chicken, turkey, trifle - there was no extra pay.

We worked 365 days of the year, from 5.00 am to 6.00 pm. On Sundays we finished at 11.00 am to go to church and started again at 3.00 pm and finished at 6.30 pm. On Good Friday we finished at 11.00 am until 3.00 pm so that a married man could take a load of muck home to start his garden. On Boxing Day we had between 11.00 am and 3.00 pm off, so we'd take the ferrets and go shooting. Christmas Day was the same as Sunday. I never had a day off until the end of the War. You had to be there. When it come 1954 they gave us a penny an hour rise and a week's holiday. All the farmers said they was going to go bankrupt, but they're still farming today. Eventually we started at 7.00 am and worked until 5.30 pm.

If you got hurt you never got any money and you had to pay the doctor if he came out to you, so you didna go. I used to break colts in. I had all my fingers broken with horses.

There was no machinery when I started work. Odd farmers had tractors. Then in 1940 the Fordsons came in - the classic. I used to go to strike 'em up. Break your flippin' arm! There was a mowing machine pulled by horses and in the summer the wagon used to turn out at three o'clock in the morning. We used to have some good hot summers so we'd turn out at 3 o'clock, before the sun got up, to do this mowing. We'd go home for breakfast ready for turning by hand and badging all the edges of the field - cutting by hand all the bits that were left. There was no leaving these bits. We used to make hay with them. When we was harvesting there was no hay left on the field at all. There had to be none left on the edges. I don't know how much it was for an acre of grass. They used to strike off with a hand rake and turn the field - ten acres - one behind the other and they used to walk at speed. They'd give it a flick and the hay would turn over. They would do so much then go back. After it was turned we'd rake it into rows and rook it. Some called them rooks, some called them quarts, we called it quailing. Then the wagon would be loaded. They would take two loads to the stackyard. There'd be two stacking and a man unloading in the stackyard all day. It was a terrible job. Eight of us was employed when I started. There was 220 acres and 15 shire horses.

We used to go ploughing with three horses. The loose horse had to be away from the traffic. There were three horses abreast. You got the reins on the two outside horses and the other was fastened to them. With a pair of horses we'd plough an acre a day. In a straight line it would be about 14 mile. It was freezing!

'Now then,' says the farmer, 'I'll show thee how it's done. Six furrows one side, straddle the middle and six on the outside. You put your hand in the bucket and you come from the back straight forward and your hand goes across in front of you. 'Ave you got it?' The fertiliser went out like a fan. You had to sow it correctly, no zebra grass - that's where you have dark and light marks where you've put fertiliser down. I used to have 6d an acre for sowing fertiliser on corn. It was always in July, after a thunderstorm. I could rattle up a twelve acre in a day - sulphur, sulphur phosphates and potash. We had to mix it. There was one that everybody used to love when it was snowing - half ton to the acre, Bassetts Slag. It was black stuff, iron filings. It took a month to get it off you. You can't get it today. We used to sow it when there was snow on the ground because when the snow thawed it took it into the ground slowly. It didna go straight in. We got it from Shelton Bar in a one and a quarter hundredweight bag. We'd get covered in it. We'd go home and get a dry bag and rub ourselves with that. You couldn't wet it or you'd never get it off. You'd rub off as much as you could then wash yourself. It was a dirty job. It wasn't classed as dangerous in those days. It was bad for your lungs.

Gas lime came from the gas works and it was the best. We'd pick up a pound piece and leave it on the ground for about a fortnight and let it slack down. We'd chuck it all over the fields to sweeten the ground. We shovelled it on. We used a lot of Bassett Slag, gas lime and horse manure. The gas lime used to swell up. You'd get three or four bucket fulls from that one lump. It'd burn all the skin off you. I used to go around and burn the cattle when there was foot and mouth. We put it in the pits. You wouldn't have no moss on your lawn if you used gas lime. In the Spring, in the corn fields, they'd put the sheep in to bite it all off, then we'd shift the sheep off and go and 'arrow it. Any showing we'd have to 'arrow it again. It used to come up again three times thicker and stronger. Today it's just sown and the gate shut on it.

I was the first to crop spray fields. You weren't allowed to let anything go down the grid in them days. We rinsed our containers and tipped them up, downside of those trees where the roots are. This was how that tree came to blow down at the end of Highway Lane. It was dead.

You weren't allowed to cut the hedges in July because of the birds. We started in the first week of August - Stoke Wakes Monday, always. We did all the footpaths. We got paid 3d a chain for hedge cutting (22 yards). You had to have a tape measure as some chains had big links in 'em. From Keele Station to the Hawthorns was 25 shillings - cut both sides, top and bottom, rake up all your stuff and burn it. Pepper Street, Highway Lane and Quarry Bank were all 25 shillings, both sides and do the footpaths. It was all done by hand. Every year we used to clean off the beech hedge that's on the footpath now. The gardeners started dumping rubbish on it so we stopped. The footpath was just clay and sharp stones cut like a curb. You can still make it out today. You didn't leave no 'sparrow perches'(twigs sticking up). They wouldn't pay you for that.

You had to have a scythe. Come a day it was raining, the farmer would say, 'It's too wet t'go outside. Put a bag or two on and go thistle mowing in the Gnarley'. You didn't have a coat, couldn't afford one, so we took some sacks, made one like an apron around you, then another around the shoulders with a tie in and then we'd knot the corners in the other one and put it on top of our heads like a helmet. Off I'd go thistle mowing in the field, thundering and lightening, with a scythe!

The thrashing machine used to come on the farm - a steam engine pulling this here traction machine box. They used to set it down level for thrashing, turn the lynching around, put the belt on. They could set it to a fraction. There was always a twist in the belt. They'd just touch the lever and it'd be off. Your fingers could be gone like that! The bales were all about one-and-a-half hundredweight, and up in the loft you'd have to carry 'em. One man did nothing only coal stoking, another did the water to drive the machine. There was one bond cutting (cutting the strings) and one behind the box that made the batting (two strings around the straw). We chucked the bails on the wagon. There was a chap stacking the straw. There was two on the stack chucking into the box, another bagged the chaff - no waste, not even a bag of chaff. We'd be singing away. Then, they'd drop a shovel of coal in and Whoom! You were choked. We'd swig a drink down but we never stopped. How we never got ruptured I don't know; we used to get up off the floor with one-and-a-half hundredweight on our backs. I was only eight stone then and I used to carry above twice my own weight up the loft.

When you went hay harvesting you worked until eight or nine at night. We used to say, 'Dew's rising'. How could we tell? The pitch fork as you used, used to strike as your hands came down it and made a whistling sound. It was the dew on it. Anyone walking on the road as heard it could tell it would be a fine day t'morra.

One Friday night the farmer came and said, 'Load the wagon, it's gunna rain t'morra'. There wasn't a sign of anything. We were at it from five in the morning until half past nine at night, working by hand. At half past nine we had to go and milk us cows. On Saturday morning there we were asleep on the chair, too tired to go to bed. We had the eight acre, the five acre and part of the six acre still to get in. We didn't stop. We had us dinner in the fields. We tied the horses up to the hedge and threw them some hay to eat. It was past one o'clock. Next thing, Alf says, 'There'll be no dinner t'morra'. He's looking at his watch. It's eight past seven! The horses were being eaten with horse flies. On Sunday Alf went to church, he was church warden and very religious. We was too tired, we didna go. At three o'clock in the afternoon, there was lightening and it blasted well teemed down. The thunder was follering the lightening. Five cows was killed in the field. 'That's because you weren't at church', Alf says. He was playing hell. You didn't get any insurance in them days.

They showed me how to build a corn stack. Start off, no heads of corn on the floor - not a grain had to be lost on the floor, you'd get the sack. You'd start with two bundles in an upside down 'v' shape, the heads were on the top so the butt ends were on the outside of the stack. That way the water'd never go in. You went round and round this shape with more bundles. Each bundle was tied with a string. The new row came with the butt ends fitted onto the string of the bundle underneath. You went up and up, round and round 'til you got to the eaves. The eaves were eased out to about six inches so the rain could drain off. If the eaves were too short we'd say, 'Eaves na tight, isna right', and you'd push it out just a bit and go on until you'd got about a foot across the top. Then you'd put two heads of corn on the top and there wasna a head showing, only them two. You'd put a boss head on the top (a row of old straw right along the top and them were fastened in by a peg in the stack on each side, so as the water didna pull the pegs. The stack was now the same shape as a house. It was about eight by six yards. Then you had to thatch it. You were shown only once how to thatch. Seven strings they used and they all had to be put in. The canes went up bank so that the water didna follar it. We used a stacker's knot and you run it round and round and shove the peg in all the way. One person did a stack - shift your own ladders, make your own straw, all your own pegs, carry your own stuff up on the stack. Your knees ached, your legs ached, your belly ached! You had to keep going.

When you were getting the fruit in - damsons, plums, apples - you had to sing, whistle or talk then he (the boss) knew you weren't' eating 'em. That was the rule. He'd have every damson off the tree! One year there was a tremendous lot of damsons, they were making wine of 'em. Mrs wanted some sloes for sloe gin. It was frosty and I was sent. There was a row of trees back there. My hands were chapped and frozen stiff. I come home. 'Ay lad, there's nay need to worry about that', she says, 'shove 'em in a bucket of cow's water!'

We did all the shows - Keele, Betley, Whitmore, Longton. I went hedge laying and GD did ploughing. We took our own tractor. In hedge laying we had eleven yards to do - clean it out, fork out all the rubbish, layer it, stake it, level it and ditch it - all in four-and-a-half hours. Before you could start you cut all the rubbish out. You then cut them (the branches) at the bottom. It depended what the Judge said when you were laying, whether it was 'on' or 'off'. 'On' laying was very difficult; 'off' laying wasn't because you laid your thorns off your cuts. 'On' laying you went straight along the hedge on top of it and you had a job getting your stakes in because the thorns were in the wrong place. The lower down you cut it, and you cut 'em off straight, the better. All the underwood is cut off. That dries. Anything as grows you keep the head up or it dies. One side is left rough, the other is smooth, and you cut it and layer it down. Every year I always won the best growth - £4. You weren't allowed a measure or a saw. You didn't cut the side, you know, as the thorns grow out of the side - you left them on one side and the other had to be left smooth. The Judge would say three foot four inches or three foot five inches. You were disqualified if you used a measure or a saw. You used your stomach to measure.

I've still got my tools. I could go through a two inch branch with one cut. Anyone working hedges or trees hones his axe with a stone. You whet your scythe for a rough for cutting grass. To sharpen an axe you go round one side. One side is roughed up and the other is smooth. My speciality was hawthorn hedges, but I did them all.

A pitch fork is the worst thing for sore hands - hand rakes and scythes too. Before we started a season we got linseed oil and we soaked the handles from top to bottom. When they dried out we'd work 'em all day and never get sore hands. I didna wear gloves. If it was snowing we'd rub snow into our hands. You never got cold hands all day.

The smog used to come across, it was flippin' wicked. We'd be in the Quarry Bank field feeding the sheep. I was the shepherd at 2/6d a week. There were 200 sheep here, 200 on the aerodrome and 300 at a place near Uttoxeter. The farmer used to take me three times a week in his car. 'E always found that something had been killed by aircraft. There was about 15 horses, 80-90 pigs and 5 breeding sows. There was a hell of a lot of poultry as well. They shifted me off sheep to horses.

I looked after the hens too. One day the farmer came and wanted hens picking out. They took 'em out and there they were, he and his son, breaking their necks. The others they took home and they won the gold cup from Harper Adams College.

Cows had salt and Epsom salts in their corn to keep them fit. You had to mix their corn exactly - a tremendous amount of cod liver oil, salt and Epsom salts. You did everything by hand. The cows were fed cornflakes, rolled oats, bran sharps and flour, turnips and ox cabbage. We used to eat a hell of a lot of ox cabbage in the winter with a round of bread. That's what you could grab.

Monday was auction day and Saturday was market day for eggs, chickens and milk. They couldn't sell potatoes at one shilling a hundredweight. A rabbit was a shilling and eggs were two for one penny. Couldn't sell 'em, nobody'd got the money to buy. You couldn't sell the milk neither.

We used to poach from one end t'other. The only thing we had in us life before the War was to catch a rabbit or pheasant for us dinner. When we went pheasant catching we listened to where they had gone up a tree. We'd get a rabbit hang - a long stick with a wire noose on the end - stand under the tree. He'd be watching us, shove 'is neck out and with the rabbit hang, bong! break his neck, bring him down, put 'im in your pocket and bring 'im home. Rabbit hangs aren't allowed today.

I used to walk down the road and this farmer had a lot of turkeys. I found this turkey laying away. I watched it sneak down the hedge. They can go miles. I wouldn't disturb her but I'd watch her and then go down. I'd leave one egg behind and bring home what was spare.

I used to have two ferrets. On a Sunday, night time, we'd go up to Keele with our purse nets. We used to scan all the way around a day or two before to find where there was a bolt hole. You went there, put your purse net over it, pegged it. The purse net was a net with string around it. When the rabbit went in it pulled the string tight. We'd go around quietly and put a net over every hole you could find then turn the ferret loose in. The ferret had a collar on and you'd let him out on a yard knot. We'd sit and wait. You could hear them. Then we'd pull the ferret out and the rabbit.

If there was a lot of rabbits we'd take their insides out to lighten the load. Six a piece was as much as you could carry riding a bike. We'd give 'em away, we didn't want 'em all. We'd got no deep freeze so we'd give 'em to the old folk in the village. We'd hang it on the door knock.

All the farm workers ran the gauntlet against the gamekeepers at Keele. There were big poachers around. There were aviaries where the tennis courts are now at Gateside Corner. There the wall is quite low. I'd be up on the horses working and the poachers would come. We used to have signals to let them know where the gamekeepers were.

We always carried catapults. If we saw anything, bang! Around here there was thousands of rabbits, until myxomatosis came. Then the War came and the game keepers finished, and the army finished off the lot.

The last time I went poaching was towards the end of the War. We left our bikes and got over the wall. The sirens went. The aeroplanes were sounding and this flare dropped. You could see for miles. We jumped back over the wall, I don't remember how. There was a whistle and then a big bang. A bomb dropped on 'Castle Thistleberry.

If the farmer caught you taking a turnip home he'd sack you. The kids, when you were coming home with a load of turnips would shove a brick under the wheel and some would fall off. We'd be coming down, two horses chained, one in the shaft, singing away, mucked up to the ear holes, more sludge than there was on the fields splashed all over, then bump! off 'ld come a turnip. Take no notice, keep going.

ON THE BRIGHT SIDE

Come Christmas we were plucking and dressing turkeys. The turkey lice were the worst. It was one penny to pluck a chicken, tuppence for a turkey and threepence for a goose. Geese are very bad to pluck. The farmer was killing 'em, we was plucking and the farmer's wife was dressing 'em. When we finished we'd fall into the feathers fast asleep. We'd be there next morning.

They took the birds to auction in a pony and trap a day or so before Christmas. About two days before they'd take the live poultry down, then the dressed poultry. If the farmer didn't go to the town to sell them, he'd got no money, and we didna get paid.

As a farmer he was the best there was. He was little and bow-legged. In the summer he'd have his trousers rolled up to his knees and a handkerchief with a knot in each corner tied on the top of his head. We played tricks on him. One day he came up to the field playing hell. We hadna done enough work. He'd just had a new Alvis car. He got out and went stalking across the field. I got a turnip and rammed it up the exhaust pipe. When he come back the car wouldna start, so he had to go and send for someone. When he was away I pulled the turnip out. When he come back and got in the car, it struck up ready to go.

THE WAR YEARS

I remember one Saturday morning, my dad was sowing wheat on the five acre by Heath Wood. The farmer says, 'Take this colt and I'll come up and help you break him in'. He'd never had a collar on his head before. Just as we were ready, Highland Laddie struck up at Keele - bagpipes, drums. The colt fought and kicked and jumped. I said, 'I'm off 'ome, I'll do it tomorra!'

An air raid shelter was put in by Drive Lodge. Bombs dropped on Chesterton. A plane crashed on Locker's farm and another on Woore cricket ground.

There were thousands of troops at Keele of every nationality. They took the Toll Gate down in Keele. When they left they went three abreast from nine in the morning until 4.30 in the afternoon, to Silverdale Station. There was at least seven bands.

THE WAY WE WERE

When we came here there was a big timber yard at the end of Highway Lane. It was all part of Keele estate. There was a big drying shed where they used to cut up the trees and saw the planks into different sizes. Across the road was the wheelwright's shop - George Oakley. He was magnificent at making wheels and carts. He used to make them for the estate and mend the carts for the farmers. He had a job to walk. Then there was a smithy - Jim Cheadle and Alf Podmore. This would be about 1927. There were no houses across the road from the smithy. That was the nursery where they grew all the trees for the estate from saplings. There were no houses by the Workhouse either.

RECREATION

When the Sneyds went to church they went from the drive, across the green along that path over the green to the main road. Sneyd Walk it was called.

On a Sunday after work we'd come down to play football on the field in front of the houses on Station Road. With one football they used to come from Onnerley, Madeley, Leycett, Scot Hay, Silverdale and Newcastle. At a quarter to ten at night you wouldn't see a soul because we all had to be in bed by ten o'clock. If you weren't in the farmhouse by ten you were locked out. That was the rule. And if you weren't on the farm at five in the morning to start on the milking, you could go back because they wouldna pay you.

We used to be darts players and we had a good team. We had to be at the pub at seven, but we didn't finish work until six so we had to run. The landlord put a do on for us at Christmas, bread, black pudding and salt. The pub at Silverdale said he'd give us a pint each to play and a pint if we won. The Landlord at Madeley promised us two pints and two parties if we played for him.

Then I went dancing.

Keele village c1903, the Sneyd Arms on the right

J. HULSE.　　　　Jos. BOOTE　　　　H. SHAW　　　　D. KENT

Wm. BOOTE.　J. WEBB　　G. POOMORE.

JAMES

CHAPTER TWO
ON THE ESTATE

BEGINNINGS

My parents came to Keele in 1899. I was born in 1909 in a semi-detached cottage in Station Road. It had two bedrooms and two rooms downstairs, a scullery and a pantry. We had an outside lavatory and one tap for running water. There was one coal fire. Gas came later in about 1930. It was here much earlier but the mains stopped at the Hawthorns. Mr Sneyd brought gas here when he rebuilt Keele Hall. There were two gas engines and a gas lamp by the workshops in the village, which were opposite the old post office, by Rosemead cottage. We rented this house from the Sneyds at £6 a year - 13/5d a quarter, including rates. Although my father worked on the railway, my great grandfather, on my mother's side, worked as a joiner on the Estate. My great grandfather lived at Whitmore and worked for the Sneyds, who owned a lot of land at Acton. He came to Keele for the last ten years of his life and lived at Keele (entrance) Lodge. The rent was one shilling per annum. He was responsible for opening and closing the gates at the entrance.

Our house was lit with paraffin lamps. Coal was brought around once a week or fortnight, by a horse and cart, from the local collieries and you had as many bags as you liked. A bag would cost 10d or a shilling a hundredweight. Paraffin was brought by a truck with a tank on the back. We had a range for heating and cooking. We boiled water on the fire and we cooked on the fire in an oven on the side. When gas came we had a gas stove. There was a washing boiler. On Saturday mornings we bathed in a tin bath in the scullery. Electricity came in the 1950s.

My father worked on the railway from seven in the morning until five at night. He was responsible for different lengths of the railway line - from Silverdale Station to nearly Madeley Road Station (on the Market Drayton line) and especially for another piece on the Audley line. His job was keeping the metal in good order, fencing, tunnels, etc. He had four or five men working under him. He had half an hour for dinner and he worked until mid-day on Saturdays. The pay was 30 shillings a week which was a good wage at that time.

My parents lived in Station Road when they got married. Before that I lived in Middle Lodge (Drive Lodge) on the estate drive when I got married in 1939. The estate men went to work on the cottage before we moved in, so we had a bathroom, water and a lavatory put in. They did the place up inside out and from top to bottom. It was an estate cottage and was later sold to the University. The University wanted me out of the Lodge up the drive and as the house in Keele Village became vacant on the death of Mrs Adey I moved there.

People drank tea morning, noon and night. We had Bournville cocoa - but not very often. We had coffee on Sunday mornings which we made in a jug. We had three meals a day plus supper - breakfast at quarter past eight, lunch between twelve and one, and tea between five and seven o'clock. We had porridge for breakfast and bread and milk. There was none of these flakes. The bread and milk was put in a basin. The milk was hot and poured over the bread. For dinner we'd have beef or mutton, potatoes, cabbage, plus a pudding, that sort of thing. For tea we'd have bread, butter, tea and cake. Supper was sandwiches or biscuits and a cuppa. The main meal was at lunchtime. We'd also have meat and sausages cooked in front of the fire. The butcher, Mr Saunders from Silverdale, came on a Friday with the meat. In the week my mother would buy sausages or liver. We grew potatoes in the garden and a lot of our own vegetables. My father kept a lot of fowl so we had plenty of eggs. My mother baked cakes.

We went to bed pretty early in those days. We were in bed by ten.

I went to school in the afternoons before I was five, just to get used to it. I wasn't too keen on going. I remember Mrs Clayton. She took the 5 to 6 year olds. We started at nine in the morning and went on until twelve, then home for dinner, then from one o'clock until three. The older ones stayed until half past three. I went home for lunch; we had an hour. There were two playtimes in the day. We had drill and sometimes a nature walk down Two-Mile Lane, off the Whitmore Road and Highway Lane. We had exercise books but the little ones had slates. We learned our alphabet and figures. There was a thing you slid beads along to count. The Rector used to come to the school quite often - he'd give a talk on some religious matter. We were taught the Catechism. The Headmaster, Mr Ashton, followed by Mrs Cooke, would come up behind you and rap your shoulders with his cane - no hesitation - if you did your sums wrong. We expected it in those days.

Had I stayed in Keele School, I would have left at 13. I sat an entrance exam for the Orme Boys' School, at Newcastle, but my parents paid. It was unusual to go to secondary school if you were a working man's son. I went to the Orme by train at first, then I biked it. School didn't finish until 4.30 pm so I didn't get home until five. It cost three guineas a term and you had to pay for your own books, of course. If you passed the entrance exam, you went free of charge.

I was a choir boy and a bell-ringer at St John's Church. I was confirmed there. I started in the choir when I was nine or ten. Arthur Green was the choir master and organist and he worked for Silverdale Co-op Society. The charge for the bells was two or three pounds split between the six of us. We had choir outings to Rhyl on the train. We sang on Sunday mornings and evenings. I started bell-ringing when I was 17 or 18.

I remember Keele church when you couldn't get in - Harvest Festival evening - so many people, they'd have to turn them away! There were forms and chairs down the aisles. It was full during the week too. You had to keep showing up or the vicar would be after you. Perhaps he'd have a word with the Agent on Keele Estate. In his younger days that vicar was good. They'd come from Madeley and Silverdale. The service would go on for about an hour and a quarter. On the Thursday before Harvest the Estate men would knock off about three in the afternoon to get ready for the service in the evening. The sheaves of corn etc, used to be tied to the pillars. People would give flowers and fruit. It was all given away at the end. We didn't have a harvest supper in those days.

It was implied that you would go to church if you were employed on the estate. This eased off after the Second World War, but most went. There was a chapel once in Keele, in Pepper Street. It was turned into two houses. I remember my mother saying that nobody went much because at that time Sneyd had built his new church at Keele. If you went to chapel it meant that you didn't support him. The church was opened in about 1871. Being Sneyd tenants, they went.

THE WORLD OF WORK

My sisters were working on the domestic side. They got jobs by word of mouth. They used to come home one half day a week and they had a half day every Sunday. They had to be back by ten at night.

When I first left school, I applied for a job on the railway but I didn't get it. There weren't many jobs about - I applied for about two or three. There came a vacancy in the Estate Office at Keele, so I applied. My sister knew the Agent, Mr Scott, so she had a word with him. I went to the office for a bit of a test and I got the job. At first I worked at the Hawthorns which was the Estate Agent's office and house. The hours were nine to five weekdays and half day on Saturdays.

The Agent was concerned with about 3-4000 acres. There was Keele, Silverdale, Knutton, Red Street, Chesterton, Peacock's Hey, Talke, Bradwell, all that area, and on the other side of the

Potteries there was Sneyd Green, Birches Head, Milton, Abbey Hulton - there was a few thousand acres there. At one time there were 15,000 acres. There was the Norton Bridge Estate - 2-4000 acres, and Mow Cop estate. The Sneyds owned land around Whitmore and Acton and the Mainwarings owned land at Keele so they did a swap and to square the deal Mr Sneyd paid the Mainwarings the sum of £700. A lot was sold in bits and pieces for building. There was all this land around Cheshire, the Nantwich area, too. That was sold in about the 1870s. Just after the War a lot more was sold.

When I worked at the Estate Office I did book-keeping, collecting rents, shopping in Newcastle. One job I had to do was to go to the school house and there on the steps would be a can of milk. That I had to take to Arthur Goodwin. I used to do the Sneyd books and people would come to pay their rent. The companies were in private hands but on Sneyd land. I was the office junior. I was paid ten shillings a week (1924/5). That was quite a reasonable wage for a boy starting in an office. As I went on, my duties were increased. There were no (pay) scales or anything like that.

In 1921/2 the Keele Hall gardens went commercial. We started advertising and we had a stall at the market in Newcastle selling produce. Market day was three days a week in Newcastle, in Tunstall and Market Drayton. A lot of stuff used to go off by rail or post. We advertised in the horticultural papers.

In 1931 when Mr Scott left we moved up to the Estate Office in Clock House. There were some perks for some working on the Estate. It was a 52 week a year job. There was a pension scheme - five bob a week then. If workers were ill, sometimes their wages were paid by the estate or they had sickness benefit from the Friendly Societies. Most of the workers lived in Keele although some came from Silverdale and Newcastle.

After Keele Estate was sold up I was offered a job by the Estate mining consultant in Newcastle, Mr Bates. When Mr Bates and his practice was sold I was offered a job by Knight and Sons, Solicitor's of Newcastle. I stayed there until I retired.

It was difficult after the War to rent houses. The farm labourers' cottages were tied - some of the young chaps were fed and housed by the farmer. If a chap had £100 saved up in those days and the girl £50 they were doing pretty well. Farm workers earned about 30 shillings or £2 per week. Girls in service got ten or twelve shillings a week and they worked all the hours God sent. I think they had one evening and a half-day per week.

CHANGES

Colonel Sneyd died in 1949 and his nephew (and heir) in 1950. The Estate was sold off to pay death duties which were about £600,000. Ralph Sneyd was married three times. He was a bit of a gay blade. He enjoyed fishing, shooting and wine, that sort of thing. He built the racecourse at Keele and spent thousands on that. I don't think it went for many years before it was all sold and things were moved to Uttoxeter. He also had a station built at Stony Low on the Market Drayton line.

Between 30 and 40 men worked on the Estate - building, woods and garden staff, blacksmiths, and in the stables. There was a Butler in the Clock House. A Mrs Dempster followed the Grand Duke Michael as a tenant at the Hall. She had a Rolls Royce and a carriage and pair. She came in about 1920/21. A Mr Robert Heath came for a short while afterwards. Ralph Sneyd started using the Clock House again in about 1932. Keele Hall was empty and was last used around 1903. There was a sale of books and pictures and furniture to pay off death duties.

When the Estate was sold the workers were made redundant. There weren't many left, most had gone. The University employed a few of them. The gardens carried on for a while to grow vegetables for the students, but they found that it was cheaper to buy. The gardens were then rented to Stoke-on-Trent Corporation and later sold to the University.

THE WAY WE WERE

The roads were poor. My sister was going back to work one evening on her bicycle. It was dark and she fell in a pot-hole and broke her arm. She could never straighten it again. In winter the roads were full of sludge and potholes and in the summer full of dust. You couldn't walk down them hardly. Mr Bloor would have 50 to 60 cows going up and down the road in summer, morning and night. The carts would bring straw down to the Potteries from the Cheshire area. We used to run behind and jump on these wagons. We used to run after the motor lorries as well. We played football in the main road - there was very little traffic so we were quite safe.

Very few people had cars then. Most had a bike. The railway had a good service to Newcastle. There were two trains on a Saturday and in the night you couldn't get on the station because of all the chaps from Leycett and Madeley Heath. Newcastle was quite a focus. Then the buses started. Crosville came pretty soon after the First World War. Anyone could run a bus then and several started up. A chap in Madeley called Clarke was one - Clarke's Comfy Coaches.

Colin Green had an old army ambulance which he used as a bus and we sat on a carpet on wooden boards on each side. David Shenton who kept the Sneyd Arms had a little charabanc thing. He called it Dolly Grey and he ran it from Newcastle to Keele. The conductor walked on the outside to collect the fares. It cost fourpence to go from Keele to Newcastle, which was a lot of money in those days. It stayed at that price for years. They were taken over by the Crosville Bus company.

I was 21 when I learned to drive. I didn't have any lessons, I just watched what the chap was doing. The roads were pretty rough - rough surface and pot-holes. There were no traffic lights so you just stuck your arm out if you wanted to turn. I never had an accident! The car was an Austin 7 with a canvas top. It was an ice box in winter. You had to double de-clutch to change gear so there was a lot of grinding. Top speed was about 40 mph. Petrol was about 7d a gallon and the car did 40-50 miles to the gallon.

The Estate owned several cars for the workers. Colonel Sneyd had a two-seater, a sporty type, no hood or windscreen. It had two big levers outside the car. One was the brake and the other was the gear lever. This was early 1900s. Then he went into the early Cubit cars. Only people with a bit of cash could afford them.

I bought my car in the Estate sale in 1950 - it was an Austin 12, a 1936/7 model. They were built to last in those days. It was black, a lot of room in the back and it had a canvas top.

STAYING ALIVE

There was no National Health Service when I was young. There were the Odd Fellows, the Pearl and the Forresters. My father was in the Odd Fellows and he paid 6/6d a quarter. This covered illness. The collector, Mr Cadagan, was based in Church Street, Silverdale.

I had my tonsils out when I was seven. I went in the afternoon and at tea-time I could come home. I remember coming back on the train. My mother carried me up and the stationmaster helped her. I was still half asleep from the effects of the chloroform. They put a bag on my face and I was out. There were no masks on the doctors or rubber gloves, nothing like that. There were no ambulances either.

In those days you couldn't just go to the Infirmary. You had to have a 'recommendation'. You didn't pay for anything but you had to have this 'recommendation' from a person who gave an annual subscription. That person was given so many recommendations according to the amount of the subscription. There were In-and Out-patient recommendations. You got Sickness Benefit from the Friendly Societies. Colonel Sneyd gave ten guineas a year to the North Staffordshire Infirmary and for that he had about three In-patient Recommendations. The number of 'recommendations' depended on the amount the employer paid. You didn't have to work for an employer to get a 'recommendation'. People went to the Estate Agent of Keele or they would know someone who had an in-patient 'recommendation'. You paid for the doctor if he came to call. For those who couldn't pay, some doctors didn't charge. Dr Gittings used to say, 'I charge those as can pay'. He only had a horse and cart to come around in in those days. He covered Keele, Madeley, Onnerley and perhaps Whitmore side. He would see the colliers' wives. I don't think the Railway had any 'recommendations'. We went to the Keele Estate Agent. Sometimes all the 'recommendations' would be used up so you'd have to wait twelve months or more.

My father was keen on Johnson's Liniment and oils. When you were ill you waited until it wore off. We went to Mr Wain the chemist in Newcastle. He was as good as any doctor. You'd tell him the symptoms and he would put you up a bottle of medicine. There were no pills in those days. The doctor used to mix his own medicines -a bit of this and a drop of that, then over to the tap. We had lemon tea and a glass of wine. Not so much whisky - it was too dear. It was 12/6d a bottle then. My father was interested in herbs. He liked dandelion coffee. He said it was healthy.

I wore short trousers until I was about 14 or 15. My mother made some of our clothes or we'd buy them from the Silverdale Co-op or in Newcastle. My mother shopped in Blockleys and Watsons (Newcastle). We also went to McKilroys, a department store in Hanley. We took the tram car which went from the Sneyd Arms in Silverdale. All have disappeared now. She had a brother in Market Drayton so we would sometimes go to the weekly market there. But we mainly used the Co-op in Silverdale for our groceries and everything else. Their headquarters was in Silverdale. I used to dash out of Keele School to give the order in on a Tuesday then they delivered it. I fetched milk from Top Farm until a chap from Betley started to deliver, so we had it from him.

ON THE SIDE
Most people kept a pig or two. My father kept two. We had them in the Spring and fed them until the Autumn. When the cold weather came in October/November, we killed one and cut it up for use in the house and sold the other one. We cured it by rubbing salt petre into the meat. I think we got it from the chemist. It was a long job - your fingers used to be raw at the ends. My grandfather, when he retired, spent many an hour at it. With the hams, you have to get right down to the bone otherwise it would go rotten. It took hours. Now they inject it with salt solution. The meat kept us going through the winter.

Several people had pig sties. Ours was round the back. We fed the pigs on meal and household scraps. I kept pigs when I first came here until about 20 years ago. I had 6 to 10 at a time. When all the restrictions came in with regard to weight and fat I packed it up.

RECREATION
I had a Meccano set, and a bicycle when I was old enough to ride one. I had an old wooden horse with wheels that my grandfather made. You pulled it along. Then I had a wheelbarrow. We didn't have many toys in them days. I took the Children's Newspaper for 8 to 10 year olds. It was just like a little newspaper. There was also the Beano, the Dandy and Boys' Own. They cost about one penny or tuppence. They were brought up from Silverdale every Saturday morning by Mrs Morrall.

When I got older there was the football team and the cricket club and a tennis club before the War. Keele Cricket Club had two teams at one time. I was Secretary and Treasurer of the club and I played. I wasn't much of a bowler or a batsman. I organised the fixtures and looked after the money. There was the baths in Newcastle and that cost tuppence or threepence on a Saturday afternoon.

The sports clubs would hold dances and there were dances in the Assembly Rooms. There was the Reading Room and the Billiards Room in the old Post Office. You paid by subscription to join. My mother belonged to the Mothers' Union. The Assembly Room dances were well attended. They went on from ten until two in the morning. There was a live band. They would hold charity functions there. On New Year's Eve there'd be a dance up at Keele Hall.

The Pavilion Cinema in Newcastle did so well they built another adjoining it, the Regal. There was an old picture house at the bottom of King Street. The King's Hall in Stoke had live performances too. When we were boys we used to go to the pictures in Silverdale on Saturday mornings - mainly cowboy films. It cost a penny but if you wanted a better seat it was tuppence. It was in the High Street. When the war came that put a stop to it.

My father was keen on poultry. He won a silver cup in a laying competition. We had a piece of land at the back, about a quarter of an acre. He kept Rhode Island Reds, amongst other breeds. He aimed at having 50 pullets put in his shed in the Autumn. They were all trap tested. All the eggs laid in a day were recorded. The best performers were kept and the rest - those that laid less than 250 eggs in a year were out. He bought the best bred cockerels for breeding purposes.

There was cock-fighting going on but it was illegal. There would be cock-fights going on in the Laundry at Keele Hall - Mr Sneyd and his friends.

The Keele Show was started in the 1800s. It was run by the Horticultural Society but came to an end in 1914. It was regenerated in the 1930s. I was Secretary to the first one and it was mainly horticultural - horse-jumping, fruit, vegetables and flowers, a Rose Queen procession. Thousands came. We had around 20,000 one August Bank Holiday Thursday. It was always held on the first Thursday in August. Entry cost one shilling. There were big shows before 1914 but the War put a stop to that. It was one of the biggest one-day shows in the county for local farmers, estate men, etc. It was held where the University sports fields are today.

Just before Christmas there was an Estate party. That was good. It was in the Assembly Rooms behind the Sneyd Arms. The Sneyds used to attend.

At home we had Christmas pudding, a turkey, a tree and the rest of it. My father was a very good poultry man and he used to rear turkeys so we kept one for ourselves and sold the rest to a local chap, together with a few chickens.

THE WAR YEARS

I remember the day the First World War ended. I'd be nine or ten. The Zeppelins came over Keele. I remember hearing the engines - that buzzing noise. In 1939 there were soldiers based at Keele Hall. The Americans and the Poles came. They cleared them off then the Cypriots came. I think one of the Cypriots murdered someone. When they cleared out the University came. The soldiers left Keele Hall in a terrible mess. The Hall was on fire about twice.

CHANGING HANDS

People thought it was a good idea, the University coming. No-one private could afford to take the Hall on, the state it was in then. The University has been a good thing except that it has come down into the village and spoiled it.

THE WAY WE WERE

The person who kept the Post Office at one time was Mr Barrett, a tailor by trade and the Sneyds used to buy the liveries for the gamekeepers, etc from him. The village policeman lived opposite the Sneyd Arms, then they took on the Lodge on Keele Road. There was a saw mill, a smithy and a wheelwright's shop here, and the painters were opposite the old Post Office. There was a joiners' yard and a paint shop and behind the Sneyd Arms was a place where horses and carts were kept. There was quite a hive of industry going on in the village. The wheelwright closed before the Second World War. The saw mill was moved to Keele Hall. The children had metal hoops which the smithy used to mend for them. We didn't have to pay. He would just stick it in the fire for a few seconds. The Agent and the Parson were the big shots in those days. They ruled the roost, you might say. They advised and helped people.

Neddy Barratt was the postman. Letters were brought here twice a day from Newcastle by a man on a bike. We had one delivery every morning. He'd come at six at night the second time. It cost one penny for a letter unsealed, sealed three halfpence and a half-penny for a post card.

There was a shop in Keele sold everything. Shop House. It was rented by Dix from Silverdale. After, a chap called George Brown had it. It closed down for a while then Ted Askey took it over. The village shop was at the end of Rosemead. It was mainly groceries, sweets, that kind of thing. The sweets came in jars at tuppence a quarter.

Keele University Library Archives

Early photograph of the Keele Estate workers c1890

Keele University Library Archives

Colonel and Mrs Sneyd with their estate employees

Keele University Library Archives

When the Keele Estate went commercial the nurseries were leased to Stoke City Council

Giant bonfire ready for lighting by the estate employees

Off the Record

Keele University Library Archives

The Keele Show

Warrilow collection *Keele University Library Archives*

Aftermath of the fire; an entire wing is devastated

Interlude: THE NEW TENANT OF KEELE HALL: THE GRAND DUKE MICHAEL OF RUSSIA

When the Grand Duke Michael arrived on Monday 10th June 1901 at Keele, he and his wife, the Countess Torby (great grand-daughter of the Russian poet Pushkin) replaced the absentee Sneyds. The role of the new patron to the village and surrogate Master of Keele Hall appears to have sat comfortably with him.

He and the Countess were immediately 'adopted' by the village, school and church. In return, the royal party bestowed on them the necessary largesse. On the day of their arrival the children of the school were reported by the Headmaster, in his Log Book, to be 'delighted of the chance of seeing the arrival of Grand Duke Michael of Russia and Countess Torby who have rented Keele Hall'.

By 2nd July 1901 the children had been invited up to the Hall and there were preparatory 'singing lessons in the school yard'. The date, however, had not been specified by the Duke and the eventual visit did not take place until King Edward VII paid a visit to the Duke at Keele Hall. In good time, on 9th July, permission was applied for 'to take the children up the drive to see the King on his arrival' and 'by kind permission of the Grand Duke, the children of day and Sunday school and their parents and friends were allowed up the avenue and so had a splendid view of Edward VII at 5.30 pm on 12 July 1901'.

'The Royal Party visited the church on 19th July and 'the smallest child had a splendid chance of seeing the King and Party'. The open air concert was finally given on the lawns of Keele Hall on 29th July 1901 with the village children providing the entertainment. The programme was as follows:

> The Russian National Anthem
> Hoopdrill
> Infant Action Song
> Dumbell Drill
> Action song
> Recitation
> Maypole Song
> God Save the King

Wednesday 16th October was the Duke's birthday thus, 'by special request of His Imperial Highness the Grand Duke Michael the children had a half day holiday and he provided bonbons. The bells were ringing all day'.

The Imperial Party visited the school on Wednesday 16th October 1902 at the Duke's special request. On this occasion the children were 'invited to a garden party at the Hall to be held on his return from the Coronation. Unfortunately, owing to the King's illness, the Coronation was postponed, as was the Duke's treat.

Perhaps as compensation, on 8th July 'a gift of about two dozen illustrated papers on current events' is gratefully acknowledged by the Master. "The children", he wrote, "are delighted and this is a further example of the kindness of the Grand Duke". It could, of course, have been that the Countess Torby and her staff were simply turning out the cupboards.

The following year, Thursday 22nd July 1903, 'the Grand Duke postponed the fête (now an annual occurrence, it seems) 'until Thursday pending the arrival of Prince Nicholaus of Nassau and Countess Merenburg Stoekle'.

But all was not champagne and croquet for the Duke. By 1904 he had been made Chairman

Courtesy Racing Illustrated

The 1896 October Steeplechases - the crowds gather in the stands to witness the start of the Keele Hurdle Handicap.
The race course was built by the Sneyds, together with a railway to bring both horses and visitors to the track

Keele University Library Archives

'Sasha" with friends at the Keele races

of the Managers' Committee of the school and meetings were taking place regularly at the Hall. He and his party regularly visited the Keele Show, the Royal presence making it an important event in local diaries, no doubt.

Unfortunately, all this good work was cut short when on 7th March 1910 'the Grand Duke Michael came to the school to bid farewell as he was leaving Keele Hall'. The blow was somewhat softened when 'every child which had been in the school during his Chairmanship of Managers was presented with a beautiful silver medal'. The Royal Party, it seems, were decamping to Ken Wood where they became tenants.

The last record of village contact with the Duke was 21st October 1914. The Headmaster of the school writes, 'knitting mittens for war effort fund'. By 9th January 1916, '25 pairs of mittens were sent for the children for Grand Duke Michael'.

No mention was made in the Master's Log Book of the death of the Duke which was recorded in The Times, on Saturday, 27 April 1929. The Times, then ever the master of understatement, listed some of the Grand Duke's achievements: 'elected High Steward of Stafford 1903'. And, as the Duke was a keen tennis player and golfer The Times describes him as 'a man of such powerful physique that he had to have clubs with very long shafts and thick grips. He was a familiar figure at the Riviera courses'. The Duke was also remembered for entertaining 'magnificently at Ken Wood. A great Ball which they gave in 1914 will be particularly remembered for the king and queen were there, as well as a numerous company of social and political distinction'.

'Also, in October 1914, at the suggestion of his daughters and two of their friends, he established a movement for sending quantities of warm gloves and mittens which proved a great boon to the men in the trenches'. It is hoped that there wasn't too much disappointment when the consignment of children's mittens from Keele school arrived. The Grand Duke died, possibly as he had lived, in his sleep, at York Terrace, Regent's Park. He was buried in Hampstead Cemetery.

THE KEELE ESTATE

On 8th September 1951, the *Staffordshire Weekly Sentinel* published notice of the sale of Keele Estate. It was to be sold in 171 lots. There were three public houses which were the Sneyd Arms, Keele; the Sneyd Arms, Silverdale; and the Jovial Colliers, Knutton; 31 farms to the west and southwest of Newcastle; woodland freeholds and numerous residential properties in Silverdale, Knutton, Leycett, Scot Hay, Wolstanton, Chesterton, Madeley, Hanley and Tunstall. The *Sentinel* also reported that parts of the estate had already been sold off in previous sales and these included the Norton Bridge Estate, Mow Cop Estate and the Willaston Estate. The *Estate Catalogue* for 31st October 1951 states that the Keele Estate was, at the that time, 4,407 acres and included valuable accommodation land, allotment gardens, numerous cottages and village properties. Most of the cottages at Keele were offered to the tenants on a first refusal basis. The majority of tenants purchased the homes and farms they had rented for years. Those properties not purchased by the tenants were offered for sale in the auction. On 3rd November 1951 the *Sentinel* reported that the sale had realised £332,785. The Sneyd Arms, Keele, was sold for £7500 and the Sneyd Arms, Silverdale for £7000. The Estate when sold to the County Council for a University College, was estimated to have cost, with repairs, in the region of £160,000. The eventual sale of Keele Hall, for a University College, together with 154 acres, was sold for around £32,675 (Mountford 1972).

Keele University Library Archives

Some examples of the fine silver owned by the Sneyd family, which was sold in one of the great sales (1924) by Christies. The sconces and candleholders were described by Christies as being from the reign of William III and Queen Anne. They are said to have 'possibly' been made by Phillip Rolles circa 1697/1700.

Grand Duke Michael of Russia

Keele University Library Archives

The entrance to the estate at Keele, Whitmore Road end. Villagers were allowed to look but entrance was by invitation only, unless they worked on the estate

The Grand Duke with family and friends on the terraces of Keele Hall

Going to open the Keele Show in 1905

Keele University Library Archives

Setting out from Keele Hall to meet the King

Warrilow collection *Keele University Library Archives*

The King and the Duke at Whitmore

CHAPTER THREE
DOWN THE MINE

BEGINNINGS

I was born in 1904 in this house. As far as I know, I'm the oldest one born in Keele. My father worked on the Keele Estate. He had a pony and trap to look after and he did the Boss's garden. Church Fields was an orchard then, so he had to do that too. There was another orchard where (old) Berachah House is now. I understood that it was the villagers that had Berachah House built for the parish priest. The University Chaplain had it, now it's in private hands.

My mother's father was born in Keele and as far back as I can go, I think he worked on Heath's farm. They lived in that old black and white cottage down Keele Road, Rosemary Cottage (it was rebuilt in the 1980s). He came to live in the bottom cottage opposite the present Post Office. My mother went to work at Keele Hall, in the laundry, when the Grand Duke Michael of Russia was living there.

I only knew one grandmother (my father's mother). She would come and stay with my father here at Keele for three months then she would go to another brother for three months. She was on the pension - five shillings a week. She used to give me and my sister a halfpenny. We called it the Saturday Halfpenny. I was going to school then, I should be about seven or eight.

I went to the village school in 1909. I was five. The headmaster was Mr Cook. I started in the infants with Mrs Clayton. The middle classes had Miss Knight. We had lessons in geography, history, that sort of thing. We had desks for two. The teacher had a blackboard and we had exercise books for arithmetic. When we first started we had slates. The teachers were pretty strict. They had the cane in them days. I had it many times! We all kept pretty quiet. We had examinations about once a year. Them that did go to secondary school probably sat a test. Them that were well off went to the high school. My parents couldn't afford it so I left school at 14.

King Edward VII came to visit the Grand Duke Michael at Keele Hall. Opposite the Sneyd Arms, they put up a platform and they had all us children out of school going on this platform to wave to him. He came in a car from Crewe Station.

The Grand Duke used to give all us children in the village a treat up at the Hall. It was a tea party. One year we had it outside and we played games on the side of the lakes. I know I went twice, it must have been 1909 and 1910 - he had to leave in 1910. He had to go back to Russia because they had a Revolution there. His two daughters didn't. One married Colonel Werner - her name was Lady Zia. My mother told me all about them. After he left, the Hall was rented to a Mrs Dempster from Chester way. My father had a medal from the Grand Duke when he left.

The village school was a church school. When there was a confirmation on the girls used to go into the school and get dressed in white and then go up to the church. I was in the church choir. I wore short trousers just below my knee and a jacket for going to church. We had an outing when we went to Dovedale with the choir - there was a donkey or two you could ride on.

The Sneyds were good church people. There used to be a path, near the wood at the end of the drive, that led onto the road. They would come along this path, through the wood and through a gate and over the road to the church - when they walked. We saw them in church. There were three pews behind the choir for the Sneyds, separate from us. The church was full in them days. People often went at night time of a Sunday. You had to go, if your mother and father said.

THE WORLD OF WORK

About two months after I left school I got a job. I'd only got me mother. The Vicar, Reverend Grimwood, he was there then. As it happened the manager of Silverdale Colliery used to come to Keele Church and so the Vicar had a word with him. He come and told me mother to send me to Silverdale Colliery on the Monday morning at six o'clock. That's how I started work. The manager was Mrs Bates' father-in-law. When he finished at the colliery he came to live in Keele, in The Villa.

My first job was on the top with the joiners. You weren't allowed to go down the pit until you were sixteen. I was repairing wagons and that. They put me in the fitting shop on the screw machines. They did the threads up so you could put the hubs back on the wheels and you could use them again. Then they transferred me to a small drilling machine. I worked my way up to the large drilling machine and then the lathe. I went through all the fitting shops until I was 18 or 19, then they said, 'We'll have you on the bench'. It wasn't long after that that I went down the pit with someone. I could have gone to night school but I didn't. I learned everything at the colliery. I was working with metal and we did everything with our hands. I was a foreman when coal was nationalised in 1947. I wouldn't mind going through it all again. There were some rough times, but I enjoyed it. I'd choose the same again. I stayed in the colliery for fifty years. When I was sixty, the engineer who was about the same age as me, eased off me a bit. He'd get the young ones to do things. Life's easier in the pit today. It's all machinery.

I started work at six in the morning and finished at five o'clock at night. We had half an hour for breakfast and at dinner. The men thought it a waste of time having an hour for dinner, so they cut it to half an hour and we finished at half past four, which was better. It was six days a week and we worked half days on Saturdays until one o'clock. As I got older, I had to work weekends. We were paid time-and-a-half for that. I started at 7/9d week, then it went up to 15 shillings. Then something came out in the 1920s called the Sankey Award, and our wages went up to 25 shillings. My mother did a bit of washing, so we managed. She only give me sixpence pocket money out of my wages. We had only three days holiday, at Stoke Wakes, and two days at Easter. We didn't get two weeks off at a time. We worked while the potters' holiday was on and the pit was closed, because the machinery needed doing every twelve months and we could only do it when the pit closed.

I walked to work until I could afford a cycle. I used to go out of here at half past five of a morning. I had a drink of tea and I took sandwiches - cheese, potted meat - and a piece of cake. Jam was the best thing. The pit men all went for jam. Oranges and apples we had. You could smell if there was an orange about down the pit. We started off wearing slops, a brace and a bib. We did away with those later and had overalls. We had to buy our own. Sketchleys asked us if we'd pay 2/6d out of our wages and they would supply us with three sets of overalls and they would clean them for us. We paid for everything. You could buy the shoes and gloves from the pit - they were about 2/6d and the boots about £2.

I worked on the coal face repairing machinery. You had to take plenty of tools down with you because you couldn't come up if you wanted anything. It was half a mile from the pit bottom. If the belt was running, we'd throw the tools on the belt and we'd get on the belt and lie flat. We weren't supposed to, but it was a long way to walk.

When I started they didn't have all this machinery on the coal face. It was all by hand -picks and shovels. If two men got a couple of wagon loads out of a shift they'd done well. There were pit ponies at the beginning but they soon disposed of them.

There are a lot of springs at Keele. There's a pool as we used to call Springpool. We used to get water from there to the colliery. If the pumps stopped there would be flooding. I've been up to my knees in it. There were three big pumps at the pit bottom pumping it up the shaft. There were a lot of little pumps pumping the pit bottom. The firemen were responsible for safety - if they thought it wasn't safe they'd withdraw the men until it was put right.

The main accidents were the roof falling in, gas, fire, that sort of thing. If there was any gas on the coal face the firemen would get you off and the fan would get rid of it. Leycett was a dry pit, but Silverdale was always wet - all these springs underground.

I had one accident. The machine caught me on my stomach. The ambulance was horse drawn and I was taken to the infirmary. It must have taken half an hour. I was in bed for a fortnight and me mother had to get in touch with the pit and they sent a recommend to the hospital. Everyone who worked at the colliery had one penny stopped out of their wages and the money went to the North Staffs. Infirmary. If you went into the Infirmary they would ask you if you could get a recommend. The recommend covered employees of firms. The firms would give so much to the hospital then they got so many recommends. They could then recommend their employees to the hospital if they became ill. The National Health Service didn't come in until the 1940s. I don't know how we managed it.

There was a miners' union, but we were in the craftsmens' union. The unions weren't as active as they are today. They didn't bring men out on strike unless it was essential. We did have a strike in 1921 - a long one. We were off for six months. I think we went back and got nothing, you might say. I think we were striking for more money.

I lost my father in 1923. My mother paid five pounds a year for this house. The old big house in the centre of the Hawthorns used to be the estate office and the Estate Agent lived there. My mother got the job of cleaning the offices. She used to have to go out at about half past seven of a morning and clean the offices and light the fires. She did that for quite a long time.

The first week's wages I brought home was 7/9d. It would go a good way. At 14 it was an average wage. It went up to 15 shillings as I went on.

MAKING ENDS MEET

We kept our own fowls and my father always got a good cockerel for Christmas dinner. We didn't have turkey and all that. We grew our own vegetables - taters, carrots, peas, beans. My father was a gardener really. My mother made jam from the fruits we grew in the garden. My father liked pickles, shallots, that kind of thing. The food went into the pantry, we didn't have a refrigerator. My mother made plum puddings. She'd boil them in the copper in the garden over a fire. She'd put five or six puddings in, with a rag on the top of each one. Later, we had a boiler on the backside of this wall. She would put a board with puddings on and boil them in there.

They used to deliver bread from Silverdale. They baked their own bread and brought it up by horse and cart. As regards milk, we used to fetch our own from Summerfields. My job when I came out of school was to get the milk every day - halfpenny for a pint of milk. The farmer from Bromley Green on the other side of the M6 used to come up with a horse and float and deliver milk. Over time, the Lockers took over this.

We had two pigs. There's a pig sty down there (at the bottom of the garden) and an ash pit. My father would buy two piglets and rear them. In Pump Bank Mr L had two pigs, Mr W had two pigs. When they were ready for killing we used to kill them in the Coach House of the Sneyd Arms. They would share out the pig between them.

They had a bench and a big iron bath. I can picture my father now. He got a rope around the pig's neck, taking him down the bank to the Sneyd Arms. He used to get about four men and the butcher. These four men had to hold the pig on this bench while the butcher started to kill it. When they'd quietened the pig down they'd roll him into this bath of boiling water from the hotel. Then they scraped all the hairs off. It was dead before it went into the pot. They slit its throat and then they hung him up in the ceiling before cutting him up. I used to go to watch. It was fascinating, when we were children. We never used to waste anything off a pig. We made lard, scratchings, pig's hodge - something to do with the bowels, my mother boiled it and we ate it, some salt and pepper on it. I didn't. Then you got the hams, head and brawn. There wasn't much waste on a pig. I think we put the bones on the fire.

If somebody give me a penny I'd go to the shop and get a penny jelly. You could get five Woodbines for a penny. Sixpence would go a long way. You could get a pint of beer for a penny or a penny halfpenny. It cost 2d or 3d to go into Newcastle on the tram. You could get a dozen oranges for 6d and I'm told you could buy two dozen eggs for a shilling at the market in Newcastle.

HEALTH CARE

My father was in a Friendly Society. There were the Odd Fellows and the Prudential. My mother used to take me to Silverdale to see the doctor and I think the bill came to 7/6d. The doctor used to make his own medicines in those days. The doctors from Silverdale and Madeley used to walk up to Keele. They didn't have a car in them days. A lot used to doctor themselves. We had lemon tea for colds, cod liver oil, that sort of thing. There was a lady in Pump Bank and she used to do this herb beer - dandelion and nettles, that kind of thing. She used to sell these bottles for a 1$\frac{1}{2}$d or 2d. We'd put a cork in and string around the neck. My sister, she was about ten, had meningitis, diphtheria, scarlet fever, and she had to go into isolation. You had to look through the window at her. Scarlet fever and measles were pretty common then.

THE WAY WE WERE

I walked down Quarry Bank to Pepper Street to get the tram. Keele Station was by the bridge as you go into Madeley. I don't remember the station in Whitmore. It wasn't a people station it was just a siding with a platform. They used to bring race horses in wagons and they had to walk the horses down the Whitmore Road. There was a drive near Racecourse Farm - it's called Stoney Lowe now. I don't remember Keele Racecourse or the races, though.

I remember the tramcar. We had to go to Silverdale and they used to turn round at Silverdale and go to Newcastle and Chesterton. Some went to Stoke and some to Burslem and Hanley - all out of Newcastle in the Iron Market. When you got to Nelson Place it was Hanley or Stoke. Burslem, Silverdale and Chesterton had to come out from the Iron Market and come down Church Lane. The tramcars had posts and wires. When you got to Silverdale they would have to unhook them with a pole, walk around and hook them up again. The trams were single decker with two compartments. People used to have to stand in the gangways at times. The driver went from one end to the other when the tram was turned around. They were still running in 1926. They started before I was born, I think. There were long seats down each side.

If you stand at the yew tree and look down the village towards Madeley, it hasn't altered. All that they've done is brought the shop and post office up onto the garden. The lady that lived in the cottage (next door to the current post office) let the builder have the garden because she wanted a bathroom on her house. There was a five ton weighing machine by the yew tree on the Madeley side, and my father had to look after that. It was used by the farmers from Cheshire and Shropshire. They used to bring the wagon loads of straw and they used to weigh it here and then they weighed it at the pot bank. It was used for packing ware. They used quite a lot.

Keele has expanded down Highway Lane. In my day, Highway Lane was called Workhouse Lane. The first house to be built there was Janet Locker's father's house. The Lockers and the Summerfields were in the village when I was born. Mr Locker's great grandfather used to live in Keele Farm House. The Village Hall? That used to be the wheelwright's shop. Go further along to Pump Bank - those houses were there then. Further on there is a garage with a flat on top - that used to be the blacksmith's shop and the blacksmith's house. You carry on right to the top to the four cottages, that was where the workhouse was. There were railings on top of the wall, all the way along. On this side (left-hand side facing Newcastle) was all wood. Higher up the drive in the University where the staff flats are (Church Plantation Flats) there used to be all scotch firs and that's where all the pheasants in their coops and broody hens used to be reared.

The Sneyds used to shoot all around - Springpool Wood, Bear's Rough, down the Two-mile Lane. They went shooting once a year - pheasants and rabbits. Gentry would come with guns - them that owns the pot banks. They used to decide where they would have their lunch. The man who kept the pub used to have to get the lobby (stew). He took this to wherever they were going to put up for their lunch. The estate men were the beaters. They had them up in the air then the Colonel and his party used to shoot them. They had some pheasants I can tell you! A lot were given away. We would get a rabbit or two.

When Keele estate was sold up, a Mr Swan, a solicitor in Newcastle, bought the Middle House. He had it altered to suit himself and he bought two gardens off the cottages, to extend. As years went by, he moved the shop higher up and went and bought on the other side of the road where the old shop used to be. He sold the Middle House. The Middle House was only ever used as a post office. The shop was always on the opposite side of the road. The old shop was a lock-up with a house attached. The man worked on Keele Estate. He got a big garden so they built the new shop and post office on the garden.

I remember one Christmas I thought I was going to have a tricycle. But when Father Christmas come, there was no tricycle. I wasn't disappointed. My father only got 18 shillings a week on Keele Estate. Mind you, you didn't have to pay much rent then.

RECREATION

On a Sunday night in the summer time, about five of us would go out to Whitmore - meet at the yew tree at about six o'clock and walk to Whitmore, have a drink at the Mainwaring Arms and walk back again. I was about 19 or 20 then. I didn't get married until I was 30! I played cricket with Keele (club) in my early twenties.

My mother did a Keele Show - she did some bread and got first prize. There was a bit of confusion amongst them, though. My mother always had her things (ingredients) from Dick Watson's. Because she won first prize, everyone wanted to know where she bought her flour. So, they made a ruling that next year everyone must get their flour from Dick Watson's.

I played billiards in the reading room many a time. I paid 2d for a game. All the men went there. Some older men went to read the newspapers and play cards. We didn't get any women in. They used to have a lot of whist drives and dances at the Assembly Rooms. The Rooms belonged to the Sneyd Arms. I've been to whist drives there and there'd be about 30 tables. They used to come from Madeley and Silverdale. Then they formed the Mothers' Union and the WI and the women used to go to them.

We started off in the Assembly Rooms with a piano. Alf used to come up from Silverdale to play. As time went on he had a violin with him. There were some good dances there. They were generally in the week, on a Thursday. We'd pay 1/6d or two shillings. You could go to the whist drive at seven o'clock - they used to last until half past nine - and you could stop on for the dance. That used to go on until half past eleven. I was in my teens or early twenties then. A lot used to come up from Madeley. They didn't sell beer in the Assembly Rooms, just tea and coffee in urns. There were counters at the top for the drinks, sandwiches and cakes - homemade. We performed in the concert parties in the Assembly Rooms. Everything happened there, at the back of the pub. We had dances. The other place was the old post office Reading Room, where we used to have meetings.

MAKING ENDS MEET

We had more coal from the woods at Leycett than we had when we was working. We found a

seam of top coal there. We went out onto the tip at Leycett. There were railings all around it.
We got this lorry and we'd get bags of coal for the fire every day. We had nothing else to do when
the strike was on.

My father got badly hurt in the pit. He was a fireman. He hurt his head and he never
recovered. I was nine when he died. We didn't get no money for it then, not a penny. This cottage
was a farm cottage and it belonged to Downe's farm which was then part of Keele Estate. When
Colonel Sneyd was here he used to come to the cricket meetings. He used to think he was the
Gaffer. That's how I got my house. I was a miner and everyone else worked under him. I didn't.

HT was a relation of ours from Whitmore way. She came to our house to live when I was
born. She looked after us. We used to go on Sunday, walk down across them fields to Whitmore
to take her washing and bring some back. I would ride on my father's back.

I have a photograph of me taken during the 1921 strike. I'm holding this pike up, by the
Pool at Madeley.

Author's collection

The Middle House, Keele, as it is today

Interlude: READING ROOMS AND RECREATION

Newsrooms or reading rooms as they were euphemistically called, were plentiful during this period. They were set up to offer an opportunity of increasing knowledge at a time when books were expensive, libraries were inaccessible and when there was insufficient cash to spend on the printed word. These Reading Rooms thus offered some 'opportunity of seeing newspapers'.

Clearly these objectives were not mutually inclusive. The terms of membership for those wishing to read the newspapers of the day was fixed at a lower rate 'in order to bring within the reach of the operative classes, for whose benefit, mainly, they were established - to enable them to become acquainted with the current news of the day, without having recourse to places of resort, the immoral tendencies of which are all too well known.'

Whilst the intention may have been to edify the working man, their 'gate-keepers' were of the opinion that an educated workforce might have been counter-productive and dangerous for the Masters. Consequently careful control was exercised over some of the written material in Reading Rooms. At Keele, the Agent held a firm view that 'instead of doing good to the hardworking man the Reading Room would become a mere political club for tailors etc of the neighbourhood' (Phillips 1986:120).

Instead it was agreed that 'it should be managed in a quiet way by one or two parties and that Sneyd ought at the very least to 'control the publications'(ibid:120). 'Radical publications' were therefore not available to the Keele reader!"

For those who preferred a more physical form of recreation the Keele Cricket Club provided an alternative outlet - watched over, naturally, by a careful Estate Agent and a paternal Sneyd.

THE CRICKET CLUB

A Keele Cricket Club was operational before 1936. However, on Wednesday 18th March 1936 a meeting for all those interested in cricket was convened in the Reading Room, Keele Village, to set up or reconstitute a Cricket Club for the village/parish. Mr E C Lawton stated at the meeting that 'as the old Cricket Club had been wound up .... a Cricket Club be at once organised'. Mr Goodwin, the Sneyd Estate Agent explained that he would have 'in hand a sum of money after clearing up the accounts of the old Keele Cricket Club', and that a resolution had been passed at the meeting 'authorising him to hand over such a sum of money to the new Club'. It was proposed by Mr T C Macham and carried unanimously that Colonel Sneyd be asked to be President of the new Club. The minute book records that 'Mr Goodwin stated that he had discussed the future of the Cricket Club with Colonel Sneyd and Colonel Sneyd had agreed provided he was assured that:

1. The Club would be run on a businesslike and sportsmanlike manner.
2. The following were to be the terms on which the grounds were to be used:
a) The Club to be more or less under Estate control.
b) No persons living outside of a two mile radius of the Reading Room be allowed to become a playing member unless their application had received the approval of Colonel Sneyd or his agent.
c) The Captain for 1936 was to be Mr T H Bailey and Mr Bailey was to elect his own Vice Captain. (He appointed Mr Glover.)
d) Only one XI was to be played this year and the knock-out competition to be postponed for 12 months.
e) The Secretaries were to be Mr W Bedson and Mr G Ballance (two being necessary as Mr Ballance would not be with the Club on Saturdays).
f) Colonel Sneyd does not insist but he does suggest that for this season Mr Goodwin be elected Treasurer.
g) The meeting was to elect a good and strong Committee. Anyone agreeing to be on the Committee would be responsible to Colonel Sneyd should he fail in his duties as a Committee man. The committee elected was: Captain: Mr G White; Vice Captains: F Lawton and T C Macham with power to add.
h) New Minute and Account books be started and were to be lodged at the Estate Office so that Colonel Sneyd could inspect them when he was at Keele.
i) Membership was to be 10 shillings per annum. The President would write to certain gentlemen asking for their support. Playing members five shillings to be paid: 2/6d by the last Saturday in April and 2/6d by the last Saturday in May. Playing members who defaulted would be taken off the list of members and not allowed to play.
j) The Tennis Club would in no way be connected with the Cricket club.
k) The present boundaries of the Cricket Club would remain as at present.
l) Colonel Sneyd would have the right to terminate the Club's occupation of the ground and the pavilion by giving three

months notice on any Quarter Day. No compensation to be paid to Colonel Sneyd.
m) In case of dispute the matter would be referred immediately to Colonel Sneyd or to his agent. Mr G Lea was to act as groundsman at £4 for the season provided the mowing was done at least once a week if necessary.

Mr G White agreed to do the necessary mowing on payment of £2 for the season. Ten pound was agreed for the motor mower. Fourteen teas were to be provided to members of each visiting team free of charge. Mr Askey agreed to provide the necessary teas at sixpence per head if the Club would guarantee 26 teas at each home match. No payment would be made by the Club if the match was cancelled. The terms possibly weighted from past experience, were accepted and a Working Committee Meeting took place on 23 March 1936. Colonel Sneyd was present and he agreed to be President if all his conditions, outlined by his Agent at the first meeting, were accepted.

There were now 17 definite members. To encourage younger members it was agreed that 'two shillings be paid by persons up to 18 years of age'. Colonel Sneyd agreed to purchase the motor mower for ten pounds. The Captain and Secretary were to oversee any new purchase of necessary equipment and the repairs to the old. A letter concerning the teas, received from Mr Glover, was read to the meeting. Mr Glover thought that 'the teas should be managed by the ladies of the village so that any profits would go to the Cricket Club'. After some discussion it was agreed that 'the arrangement with Mr Askey be adhered to'. Colonel Sneyd said that instead of giving a practice net he would give two pounds towards the Tea Fund and provide a partition for the pavilion. It was proposed that the groundsman be paid two shillings for every wicket he prepared for a night match. At the Committee Meeting held on 22 April 1936 the following playing members were selected: H Bailey, G White, G Lea, F Capper, H Lawton, J Glover, G Ballance, W Bedson, T C Macham (Vice President), T Askey, N Watkin, T Henderson, A Watkin, Ed Askey (Vice President), R Smallwood, G Moss, P Jackson, H Holroyd, J Hazeldine, C Rowley, G L Myatt. It was also agreed that Blackfriar's Garage tender of £11 'for conveyancing to away matches' was accepted. It was also agreed that practices be held every Wednesday night a 6.30 pm. Mr Goodwin offered to pay membership for the first five young members to send their names to the Secretary. It was also proposed that cigarettes be raffled at each home match (as last season).

At the Meeting held on 27 April 1936 it was agreed that members contribute one shilling to the cost 'of conveyancing to away matches and sixpence for home matches'. John Askey, Gerald Askey and Eric Askey were accepted as young members to the Club. After this, regular Committee Meetings were held to select players for the arranged matches. The Club branched out to include whist drives and dances, at the Assembly Rooms, to raise funds (and no doubt to placate their wives and girlfriends for the long hours spent on the cricket field and at the Cricket Club). At the Annual General Meeting of the Club held on 22 March 1937 there was a balance of £25-5s-0d which was pronounced to be 'satisfactory'. Colonel Sneyd was re-elected as President and Mr Goodwin was re-elected Treasurer. The Captains and Vice Captains were E C Lawton, G White and Ed Askey. Mr Lea and Mr White were re-elected as groundsmen. Mr Askey would continue to produce teas on the same terms as last year and Colonel Sneyd would supply two guineas for the Tea Fund and Mrs Goodwin, ten shillings.

It was also suggested that the knockout competition be renewed and the Secretary was to write to Mr T C Macham asking 'for the return of the Cup for displaying in two or three shop windows in Newcastle and to see what entries came in'. Throughout 1937 there were regular home and away matches played. At the Annual General Meeting held on 14 March 1938 the financial balance stood at £34-14s-3d. Colonel Sneyd and his Agent Mr Goodwin continued to take an active interest in the organisation of the Club. Club caps were purchased from Messrs Densem and Sons of Newcastle at four shillings each. These were 'green caps with two white hoops and a white band across the peak'. The Club contributed to half the cost. On 24 June 1940 the Meeting was held in the Sneyd Arms where it was proposed that the remainder of the fixtures for the 1940 season be cancelled 'on account of being unable to raise a team owing to members being on military service, working overtime etc.'.

On 14 January 1943 a letter from the Chairman of the Cricket Club Committee was sent to the National and Provincial Bank of Newcastle asking to disband the Club forthwith and any funds to be transferred to the Keele Air Defence'. At 30 March 1940 the Club balance stood at £78 15s. 11d - the healthiest it had ever been.

CHAPTER FOUR
PLAYING THE GAME

BEGINNINGS

I was born in Finney Green in 1928. Only about five families lived there. I went to school in Leycett. The Headmaster was cricket mad and he'd be off taking the boys down to the Leycett cricket ground. The girls had to stay with Miss Smith and do needlework. Jim and Cedric later became much involved with the Keele Cricket Club. Jim was the star bowler and Cedric, his brother, was the star batter. Jim joined the cricket club before I ever knew him. He was about 16. The cricket ground was on the field by Chapel Cottages, called the Gnarley Field. That would be after 1950. The Club was going after the War, in 1950. Mr Downes let them have this land to use as a cricket pitch. He also let us have a bonfire and let off some fireworks in the field at the bottom of the garden.

THE WORLD OF WORK

My father worked for the Council but he was a fireman at the Leycett Colliery at one time. If he stayed in the pit he wouldn't have had to go into the army. Jim worked with my father, at the time up at the brickyard. Later in his life, Jim worked up at the University library, part-time. He enjoyed it up there. I went to work in the Enderleigh Mills when I left school. After, I went to the cotton factory in Liverpool Road and then to Rists before I went to the Post Office and became the post lady. The Post Office was in Juniper Cottage then. I used to have two bags when I started out. They were heavy. When I first started, they said it was only deliveries to the academic staff. Then they put the caretakers on me; then I had to deliver to the shops and bank and when they said I had to deliver to the students union and the book shop - not just letters but packets too - it was too much. They then started to take it to Keele Hall in the van. When I was 55 or 6 they said I could have a bike but I didn't want one then. I hadn't had a day off in 12 years.

GETTING STARTED

I met Jim at one of the dances at Keele. I was about 19 and we married when I was 21. We came to live here, in this cottage. It was an Estate cottage. We'd got a friend who lived in Station Road. Her father lived here. She came to say that her father was going to live with them as he couldn't manage on his own any longer. She said, 'There's a cottage coming vacant, why don't you write and see if you can get it?' So Jim's mum wrote to Mr Bedson and he said he hadn't had any official notice yet about the cottage being empty but he'd had about 70 after the cottage, already. He said he would consider us if it came up. The morning that we got married we had this letter from Mr Bedson saying that we could go and get the key. He'd kept it back on purpose so it was a surprise for us on our wedding day. Jim's brother went to get the key. It was a great big key. Eventually we had the cottage modernised and we've been here ever since.

When it was sold to us, it was £90. We'd rented it from the Estate for about eighteen months. It was unusual to live in an estate cottage and not work on the estate. I don't know why we got it. Jim was born in Keele Village - and he was in the cricket team. I remember when the estate was sold. I didn't go to the sale but Jim did. It started at £50 in the auction. People didn't want to buy it if there was young people in it. They wanted property with older people, so they weren't interested in our cottage. We still had to bid for it though.

We didn't think we'd be staying here long. We bought it really as a stop-gap. We'd saved a bit of money. Our neighbour was a builder and he came round one night and said, 'I don't want to live next door to anyone else, we've been so comfortable with you. How about us both having the cottages done up?' Let's get some plans out and have it done'. We asked for a day to think about it. We said yes. After the cottage was done up I didn't want to move. That was in the 1960s.

THE WAR YEARS

When the air raids were on we had to get up some nights and go across to the farm and sit in the cellar all night. The Hollins's were there then. There were quite a few air raids in this area. One night we were getting ready for bed and the sirens went and they dropped seven incendiary bombs on the pits. They said it was the men changing shifts who had lights on their helmets that gave the signal. I don't think there was much damage. I remember one Saturday afternoon when we were just putting the black-out up and shutters on the windows and this plane came over very, very low. We knew it was one of theirs. It went to Chesterton and seven were killed there. It was daylight. The German planes made a funny noise - the engine kept starting and stopping.

MAKING ENDS MEET

We had food and clothes coupons. We had to really think what we needed most. Shoes was the most important things for us at Finney Green because we did such a lot of walking. When we went to work it was a long walk to the bus stop. We used to buy material to make clothes. We grew a lot of our own stuff. We'd got a large garden so we used to bottle fruit - there were no freezers then. It was something that we did. We had chickens and eggs and our own pig. Someone used to come up and salt it for us. The cottage in Finney Green had a large pantry so we had meat hanging up. We grew potatoes, a lot of turnips and cabbage. All vegetables, really. Meat and potato pie would be typical in our house. We always had a joint for Sunday Lunch and it had to last until Monday. My granny made bread and it used to rise by the side of the oven before we put it in. We'd have the one pig and when it was big enough to kill we'd get another. We'd buy the little ones from the farm. We used to buy the milk from the farm too. We would take the jug across and fetch it ourselves. We had to go at certain times. We couldn't go after 5 o'clock because they couldn't disturb the milk. It had to be a few hours before they could let you have it. We paid tuppence for a pint. We always had a quart. They never measured it, we just took it. We got it from Pepper's Farm. The cottage we lived in belonged to them. It was a tied cottage, although we never actually worked on the farm.

ENTERTAINMENT

We had the run of the farms at Finney Green. And the railway. There was four girls and no other children up there and we'd sit in the station and trains would go backwards and forwards to Leycett Colliery. The Guard got to know us and he'd throw us biscuits. We said we were the Railway Children. We knew what times the trains came. They went to Market Drayton. There was a spring down there where we used to drink the water and lots of blackberries. There were dances up at Keele at the back of the pub in the Assembly rooms. We used to go every Saturday night. I'd be about sixteen then. A man from Burslem would run these dances. I think all the village people went. We got in with boys. There would be all these coloured lights flashing and a record player. Then the soldiers started coming. I think they were Americans or Polish. Jim's sister married a Polish soldier who was stationed at Keele. I wasn't allowed to go out with soldiers - they were too old. We paid about a shilling for the dance. Then we'd slip across to the pub, the back way, to have a shandy, on the quiet. There was an interval at about nine o'clock. You could get a cup of coffee or tea there but nothing else.

There wasn't much to do. We went to the pictures. There was the Roxy in Silverdale. We'd walk through Holly Wood. We'd go to Newcastle on the bus. It was sixpence return. We went to Stoke Football Club on the train from Keele Station. The station was at Station Drive. We went every Saturday, Jim and me and we always took my Dad with us. We always had a family holiday in Rhyl. The Keele Show was running and we always went to that. We took part in races.

I've heard Jim talk about the racecourse but I think it went before I was born.

THE UNIVERSITY COMES

People weren't pleased at the time. It was a quiet village. I was only young so I didn't think about it. The big thing that ever happened to Keele was Knightscroft being built. I remember Hawthorn Cottage in between the Assembly Rooms and Knightscroft on the left hand side going up to Knightscroft. I think it belonged to the University. It got knocked down. I remember the Horwood flats and houses going up and Springpool. I'd just started on the post. Half the Church Plantation flats were up. I remember Princess Margaret coming. I used to have to go to the Clock House with her post. The police were around whenever she was in. I went one day and this policeman took the letters off me. I said, 'I'm sorry, I have to put the letters through'. I took the letters back off him and put them through. I had to. I saw Princess Margaret once. I was at the back of the Library and she came down in a car. She did wave. I was waiting to cross the road. I remember Lord Lindsay. His daughter-in-law used to live in the Lodge. She worked in the Refectory. I remember the Taylors and Campbell Stewart and the Harrisons. They all made a fuss of me.

Courtesy Mrs E Spragg

Keele's 'lovely, friendly English Postman!'

Courtesy Mrs E Spragg

Star Bowler Jim Spraggs takes a rest during one of the cricket matches at Keele

Courtesy Mrs E Spragg

On the morning of our wedding at Keele Church we had a letter telling us to pick up the key for our cottage. It was a surprise for our wedding day

Interlude: EDUCATING A VILLAGE

Few interviewees remembered, in any great detail, their schooldays. Thus, forming a clear picture of their school life was difficult. Fortunately, the Master's diaries from the school almost filled the void. These daily diaries were begun in the 1860s. Whilst these, too, are often sketchy, they do provide an interesting backdrop to the education reforms of the time - payment by results, for example, a scheme which was introduced in 1861 and adopted in the revised Code of 1862 as a result of a Royal Commission which, under the leadership of the Duke of Newcastle, recommended that 'grants should, in future, be dependent upon the standard of the work tested by the HMIs and attendance attested by the school registers'. It is obvious from the pre-1900 diaries that this placed a great burden on staff and children, whilst giving room for manipulation of the figures by unscrupulous Heads. The registers became important and any alterations in them could suggest false claims to government grant. The system was still operating in 1900 accounting for the regular and dogged record of absences, illnesses (some of them unspecified) and weekly average attendance figures, which later turn to an obsession with 'numbers on the books'. In the later diaries there is less emphasis on standards of education attainment, and HMI visits are fewer (when compared with entries for the 1860s).

Interesting themes raised by the diaries are patterns of illness and epidemics; weather and its effect on attendance; health; staff movements; and local and national events of importance. On offer is also an insight into how an Estate school - created by the Squire and overseen by the local Vicar and notable tenants of Keele Hall - was run. Whilst not all children were reared by the school as fodder for the Estate, children were regularly poached from the school by the Misses Sneyd and the Estate Agent, to work below stairs (or in the Lady's chamber if they showed promise) or on the land. For the Estate, the school was, therefore, a shrewd investment especially with its strong emphasis on needlework for the girls and woodwork for the boys - in addition to the long hours spent on the 3Rs.

The Balfour Education Act of 1902 compelled nonconformists to support Church Schools via local authority rates and created state responsibility for secondary education via the Education Committees of the County Council (Seaman, 1966). Children could now be educated beyond the elementary level for comparatively low fees and provided they 'passed' a stiff competitive examination at 10+ (ibid), although many state-educated children were still attending schools which catered for the 5-14 age range. Keele School was such an establishment. After the Fisher Act of 1918 some secondary schools were encouraged to undertake sixth form work to prepare pupils for university. The 1944 Education Act abolished fees in secondary schools and reorganised schools into three categories; nursery education which would be voluntary; primary schools for those aged between 5-11years; and secondary schools for those over 11 years. The Act also redefined the purpose of compulsory school attendance so that is should be 'efficient full-time education suitable to their age, ability and aptitude'. Previously, other Acts had stipulated only that compulsory attendance should be for 'efficient elementary instruction in reading, writing and arithmetic'. The County and Borough Councils would be responsible for the education of children. The Fisher Act also provided universities with an increased government grant and £8 million was made available so that ex-Servicemen could receive a university education if they wished. State scholarships enabled secondary school children to take advantage of a university education. The diaries reflect some of these statutory changes to the education system, and record how difficult it was, in practice, for a small village school to meet all its statutory obligations.

The diaries also reveal how uncomfortable school life was, especially at the turn of the century. The rooms were cold in winter and stifling in summer. The days were long, the teachers strict and the diet of learning somewhat stodgy. In 1913 the first Director of Education, Graham Balfour listed subjects on the curriculum, as part of a report on the progress made by the first County Education Committee in its first 10 years, 'Subjects taught were: reading - phonetic 'look and say'; singing, nature study, physical exercise,

Morris dancing, swimming (the local baths had opened on 26th October 1906), handiwork, gardening, cookery, laundry work, needlework'.

It is unfortunate that the diaries were not written with posterity in mind and there appear to be few, if any, statutory guidelines for recording information. Consequently, some Heads were more eloquent and informative than others. Sufficient is written, however, to obtain an impression of the daily triumphs and irritations of a Headmaster's lot - the 'poaching' of children by the local Board Schools of Whitmore and Silverdale, of not being paid on time by the Managers, of the school room furnaces failing in the middle of the coldest snaps, the heat of the summer and of the poor attendance owing to epidemics occasioned by poor heating, hygiene and diet.

The overall impression is that 19th century schools, in the early 20th century, were far from desirable places in which to spend the greater part of one's formative years. Learning was a painful experience, with the majority of children being prepared for the kind of working life that they would eventually lead - as farmhand, domestic worker, miner. Their schooling trained them to be silent and to take instruction without question. As we approach the 21st century, we may well demand, plus ça change?

1901

On 24th January 1901 the Victorian era came to an end when Edward VII was proclaimed King. The attendance figures for Keele village school, for January (weekly average 73.8) were higher than those for August (72.9) despite the fact that 'sickness was rampant and increasing' at the end of January. Although there were heavy snows at the beginning of February, attendance for that week was 78.3 ('62 children being present and Miss Kelly snowed up at home'). A cold snap in June brought 'sickness', yet the average weekly figures for attendance in June were 90.6, 95.1, 92.9 and 92.8 respectively.

On 4th July temperatures of '92 degrees Fahrenheit in the sun and 87 in the shade' were reported. By 19th July 'the heat in the sun was 99.5 degrees Fahrenheit'. Attendance was high - 93.8, 95.7, 95.5. The last week of August, however, brought attendance figures to their lowest for the year, 72.9. Rewards for good attendance, which took the form of 'sweets, magazines and dismissed at 3.45 pm in high glee', were also recorded.

September was not a good month for attendance owing to a scarlet fever epidemic. By 16th October 'the school was closed by order of Dr Dickson of Newcastle. All mild cases'. On the same day, 'the Master was taken seriously ill with nervous prostration and an attack of brain fever'. The school did not re-open until 25th November. The first death from scarlet fever was reported on 9th December - Florence Addy was the unfortunate victim.

The Board School of Silverdale was accused of 'poaching of Keele children' on 10th December, by an irate Keele Master.

1902

Attendance figures decline, picking up only in July, August and September. A heavy frost in mid-February brought the children to school rather than kept them away ... 'slides made ...those late can't slide'. By mid April there was 'decreasing attendance and increasing illness'. Weekly average attendance figures were 74.7 and 87.1. There were colds, influenza, and 'some children have been taken ill with sudden fainting'. By 25th April there was 'an epidemic'.

The 'bitterly north-east cold winds' of May did not help. The Master records that 'hardly a child in the school is free from coughs and cold'. Attendance averages were 83.2 and 87.6.

In June there was reason to be joyful when 'the declaration of peace closed the Boer War in South Africa after 32 weeks. 'Universal rejoicing. Holiday this afternoon', recalls the diary.

September brought another bout of fever. The record for 12th September states, 'a case of fever occurred this week and caused a small panic after the experience of last November'. By 22nd September the 'epidemic of fever is slowly spreading. Cottagers will not take proper precautions'. Yet the weekly average attendance figures for September are high: 97.2, 92.1, 80 respectively.

By October, 'depressing atmospheric conditions added to the increasing roll of fever cases', makes one wonder what is going to happen. A meeting was 'recently held at Keele Hall by invitation of the Grand Duke Michael'. For that week attendance averages are 78.2. On 9th October the school is 'closed at noon by order of Dr Dickson and does not re-open until 3rd November. The Master reports that, 'the rooms were thoroughly disinfected ... WCs whitewashed, cleansed out, scrubbed out with disinfectant'. On 5th November 'operations commenced for bringing water to the school and to the school house'. Clearly the meeting with the Grand Duke had not been in vain. However, on 14th November, one of the teachers, 'Miss Martin filed a doctor's certificate that she had developed fever after reaching Audley'.

The year ends on a happy note, 26th December being 'the annual treat for children and old folk. Over 60 attended in the Assembly Rooms'.

1903

Although attendance averages in March are up on those for January and February, the Master records that many children are absent with coughs, colds and 'some ring worm'. For the rest of the year attendance is steady at around 83.5.

July sees a 'terrific heat, 98 degrees Fahrenheit in the school yard'. Good attendance for the week of 20th July could be owing to the fact that this was 'the children's fête week at Keele Hall'.

On 1st October, together with the problem of bad weather, coughs and colds, 'the school was taken over by an authority called the Staffordshire County Council Education Committee'.

The Keele races are held on 18th February. Attendance does not seem to be affected by this event.

1904

This was not a good year for attendance - the highest average weekly percentage was 79.5 in November and the lowest 67.7 in July, despite the fact that the Master records in January that 'attendance is affected by rain and fog'.

By 3rd May scarlet fever rears its head again. 'Mrs Hughes' baby having developed scarlet fever and two scholars are absent'.

On 17th June the scholars are allowed to go 'hatless'. However, by 4th July the weather is described as 'scorching hot, 89 degrees Fahrenheit in the sun', so, no doubt, hats were resumed for protection. The Master records 'numerous cases of semi-faintings among the children' on 8 July, possibly weather induced.

Attendance is poor on 25th July (67.7) 'on account of fever scare increasing'. By 27th July, Dr Dickson had advised closing the school. Once closed the school undergoes a thorough cleansing to the extent that the Master reports on 29th July, 'We have never had such a thorough cleansing since 1885 when the Master first came to Keele'. Presumably the school opened soon after this and there is no further mention of the epidemic until 30 December when the Master writes, 'village still free of infectious diseases when schools are being closed all around'. The weekly attendance averages for December were 74.3.

1905

There were no epidemics reported for this year although attendance falls. On 9th May 'a flagrant case of defying school attendance occurred this morning, VD being employed by Mr Y to work on the land' and on 8th June 'the Attendance Officer called in connection with CA being absent on Monday morning, carrying golf clubs ... the golf man having engaged him'.

July sees 'weather 88 degrees Fahrenheit in the sun' (11th July). However, weather and illness do not account for the 'dribble of children to neighbouring Board Schools'. Unfortunately for Keele school, '...Keele children find ready admission, one Master even going out of his way to draw two boys from a neighbouring parish to his school, granting them facilities for travelling, denied to his own scholars'.

From 1905 the method of recording changes from daily attendance figures to 'numbers on books', possibly reflecting a change in Education Policy by the County, although this is not stated, nor the change explained in the diaries. It could, however, be owing to a less conscientious approach being adopted by the Master. It would seem that the latter might be the case given that in 1904 an underlying dispute with the Managers surfaces when on 30th September (1904) the Master records 'no monthly salaries, the paymaster having a better berth than a teacher. The salaries were in the Estate Office today and the teachers went away disappointed'. 'Who pays for all this extra clerical work, County Council registers, attendance forms?' demands a terse entry on 11th November 1904. More dissatisfaction is expressed on 22nd December (1904) with, 'Great disappointment is caused by the salaries for December not being forthcoming'. By 3rd January 1905 the record is hostile; 'Paymaster turned up this noon with monthly salaries, three days late which is a great piece of casualness when Mrs C's case is considered - a husband out of work since before Christmas, a sick baby and a family dependent on her earnings'. On 2nd May, 'the Paymaster made his welcome monthly visit, only one day late for a wonder'.

It does not come as a great surprise when on 6th February 1906, a clipped statement records the coming of 'a new Master'.

1906

In January there are 77 children 'on roll'. Two cases of scarlet fever are reported in June and on 31st October the death of a pupil, Eugenie Chidlow, is recorded, although cause of death is not specified.

On 22nd March 'the hounds met under the yew tree...the children given the opportunity to see them'.

In September 'Mr Shorthouse (the Attendance Officer) called and expressed himself pleased with the Keele children, informing me that the school was the best attending and caused less trouble to him than any school in the district'.

1907

The numbers on roll continue to fall from 77 to 71 on 6 September, rising to 73 by 20th September.
February sees the outbreak of measles on 15th February. By 26th February the school is closed for 3 weeks.

1908

Numbers on the roll fall to 69 in January but rise to 79 by September. In June the Attendance Officer 'visited and attendance was so good that there was no need for his services'. On 3rd September the first medical examination for six and twelve year olds takes place at school.

1909

The roll continues downwards and slumps to 62 in April. During this month one of the teachers leaves 'to become a private Governess for more money'.

In September 'whooping cough is prevalent in the village' and the Master records that he 'sent home another 6 doubtful cases this morning'.

November, 'drawing one day per week in lieu of arithmetic on the advice of the HMI', was to take place.

1910/1911

With the roll falling from 70 in April to 60 by October (1910) and 'King Edward VII died on 9th May' and 'Empire Day was not observed this year as a result', 1910 had all the makings of a bad year. To compound the Master's worries, in February measles and chicken pox were reported and in March a case of scarlet fever. On 20th December an outbreak of mumps closes the school until 11th January 1911.

In November a new Master is appointed. He arrived on 21st November and on that day introduced 'gardening, hygiene, elementary science, Latin roots and conversation'.

If 1911 wasn't a good year at least it was eventful - or the new Master was more conscientious in keeping his daily diary. In January there were 61 on the roll and average attendance figures of 41.9 'on account of mumps' The school was closed on 9th January for an extra week 'owing to the outbreak of a mumps epidemic. Chicken pox is discovered on 27th January and by 3rd February the school is closed once more. On 3rd February attendance is down to 36.4.

When the school reopens a new interest emerges - the school garden. On 15th February 'the gardening Inspector examined the ground for the proposed garden for the school'. The garden is prepared and 'a new fence is supplied by Mr Sneyd', on 7th April. On 23rd May the garden is 'plundered by the fowl of the village'. And adding insult to injury, the weather in June is not kind to growing things. The Master records that on 2nd June, crops spoiling in the school garden owing to the drought'. All this proves, however, to be a minor set-back to the project because by 2nd July 'two pecks of early potatoes have been dug up ... and distributed, 15 pounds of peas, lettuce and beans'. There is a bumper harvest in September with '10 pounds of peas, 60 pounds of potatoes, 8 pound of kidney beans, lettuce, onions and turnips' being distributed 'as soon as they were ready, the children having weighed these amounts themselves'. In October there is a late crop of 'three marrows, 12 pound, 7 pound and 6 pound', but 'the cattle in the adjoining field have taken 10 cabbages', whilst 'several rabbits have been observed from time to time in the school garden and many vegetables have been nibbled away, particularly the cauliflowers'. If the record is correct, then the school garden project could be judged a success, at least by the recipients of the produce. Unfortunately, by 1913 the Rector informs the Master that 'the garden would not be kept after 31st October 1913' and that 'cardboard modelling will be taken instead of gardening'.

It was fortunate that the harvest was gathered in early in 1911. By November, 'the lowest temperature of this room this week was 42 degrees Fahrenheit and the highest 58', were recorded. 'The children have complained much about the cold during the week in which the weather has been severe. Many cases of sickness'. The average weekly attendance was 59.9. On 20th December 'the children are scarcely able to do their work owing to the dark, wet day'.

On 16th June the school closes for a week to celebrate the Coronation of King George V and Queen Mary.

Evening classes are approved by the Managers on 24th August 1911 and it is 'the wish that special classes for females shall be formed for needlework and cookery'.

1912-1914

During these years there is a quick succession of Masters, two staying for less than a year. In January 1913 there are only 53 pupils on roll which is reduced to 51 when three children 'migrate' to Whitmore school. The weather at the beginning of 1912 is harsh, the temperatures extreme. Heavy falls of snow are recorded for 18 January (with gales) and the school is closed. In February the temperatures in the school are down to 31 degrees Fahrenheit in the morning, rising to 42 degrees Fahrenheit by 3.00 pm. An outbreak of chicken pox ensues.

By 23rd May 30 children are absent and the 'Medical Officer has been notified on the telephone'. On 5th June the school is closed for two weeks.

Although the numbers increase to 60 in 1914, epidemics are still prevalent. On this occasion it is measles which closes the school from 12th February until 2 March. Chicken pox stalks behind claiming several victims in July. On 31st October a case of diphtheria is reported.

A temperature of 45 degrees Fahrenheit is recorded in the schoolroom on 20th November 1914 and the Master notes 'There is no fire today'.

2nd December a scholar is late occasioning a long entry by the Master concerning the employment of children: 'It appears that his father employs him to deliver milk and the lad is engaged in this occupation until after 8.55 every morning. This case needs close attention as no scholar attending a public elementary school where the morning session begins at 9.00 am should be employed after 8.45 am at the very latest'.

On 23 December the Charge Teacher terminates his employment. No reason is recorded.

1915-1918

Numbers at the school continue to decline reaching a low of 47 at the end of 1917. The new Master who arrives in February 1915 (Mr Cook) leaves on 28th January 1918.

Although tacit complaints were made in the Master's diary about the coldness of the rooms during winter months in 1911, 1912 and 1914, it isn't until November 1915 that it is stated that 'the stoves (are) not very satisfactory. School room temperature is a little over 40 degrees Fahrenheit. Heavy snow so the children sent home'.

Although ringworm and scarlet fever are reported on 13th June 1915 there is no epidemic. On 5th September 1915 cases of ring worm and mumps are reported but there is no epidemic. In 1916 scarlet fever and TB are reported. In November 1917 two cases of whooping cough are recorded. Influenza and whooping cough occur in October and November but they do not reach epidemic proportions until 1922 when the school is closed.

In 1916 in the middle of the First World War, the Education Committee writes saying that 'they were willing to release boys aged 12 for the purpose of working on farms'. Whilst this seems acceptable to the school as part of the 'war effort', in 1917 it is recorded that four boys are absent acting as beaters for the game keepers', which is not. On 29th June 1916 the 'school is closed for a fortnight's holiday for the hay harvest to enable such children, as are inclined, to help the farmers'.

The Circulating Library is introduced by the Education Committee on 20th December 1916 and the school is chosen to be the 'local centre'.

Although the school garden was discontinued in 1913, in 1917 'at the suggestion of the Director, for a whole week as many of the lessons as possible will be devoted to the question of food supply and the economy in its use. The aim is not only to instruct the children themselves but to get at homes through the children and thus create a spirit of loyal adherence to the principles of voluntary rationing by convincing the public of its necessity'.

By September the children are 'blackberry picking for the Ministry of Food' (2nd, 9th, 17th, 25th).

1920-1941

On 1st January 1920 a Mistress takes over the school, ending a long tradition of male leadership.

Possibly the first parents' evening is held on 17th December 1920. The Mistress reports that 'Almost all the mothers and as many friends took this opportunity of seeing the work of the school children'.

In 1928 the Haddow Report advocates a definite break at the age of eleven plus, with classes not to exceed 40. Organisation of schools for pupils under eleven years of age will be into Junior and Infant classes with classes not exceeding 50.

STAFF MOVEMENTS

5 January 1920	Headmistress begins
30 June 1920	Mrs C resigns
3 September 1920	Mrs C reappointed
30 June 1921	Miss G leaves to be married
31 March 1922	Headmistress resigns
4 April 1922	Miss Tennant resumes as Head
22 May 1922	Miss Clayton retires
1 June 1931	V Turner in charge of infant class
July 1942	Miss Tennant retires after 20 years as Head

From 1920 onwards there are regular epidemics:

17 February 1921	Chicken pox
16 January 1922	Influenza which closes the school
14 January 1924	Scarlet fever, school closed until 3rd March.

When it is found that half the school is absent, it closes again until 7th April

10 March 1925	Influenza
21 April 1925	Although 9 cases of whooping cough recorded it does not reach epidemic proportions

20	July	1926	Measles closes the school
14	October	1926	Diphtheria is reported and all books are burned
20	March	1928	TB is reported
29	January	1932	Measles closes the infant school
1	September	1932	Whooping cough
24	January	1933	Influenza closes the school '70 per cent of children absent'

Whilst attendance was disrupted by illness, Keele school did manage to obtain extra play on 27th July 1923 'when 100 per cent attendance' was achieved. There were 61 on the roll. In October a letter from Staffordshire Education Committee arrives 'congratulating the children on the percentage for the quarter - 98.9. This is the highest ever gained by any school in the county'.

The numbers on roll continue to fluctuate between 69 on 6th January 1927 to 104 on 20th April 1936. In 1940 the numbers are increased when 15 evacuees were 'welcomed to the school'.

EVENTS RECORDED IN THE MASTER'S DIARY:

There were General Elections on:- 15th November 1922, 6th December 1923, 29th October 1924, 30th May 1929, 27th October 1931, 14th November 1935.

26	April	1923	A day's holiday is given for the Duke of York's marriage
27	November	1925	'Queen Alexandra's Memorial Service, children attend church'
3	March	1926	'The death of the Keele Estate Agent, A.G. Goodwin Esquire', is noted
28	January	1936	The school is closed after the death of George V
12	May	1937	'Coronation celebrations'

Author's collection

Old St. John's School, now a private residence

Jones' family collection

The infamous Bayliss-Thomas!

Silverdale Colliery c.1910

CHAPTER FIVE
EDUCATING A NEW GENERATION

BEGINNINGS

I was born in 1914 in Chesterton. The First World War had started. My father was a miner. As they were wanting the coal and as miners were important to the welfare of the country, he was never called up to go to the War.

My mother was rather nervous because the Zeppelins were coming over and she had two little ones to care for. Her mother lived in Silverdale so my grandfather said, 'We must have them near so we can look after them'. We came to Silverdale and lived in Sneyd Terrace. I loved it there. It was not far from the station and my father worked at the Burleigh on the Apedale coalfield. I remember as a young girl being allowed to cross the line by the crossing gates to go up to what we call the Black Bank to meet my father, who was walking home from work. When he was on the day shift, we would walk down the fields together. Father loved nature and he would say, 'Listen to the skylarks', and all that. It was lovely.

He had a garden away from home called the Acre, right down the other end of Silverdale. He used to put me in the wheelbarrow and push me down to the garden. We went down the back lane, now called Park Road. The Acre was near the brickworks. It went over towards the old Silverdale Colliery. The present Silverdale Colliery used to be called Kent's Lane Colliery.

My mother went as an uncertificated teacher and she began in the infant school. She was struck with rheumatic fever which damaged her heart so she went into the shoe department of the Co-op store in Silverdale. She would have loved to have been a teacher. She had gone to the dame school.

My grandfather was a lover of education and he paid one penny to send his children there. He was also keen on evening classes. Mother went to cookery and embroidery, my father went to the Stoke-on-Trent Technical College. He taught the pupils below him. He became a Deputy at the Brymbo Mine. He was a fireman to begin with and he later became an overman. He was offered a manager's job in the Ironbridge area but mother didn't want to move.

We went to the Council School run by Wolstanton Board. We called it the Board School. We had a dragon of a headmistress called Miss Cook - perfect on discipline; it was a well-mannered school. There were six standards. I remember in the infant school making a basket of paper shapes and I used to be frightened of cutting the wrong fold. When the gummed paper was brought out I used to ask to go to the lavatory and run home.

We had tiered desks on a platform. The main emphasis was on reading and arithmetic. There were ink monitors who had little inkwells they had to fill from a copper can with a spout. There was a time-table. We knew our nursery rhymes so we must have done singing. We did some craft and we played ring games in the school yard.

In the junior school we were put through our paces with singing on the modulator (doh, rey, me). We had to sing in time and do these exercises. We might have had a tambourine, but no other musical instruments.

I remember Miss Hassells, the standard six teacher. I can see her now in her gym tunic with a whistle. We did country dancing and we always had a sports day with egg and spoon races, three-legged races, relay and team races. We had our little sports in the school yard. The parents watched. Sometimes we had special events. My friend could clog dance. She dressed as a Dutch girl and with her arms crossed she did this clog dance. We didn't have drama but we had to learn poetry. We did drawing and knitting. We had to learn to run and overstitch and we had to knit

Off the Record

Keele University Library Archives

Keele School, 25th August 1892

Keele School in 1905. St John's Church of England School was built in 1858 by Ralph Sneyd, and finally closed in 1965. It replaced an older school

an interminable scarf.

I don't remember exams in the junior school, but I remember little tests in arithmetic and spelling. They experimented with the first assignment tests when I was at school. I shot up from standard three to standard six - you did this if you were progressing. There must have been a test for that. I stayed there until I took the Scholarship. If you wanted to go to the Orme School then you sat this Scholarship. It was the first year that Miss Cook was allowed to send girls to the High School in Stoke-on-Trent. I was chosen with Nancy Sutton to sit this exam. We both got a scholarship to Brownhills High School.

We had a wonderful headmistress in high school, Miss Wilmott. She made it usual that if possible we should go on to college or university. She would interview parents. All my friends at high school wanted to teach so it wasn't unusual - but in Silverdale, generally, it was.

We were well-mannered and no-one went out without their gloves on. Our uniform was brown and shantung with black stockings. Our motto was 'I serve', and our emblem was a tree. There were paying pupils at the school too but we all got along very well. If we misbehaved we were in trouble with the headmistress. We took the Oxford School Certificate of Education for college. We stayed on for 'A' levels if we had eight subjects for matriculation. We needed two main and two subsidiary subjects for the Higher Certificate.

I knew I wanted to teach. My aunt lived in Yorkshire and her daughter was going to Homerton. However, if I wanted to go there I would have had to have waited another year. So, my aunt said, 'why don't you apply to Bingley Hall?' I was the only one to apply. I had to go for an interview in Manchester. My father took me and my mother in the car. Miss Spalding interviewed me then she wanted to meet my parents. I think that swayed things. I got in. It was an all girls college and this would be 1932 -34. I enjoyed it. I had a loan from Staffordshire to go to college and I had to pay it back when I finished. That was hard.

THE REAL WORLD

It was difficult in 1934 to get a job. Manchester only wanted four and they chose one from Bingley Hall to be interviewed - me. The college chose me to go. I loved psychology, did well on my child studies and got A's for my essays. I started teaching in August and I came to Newcastle soon after.

The Brymbo disaster was in 1937. They were cutting to open up a new seam of coal. They'd finished it and they'd got the belt in and they were testing the belt when a spark from that - who knows, we can only surmise - set alight a pocket of gas that they hadn't detected. In those days father had a Davey safety lamp. He used to tell that in the early days at the Apedale they took canaries down. There was this big explosion. My father had just come up having finished his shift. He came up with Tom who lived next door to us. Then the explosion happened. My father couldn't come home because he was in charge of bricking up after the fire, to seal it off. My father had to superintend the materials needed to seal it off. Tom wouldn't come home without my father, so he went back down with him to help. (I heard all this from people who were at the pit top). I think father would have known that there would be another explosion, there usually was. Anyway, he went down to see what could be done and there was this second explosion which was a big one and that was it. Down with my father and Tom was the pit manager and the HMI. They were all down overseeing this new seam. Quite a lot were killed as the next shift would have gone down.

I was at school and the headmistress came to tell me to go straight home because there had been an accident. Mother asked if I'd go straight to the hospital to identify the body. It was a terrible experience. All the beds were taken, it was an emergency.

After my father died my sister and I had to pool our resources to keep the home going and to look after mother. She and my father were very close. I had to get cracking getting pennies for bread, doing the garden, that kind of thing. There was a disaster fund set up. It would be one of the first, I should think. My mother had about nine shillings a week from it and I had to go to the National Westminster Bank in Newcastle to get this. My wages then wouldn't be over £4 a week. But that wasn't a bad wage.

On the Acre we had mint, sage, parsley. We grew our own rhubarb, runner beans, potatoes, cauliflowers and beetroot. All this to ensure the health of the family. The menu was plain and good and what was needed to keep healthy.

STAYING ALIVE

To keep colds off and to keep us warm we wore a camphor bag under our liberty bodice. It was a little round block of camphor and you wore it until the camphor went. We had to preserve our clothes so we also had mothballs. We used Zambuk ointment. It was green and it cured everything. My grandmother kept all these remedies. Grandmother and grandfather always wore a bag of comfrey. It was good for sprains. And we always saved the goose oil. Anyone with a sore throat had an old sock dipped in warm goose oil strapped around their throat. My word, those remedies worked! I suffered from septic throats as a child. When these occurred I used to dread it because mother's remedy was turkey rhubarb. It was a powder and she used to mix it. It was one of the most bitter things, but we recovered. We couldn't stop off from school. We had little money to spare, but what there was went on health. There was no NHS so you had to pay the doctor.

Many people had bicycles in those days. I had one. I never worked the problem of traffic out. If I saw trouble, I'd get off and walk. Father had a bike to get to and from the Brymbo. I cycled all through the War. I used to go into Newcastle on the tram. It was a single decker and started up at the Bush in Silverdale and came down Sneyd Terrace.

The station was still operating but we only used it when we couldn't get from Newcastle, in the snow. I remember being caught with the Misses Saunders in a terrific snow. No buses were running so we went to Newcastle station and came up to Keele on the train. The Crosville bus was used more than the trains. Bonnet's bus ran from Silverdale to Newcastle. They were big sturdy buses that could take a load. There were no regulations as to how many could stand. You just piled on. It was a single decker with a bus conductor and a driver. I remember once going to Rhyl. The charabancs were going then. They were open-topped and there were doors to get into the rows of seats.

There were no big dual carriageways and you had to gauge the width of your car from the on-going traffic. I was about twelve when we got the first car in 1926. It had an open hood and plenty of room in the back. It was a momentous event. Father knew this man from Hope Street, Hanley. Over he came to Silverdale with this car. It was a Bayliss-Thomas. It wasn't new but father kept it in apple-pie order and did his own repairs. Then we ventured forth to Rhyl and Chester. There was a bit of queuing at Chester and we had to keep stopping and holding on. When this Baylis-Thomas engine stopped father had to get out and crank it. Mother didn't like this so she would get out and walk through Chester and we'd pick her up on the other side. There was a bobby on point duty and he would decide who to let through. She often got there before us.

I was doing a child study at college of a little boy in Silverdale, Frank. I asked if he could come with us on the outing to Rhyl. We sat in the back of this Bayliss-Thomas and I was in charge of Frank. I was always a back-seat driver, so I was looking out at the front to see where my father was going. Frank, meanwhile, was cocking a snoot at all the traffic behind. Everyone that passed my father honked him and looked at him. He wondered what the matter was.

It wasn't long before we changed the Bayliss-Thomas for a Triumph. You could press start it. I learned to drive in the Triumph. Whitmore Lane wasn't as made up as it is now. It was a country lane. Father thought it was good for steering practice, so off I went for my first practice. The lane didn't have a footpath or anything, just a drainage ditch on either side and lovely hedge-bank flowers. It wasn't too deep, this ditch. It drained the fields. The farm dog came out and I never thought the car had brakes or anything so I swerved to miss this dog. The car went into the ditch. My father shouted, 'My car! My car! You've scratched my car!' I hadn't scratched it but I'd learned my lesson. I didn't touch it again. We didn't have driving lessons in those days, you learned from whoever could drive. There was no driving test either. My sister was taught by my father on a disused airfield.

RECREATION

I had made up my mind to work with children, so I taught at Sunday school, before I went to secondary school, in a Methodist church in Silverdale. My party piece was 'Under the Spreading Chestnut Tree'. So for every concert and things at chapel, I had to recite 'The Village Blacksmith'. My father played the piano by ear so we set it to music sometimes. We did a lot at the methodist chapel. There was a big choir and they put on these operettas. The Sunday school would be packed for these operettas. The church had a good congregation in those days so we had to pay pew rent if you wanted a special pew.

People from Silverdale walked up through Pepper Street and they came out at the 'pop house'. They would pass the Sneyd Arms and go back along the old toll road (Quarry Bank Road). We had a regard for Keele and we used to go up in the car.

At Keele they had marvellous concert parties and there was a Keele Show. Everything was dated from 'afore' or 'after' the show. There would be the Rose Queen too.

Father came from a large family - there were 18 children. He contacted everyone at Christmas. Mother would be going to night school for cooking and embroidery so in December it would start. We couldn't afford a Christmas tree but we always had a substitute for a Christmas tree. Father's hobby was his car, and he would save up his petrol money to go into the country to bring back a nice big spray and we'd decorate that. We had a mobile of flags of all nations (we lost it when we moved to Keele) but it always came out at Christmas. We didn't have a stocking every time. The table was all put out lovely, half for my sister and half for me. We would come downstairs. I had a celluloid doll about a foot tall. It was beautifully dressed. Mother had knitted all the clothes herself. My sister had a pram and a scooter. I liked a book. When the first fur-backed gloves came out I had a pair and I wore them until the fur was worn down to the leather.

We had a party for our friends and we were told how many we could invite. There was a leaf that came into the table for that. Father used to plan it well. We had a fire in the front room - we never had a fire there too much, only on Sundays and Christmas party days. Up would come the sheet onto the picture rail and father, with a lamp, would make shadows on the sheet. We had to sit and watch whilst he carried out a mock operation behind the sheet with a big saw, his pincers and a hammer. Then we'd play games. It was mainly family and friends. We had a piano and that made it.

We always had a chicken or a goose and port. The preparations beforehand! We had to wash all the fruit for the pudding or cake. My job was to dry it nice. The table was cleared for making the Christmas puddings. We boiled them on the coal fire.

THE WAR YEARS

I can see Chamberlain now, with the piece of paper in his hand. We'd been to Llandudno and my mother said, 'Have a good look at these shops and what's inside, because you won't see the like of that much longer'. She didn't know then that there was going to be a War. Before we went to Llandudno, I'd made my favourite egg plum jam. I don't think I paid more than a 1½d a pound for them. I'd got a dozen pound. We kept a stock of sugar and I used 12 pound of sugar on these plums. My mother said, when we arrived at Llandudno, 'Have you used all that sugar? Did you get any more in?' When we got back, the first thing we did was to go and get a stock of sugar in. She had a feeling. Sure enough, not long after, War broke out. People didn't let themselves get short of sugar or eggs. We preserved eggs in big stone jars. They were stored in liquid and they kept a nice white. You could put two or three dozen eggs in a jar. There were a lot of food shortages, but we managed quite well. We also dug for victory: I grew spinach. Butter was rationed and we stock piled tinned fruit.

I had been to Germany in 1935 and 36, to the Rhineland, and everywhere we went people would be saying 'Heil Hitler'. We had the feeling then that Hitler was coming on apace. It wasn't so much of a surprise to me to know of the build-up of might in Germany. We weren't afraid, we never thought the country would be invaded or that we would be let down in anyway.

My mother would be typical of 'thinking mums'. The first thing she did was to put the deeds of the house in a tin box and wrap that up in a shawl so it was always ready - deeds, marriage certificate and birth certificates went into this box, everything to show that we'd been born and lived. My mother said to me, 'Don't worry when you come home from school if any of those Germans come dropping in those fields. We're taking our tin box under the Dunge Tunnel and you'll find us under there. Everything will be safe.'

People were very keen on getting the Anderson shelters in their gardens. Not so much in Keele, there wasn't much to bomb, although we were en route for Liverpool. We could tell the German bombers from our own engines. The German ones had a deep throb. We had to check the blackouts to make sure there were no chinks of light. We did some air-raid shelter work at school. Even if the planes were on reconnaissance, we went into the shelter. At home we had pantries under the stairs and we had a good sturdy table in the dining room. When the sirens went, I would go on my bicycle to the ARP (Air Raid Precaution) at Rosemeade Cottage. When the sirens went we had to clock in. Mother would be under the table. My sister was in bed upstairs - she never got up!

At school in Newcastle, where I taught, we had to remain calm but we had to go into the shelters whenever we heard the sirens. There were tables in the shelter and seats down the sides and we always had a lamp ready to take with us. The children learned lots of nursery rhymes and how to count backwards, lots of singing games and exercises. We had fifty in a class in those days. There were two shelters joined together at the end of the playground. Every class had a shelter and there were eight classes. They were not underground but they had thick re-enforced roofs. The school was all wood, so there would be a danger of fire.

Everyone was knitting for the soldiers. There was a wonderful spirit and nothing was too much bother. You might have been up all night but you'd be willing to go straight off to school next day. Everyone was co-operative.

The troops came to Keele before D-Day. Keele Hall was a training camp. I remember our soldiers coming back from the beaches and coming to Keele to recuperate. They did short route marches which got longer. One route came down from Keele past the house where we lived in Station Road and in at the gate opposite the Station Road houses. There they used to rest. We had a lovely apple tree and mother made me get all the apples off the tree and give them to the soldiers - our boys who had managed to get away from the beaches.

The other troops were the Cypriots. I used to cycle to school up and down the main road. One night I was coming home pushing my bicycle - it was too steep to pedal - and on Keele wall, running along the top with a knife, were two soldiers. I had never been so afraid in all my life. One was a Greek and the other was a Turkish Cypriot and there was a bit of aggro between the two. I never came that way again.

When my sister's twins were born, mother said, 'Keep to the main roads'. But not my sister, she pushes them down Whitmore Road! One day she arrived home in a state. Down the lane, sitting in the hedge was a Cypriot soldier. He was saying how nice the babies were. She wanted to keep them safe so she kept her calm and asked him about his family. She turned the pram around and he kept his hand on the pram. Then he took some photographs out of his wallet and showed her his children. There was always a fear. The Military Police told us to always keep to the main roads.

We didn't fraternise with the troops. What we did was to make our spare room available with breakfast, free of charge to the soldiers' wives. That was the only way we came in contact with them.

I remember two very nice Prisoners of War being allotted to one of the local farms. They were Polish and very nice. There was a POW camp at the Digness Tileries. I used to walk down the lane across the public footpath that skirts the wood, over the stile and there, at the top of the bank, you could see the camp. It was a tall wire compound with the POWs walking around. The two Polish POWs had the freedom of the farm. One married the farmer's daughter. We went rabbiting with them once. They would have the gun and we would go under the Dunge Tunnel.

UNDER NEW MANAGEMENT

I was very pleased when the university came. I thought it would be a lovely place of learning - an educational centre. I was always aware of the nice land that should be opened up to let more people enjoy it. I hoped there would be a good extra-mural department - I like a good lecture. Not many people from the village went up, but I went to quite a few courses and lectures and the music concerts. Magnus Magnusson came in his early career to give a lecture and an appraisal.

When the university first came it didn't come into the village. The Hawthorns wasn't built then. It was just the army huts on that nice campus. Mary Stewart came into the village. She was the President of the WI. Her husband was the first Librarian.

THE WAY WE WERE

We liked the village. I knew everybody. The church was very much the focus but not for us because we were Methodist. I went down to Silverdale on my bicycle.

We had gas in our house in Station Road. Electricity came after the war in 1945, I think. We had a bathroom with running water. The modern houses were being built on Station Road. My mother was friendly with Mr D who was a builder. He built two of them and came to live in one. The blacksmith from Silverdale came to live next door to him. They started the footing for the next two houses when Mr D died. My sister's fiancé was in the building trade. His firm made a bid for the footings and the next door plot of land. They bought it and built on it. We were interested in a modern house so we decided to support my sister's fiancé. We also loved the country. When they were sold, the houses cost £500. It was quite expensive at the time and we had to have a mortgage from a building society.

I loved every day in Keele.

Warrilow Collection *Keele University Library Archives*

The Workhouse at Thistleberry

Author's collection

The old workhouse in Highway Lane Keele, now a neat row of cottages

CHAPTER SIX
BUILDING UP KEELE

BEGINNINGS

I've lived in Keele Village for 44 years. My father was a miner in Silverdale and he was badly injured in 1910, down the mine. He had to walk with the aid of sticks and crutches all his life. I never knew him without sticks. He was about 30 when it happened and he lived until he was 84. His compensation was 14 shillings a week for a wife and five children. He became a member of the Friendly Society. He was a Trustee when he died. It was through him that all our family became members of the Odd Fellows, because of all the help they gave my father. In his day there was an accident a week in the mines, caused by the collapse of the roof. Compensation was meagre. After my father was injured he was in hospital for quite a long time. When he recovered he became a part-time insurance agent in Silverdale.

We came to Keele because we built four houses in Station Road - my brother and our works. We moved to Keele at the end of the War. I was based there during the War. I didn't go to fight because I was in a reserved occupation as a builder. I worked for the Admiralty on land ships at Clayton.

I went to a Council school and we left at 13. Mine was the first year to stay until 14. There was a benefactor in Silverdale, a Colonel Goodwin, and he paid for children to go from Silverdale to the High School. You could pay to go to Grammar School. A lot did. In 1923 I was lucky to get a job. I worked at the Co-op on deliveries. When I started I had to keep the brasses polished. I was there for about four years, then I went into the building trade at 18. My eldest brother was a builder's manager. In the 1930s there was high unemployment. But, in 1933 we became a limited company.

There wasn't a lot to do in Keele. It wasn't an outgoing village. The youngsters travelled on the railway to Silverdale for their entertainment. As a boy I had walked around Keele thousands of times, but I had never seen Keele Hall. Until the University came, it was always protected by gatekeepers, gamekeepers and woodland. You had to trespass to get to see the Hall. Miners with chest complaints walked around Keele to get fresh air. The famous walk from Silverdale was to walk out of the village up the Rosemary path and turn down Quarry Bank Road or Pepper Street. On lighter nights we went around Keele, down Two or Three Mile Lane to Whitmore. We passed the time walking and at evening classes at school.

THE WAY WE WERE

There was an annual show at Keele and the people of Silverdale came too. I knew of the Sneyd family, but I don't think they were well respected in Silverdale.

There were lots of little things written into the deeds of the properties on Keele Estate. You couldn't have a brick wall in front of your property. In a way, they were in advance of town planning. There were some deeds of a property in Silverdale which stipulated that the properties had to have sash windows. Also, there must have been someone on Keele Estate with a terrific interest in trees. I remember as a boy walking down Two Mile Lane and there was a big sign painted which said, *'Trees that are planted with knowledge and care, Are a national treasure ...'* I would be about seven then.

MAKING ENDS MEET

The Co-op started in a small way in Silverdale. You could go and have a week's groceries without paying immediately. There was also a good pawnbroker. You could put things in on Monday and take them out on Saturday.

We had a Victorian range with a coal fire and hearth and mantelpiece. At Christmas we hung our stockings on the mantelpiece and in them we'd find a piece of coal, an apple and an orange.

THE FRIENDLY SOCIETY

I believe they (The Odd Fellows) helped to fashion the Beveridge Plan for the Welfare State. The Society had a long experience of welfare. There were also the Forresters, the Shepherds and the Racobites - they didn't drink. Each year they had an annual procession. They would assemble at Keele Church with their banners and regalia and they would walk right through to Silverdale. Then they would have their annual feast. These societies had quite a hold on people. There was quite a discipline. People paid so much in to the society and if you were ill the society paid for the doctors' visits. If you didn't belong to a society it was terrible. There was the Workhouse, of course. That frightened people. There was a workhouse on the Cloughs in Thistleberry near Gallowstree Lane. I think by then the workhouse in Highway Lane at Keele had closed.

The Oddfellows started in Keele in the 18th Century but written records are only available from 1833 in the form of old Minute Books. The name of the Keele Lodge was 'the Good Samaritan'. There were two Lodge Rooms at Keele, one at the Crest and the other at the Sneyd Arms . In 1856 the Lodge was moved from Keele to Silverdale, to the Crown Inn in Crown Street. It joined up with the Lodge called 'The Royal'.

The Officials were elected democratically and their elections were formally recorded. The Lodge seemed to accept people of all ages. This is a list of some of the members who came from Keele:

Adam Mountford aged 20	Butcher of Keele
Thomas Pover aged 34	Tailor of Keele
Edward Hewitt	Tailor of Keele
S Dean aged 37	Collier of Keele
Rev G Styche aged 43	Clergyman of Keele
Thomas Steele aged 22	Blacksmith of Keele
Richard Bloore aged 23	The Yew Tree, Farmer
T Alman aged 30	Blacksmith of Keele
William Ellerton aged 29	Stonemason of Keele
Andrew Pepper aged 20	Sawyer of Keele
Henry Hemmings aged 21	Servant of Keele
John Tomlinson aged 24	Farmer of Keele
Holland Cooper aged 18	Joiner of Keele
George Stevenson aged 21	Shoemaker of Keele

The Lodges were established mainly to provide travel relief for those moving about the country to seek work. Expenses were calculated for bed and board on a daily basis. To gain entry to the Lodges, there was a universal, secret password.

The officers' names were painted on a board and there was a security box to house the rules and records of the Lodge. Indulgence in politics and religion was not allowed, neither were tobacco or alcohol. Discipline was strict and members could be expelled for bad behaviour. Those who joined wanted a better and more secure life. One of the many mottos of the Keele Lodge was 'Friendship, Love and Truth'. Anyone who didn't attend meetings was fined.

Members paid into a fund which helped widows and orphans (this particular fund was set up in Keele in 1837), the disabled, the sick and a surgeon was paid for his services to members. A payment of eight shillings was made to the long-term sick for a period of six months (this was then reduced to four shillings per week). A Funeral fund was also set up in 1833. The Lodge also compensated farmers who lost animals. In 1854 Keele Lodge set up a Patriotic Fund and most members contributed one shilling per meeting. Several members were hauled up before the Lodge to answer charges of 'disgraceful conduct' alleged against them.

A great deal of money was spent on funerals. Handkerchiefs with black borders, black funeral cards done in silk, illuminated clay pipes with tobacco would be produced for you. In the old days there was a Keele and Silverdale Burial Board. People from Silverdale had to be buried in Wolstanton. If you could afford it you were carried off in a coach and horses, otherwise it was on a trolley or on people's shoulders.

THE WAR YEARS

Someone was killed in Gallowstree Lane, I think. It was never discovered who did it. There were suspicions that it was a Cypriot (who was billeted up at Keele).

There was a Prisoner of War camp up at the Digness (where Steetley brick works is now). Some worked on the local farms. The prisoners were very friendly. One of them even married a local farmer's daughter. He was a very nice person. One, I think, became naturalised and the other still writes.

There were air raid wardens and first aid meetings. We had no street lights so everything was dark. We received evacuees who came to stay with families in Keele. I remember at least two at Keele. When the soldiers came they were stationed at Keele Hall. When this happened their wives had lodgings in Keele (village). Evelyn Laye stayed in Highway Lane because her husband was billeted at Keele Hall.

Author's collection

The Station Road houses as they are today - virtually unchanged since they were first constructed

CHAPTER SEVEN
HEALTH IN THE COMMUNITY

Health visitors came in because there wasn't any health care for children before the NHS. There was Parish Relief, but people had to pay for a doctor's visit. There was great opposition from the doctors when the NHS started up. They didn't like being told what to do. They thought they would lose their liberty.

There was a school clinic in Newcastle. Some of the doctors were very conscientious, others did just what they had to. We had a very good one, a Scot, whose father had been a miner so he sort of understood the people. He came to the clinic twice each week as we didn't have a full time doctor. The surgery used to be packed each week when this doctor came. When he came he would write a prescription for children who had been away from school for a day or so. Children weren't too well fed in those days. The mothers would take the prescription to the chemist and that saved a visit to the doctor. Prescriptions were free until the Health Act came in. When people could go to the doctor free of charge, the clinics closed. The doctor at our clinic wasn't supposed to give all these prescriptions out, but people just didn't have the money to pay the doctor.

I would get to the clinic at nine o'clock and mothers would already be there. They would say to me, 'They don't like that iron tonic, would you give it to them?' So, before I took my coat off, I used to put the little tots on the table and dose them with tonic and give them vitamin tablets.

There was a scarlet fever epidemic. You get a scarlet blush which doesn't last very long. I knew when I saw it. A child came up to the clinic. When I saw him I rang the doctor and he came over. In those days they took cases into the Isolation Hospital. There was a small one in Priory Road. We sent for the ambulance. We put him in a little room in the clinic that we had for infectious cases. The child had sat for about an hour in school before he came to us. No wonder infections spread.

We had two diphtheria cases. One child came up to the clinic in an awful state. He shouldn't have been out, but the family couldn't afford the doctor. You can smell a diphtheria case. The symptoms were a nasty rough, raw, throat. With complications it could be fatal. By 1938 diphtheria was a thing of the past. There was a lot of impetigo about. Now, with a dab of penicillin, it's gone.

When I nursed in Birmingham there were a lot of pneumonia cases. There was no penicillin so you waited nine days and you looked for the crisis. It came and the patient was better. The crisis came when the lung healed. We poulticed the patients with antiflogistine. It was like putty and it came in a tin. We put the tin in a saucepan and boiled it up. When it was nice and hot you spread it on a piece of lint and put it on the back and chest of the patient. We had to keep the patient's strength up with various broths and soft foods. They had to be kept as still as possible. That's all we were able to do. The warmth of the poultices helped. We gave injections of camphor oil every four hours. The patients had to be slept before the crisis because you couldn't sleep them through it. When they were pretty bad we'd give them an ounce of brandy every four hours. This meant that every two hours they had something. They would perspire an awful lot so they had to be sponged down. For those nine days you would go night and morning to nurse the patient.

I remember a little Italian boy I had to nurse through pneumonia. He lived in a little back street, it was cobbled, you know. The first visit I made was in the evening. We used to wear a white band on our backs. We were bike pushers in those days. I was riding my bike and trying to read the house numbers. There were two men and they said, 'This way, nurse'. They were waiting for me. You never got a bicycle pump stolen or anything like that. You could put your bike outside the door and it would be all right. The house was a council house and you weren't supposed to keep animals. With going for a few days I supposed they got used to me so one day when I went this cupboard was turned around and there was a monkey inside. It was the child's pet. 'You won't say anything', they said. 'It's none of my business,' I told them.

Diet was important. The poorest would have bread and jam and a cooked meal about three times a week. A normal diet would be meat, potatoes and vegetables - cabbage or carrots. There wasn't much variety. Because of poor infant health - rickets and that kind of thing - a special clinic was held in Newcastle to provide cheaper packets of Cow and Gate milk and vitamin supplements. A group of people voluntarily paid a midwife to come and talk to the mothers and to help once a week at this clinic. I came in 1935 but it was going a long time before that. We'd get about 70 in an afternoon. After a while the council took it over.

I remember one of the clinic attenders with a newish baby who hadn't been for a while. I went along and asked about the baby. The mother said it was asleep so I wasn't able to see it. A while later I went again. I insisted on seeing it. The mother said the baby was all right but it wasn't. It hadn't grown. She showed me the big bowl of milk she had to feed it. I told her to bring the baby to the clinic and informed the doctor. When the doctor examined the baby he eventually got it out of the mother that she had been feeding it pobs (bread and milk). The baby wasn't being starved but it was getting insufficient milk to grow. She couldn't afford the milk.

Before the War there was nowhere for premature babies to go. If there was a small baby we had to visit more often, keep an eye on them, keep them warm. We got some money together to make 'prem' baskets. The dressmaker we had made linings for the baskets with four pockets along the sides for hot water bottles. We loaned these out to the mothers. Prem. babies born at five pounds we would consider to be all right.

The NSPCC was going then and we used to inform them ourselves if children were being mistreated. There weren't many cases. I remember only one.

Some mothers didn't have night dresses or layettes so we got some of these too. They could be loaned out for five shillings. We would take the mothers on an outing. It would be the only one some of them had all year. We'd collect all year for this.

Author's collection

The Villa as it is today - now the infamous Conference Centre

Author's collection

Brooklands today

CHAPTER EIGHT
LIFE IN THE FASTER LANE

BEGINNINGS

I was born in April 1902 in Liverpool Road, Newcastle. When I was two we came to Poolfield Avenue. My father's work was in Newcastle. My father was a wholesale grocer so he used to go around the farms buying cheese so we used to go with him in the car. My father's was one of the first cars in Newcastle. My father's brother was the first. My father's was an open car and I think you got in through the back, not the side door. Before he had a car he had a high cart and he used to drive a pony and trap. I occasionally went with him, sitting side by side or back to back. If it rained we just got wet. We kept the horses at the warehouse. We had stables there.

Newcastle was quiet and peaceful. We walked in those days. We had to walk. We didn't think of riding until we had a bicycle. When we first went to school we'd walk backwards and forwards, go home for lunch and back again. And then when I went to the Orme School, for the first few years I walked. When I did have a bicycle that was a bit easier. The roads were rough. Poolfield Avenue wasn't tarmacced at all. It was all horses and carts, there were very few cars then. He had quite a big staff - travellers and people working in the warehouse. His name was Ernest Butterworth and my brothers used to get their legs pulled. People would say, 'How much is butter worth today?' I was glad to change it. Such a long name, such a lot to write.

We had two servants and they lived in the house. One did the cooking and the cleaning and the other looked after us children. They used the big range in the kitchen - coal-fired. We had a woman to come in on Mondays to do the washing. We had a coal fire in the scullery to get the water hot. We had tubs and a dolly-peg and bunged it up and down, and a great big wringer with wooden rollers. Wash-day was a great day because there was so much washing with five children. There was a big rack in the kitchen from the ceiling and two clothes horses as well - all wooden. The irons had to be heated in front of the fire. Get the fire red hot, and place the irons in front of the fire. There were no electric irons then. When we got older we did a bit but there was no need with the servants there.

We had a music teacher who came to the house. There were five of us and we all, unfortunately, learned to play the piano. My father and mother were very musical. My father was a member of the North Staffordshire Operatic Society. The house was full of music. Everybody sang except me. I had to accompany them when I was older. We had two pianos - one in the dining room and another in the drawing room, a grand one. My father was very proud of that. 'You mustn't let the sun get at it', he'd say. So the curtains were drawn at the slightest bit of sun.

I went to Miss Swann's little Private School. It isn't there any more. There were three Miss Swanns who kept the school - Helena, Louise and Jessie. We used to go to an upstairs room for lessons and we sat in two rows of desks. Then we'd go downstairs for a glass of milk and play in the backyard. I remember being chased around the backyard by one of the Mellard boys. He had a long strip of licorice and he made me cry. Miss Swan taught us to do a bit of needlework downstairs. Once a week we went up to the St George's Institute - it's not there now - to march around and do drill. There wasn't a cane but I suppose the teachers were strict. We didn't wear a uniform. It was a Dame school. We paid to go and we all went down there in turn. Lots of my friends went there.

I didn't pass the scholarship, I wasn't clever enough so we had to pay to go to the High School. I went to the Orme Girls' School. I think it was about three guineas a term and my father thought, 'What a lot of money!' I liked Art and Games. I couldn't bear Maths, I was hopeless at it. I did manage to pass the Senior Cambridge. I was good at French and German so they helped push me through. I left school when I was seventeen, and I went to work in a bank.

THE WORLD OF WORK

My eldest sister was in the bank. She left to get married. I wanted to take up languages but my father thought 'Your sister's leaving the bank so you can take her place'. It was the National Provincial then, now it's the National Westminster, in Tunstall. I was there for ten years and I hated it. We used to go from Poolfield Avenue to Tunstall by bus or tram. It took so long to get there. When the weather was nice a friend and I used to cycle and think nothing of it. We enjoyed it, it was nice exercise when you'd been sitting in the bank all day. Maths wasn't necessary. It was a case of copying cheques and so on and I could add up. There were no machines at all so we had to add up whole rows of figures in our heads. I became good at it.

I was 28 when I got married. I met my husband through my brother. They were at the Orme Boys' School together. He lived in Silverdale. My first home was in Brooklands in Keele Road. My husband's people lived in Keele. We looked all around and decided to rent a house down there in 1930. We moved into the Villa in 1940. My father-in-law was a Manager at Silverdale Colliery and he had moved into the Villa in the 1920s. The Villa belonged to Keele Estate. We knew Colonel Sneyd. When my father-in-law died in 1939 Colonel Sneyd asked my husband if he would like to move into the Villa, because he used to work on Keele Estate as a consultant mining engineer. We agreed. Colonel Sneyd came to look at it and agreed that it should be modernised for us. So we gutted it, modernised it and moved in in June 1940. It was just before Dunkirk when the troops were moving into the village and taking over everything that was empty.

GETTING STARTED

The Villa was a family house. We made the kitchen into a dining room and upstairs we had a bathroom altered. We kept logs and coal and the cat in the backyard. We left the Villa in 1963 when we built a house in Highway Lane. When Keele Estate was sold we bought the Villa. Until then we had rented it. We had an allotment up by the church and a nice garden around the Villa itself. We didn't grow vegetables at the Villa because we had the allotment. It was sold for building eventually. There were some fruit trees at the Villa and the tennis court, of course. We had some lovely tennis parties there. We used to dance and take up the carpet in the big room and dance to the gramophone. We had someone to come in to help and we had a gardener to look after things.

HEALTH CARE

I had help when my daughter was born. A maternity nurse came for six weeks. She was a little girl from nearby who came to live in and to help. It was usual to have a maternity nurse. She looked after me and the baby. You mustn't put your feet to ground for a fortnight, then you were allowed to get up. The nurse looked after the baby, did the baby's washing and generally helped. I had the baby at home. Most people did that. We paid for a nurse. We had to pay for the doctor. We had a doctor from Newcastle who used to come out to Keele.

My first accident was when I had my head cut open at Hayfield. The people at Poolfield House were making hay. There was me and three other children and we went to play in the pony and trap. Something startled the pony and he tipped us all out into the hedge. That was the first thing I remember in life, having my head stitched up by the doctor.

We didn't have a play pen in those days. I was six when my sister was born. She was in a big wooden box and I was told not to pick her up. Of course, one day I picked her up, couldn't manage it properly so I dropped her. I was sent upstairs to the back bedroom without any supper that day. She survived.

RECREATION

Poolfield Avenue was just fields all around. The road surface was rough and we used to play hop-scotch in the road. We'd draw the lines on the rough road. We used to play games like Ludo and Snakes and Ladders. My older brother had a fret-work machine and he used to make all kinds of fret-work in the shed in the garden. I was very fond of dolls.

We used to go across the road into the fields, where there was a pond where we used to catch jack sharps and frogs' spawn. We brought it home and eventually it hatched out. We kept all kinds of things - mice, rats and silk worms. The person next door showed us how to look after them. I can't remember what we fed them on.

We played games in the garden. The big cupboard was in the back hall. We used to have a table leaf wedged up against the drawers and we'd slide up and down it. In the winter we had snowballs and tobogganing in the fields at the back of Orme Road. We had a tin tray and we used to go sliding down there.

We'd get up plays, acting Beauty and the Beast. We gave a trial performance in the fields opposite. We needed a piano, so we had a piano there. I don't know if it was one of ours. Transporting it there, it fell off the trolley. We did, eventually, give a performance. My sister was Beauty and I was the Beast. We made our own amusements. There was no TV or radio then.

We went to Rhyl, that was the nearest sea-side. I remember going for a picnic and we walked to Heighley Castle and back home again. I was about twelve, perhaps. Then we walked to Beech Caves, past Clayton. Some went on bicycles, some walked. Coming back I had a lift on the step of someone's bicycle and I fell off and knocked a bit of my front tooth out. We visited Keele when we went for walks. We walked around the Two-Mile Lane into Keele. I didn't know anyone in Keele when I was a child. We made our own amusements.

We spent the evenings playing games. We had to practice a lot. My father was upstairs and we'd be practising down below and he'd thump the boards if we played a wrong note.

We didn't have a lot of pocket money, so if we couldn't afford to buy cards we made our own. We used to play Double Demon where you each had a pack of cards. There was another game where you bought and sold cereals. We had a penny a week and we saved it. We didn't do jobs in the house to earn money.

Before the War they used to have a New Year's Eve dance at Keele Hall. It was lovely - huge Christmas tree, lots of villagers and people from round about went. I think we must have subscribed something because there was a raffle and we had presents from the tree. Colonel Sneyd was very good looking and he had a very attractive second wife. They weren't in the Hall long after we moved.

My father-in-law used to go to the Reading Room when he lived at the Villa.

My husband had a ciné camera so he used to give shows there. We would ciné Charlie Chaplin films. A lot of villagers came to that. We just did it for entertainment. There wasn't much you could do during the War.

We used to go to the Congregational Chapel. We were chapel people but we changed. For some reason we decided to go to church and I remember being christened when I was six in St Giles' Church.

CHRISTMAS CHEER

We saved up to buy Christmas presents - a packet of boot laces, perhaps or a pen and pencil. Ordinary little presents. Then at Christmas we hung a stocking up. It usually had a new penny in it, an orange or a chocolate model. That was put at the end of the bed and after breakfast we had our proper or big present. I liked dolls. We had books and clothes, probably.

On Christmas Day we went to St Giles' Church. My younger brother was the soprano soloist in the choir. We always had plum pudding, turkey and mince pies. We had a Christmas tree and crackers. We didn't put up the Christmas cards like they do now. We had holly on the pictures and the decorations we made ourselves. I can't remember the Christmas tree.

At Christmas time my father always went to the Workhouse in Thistleberry. He used to carve the joint for the inmates and then come back to us for our turkey. We used to visit the people at the Workhouse. There was a long room we went in. The men were down one side and the women on the other. There was a concert on Christmas night. We joined in the singing and went for refreshments afterwards with the Workmaster and his wife. My father was friendly with the Master and he was a musician so he got a concert party going. That's why we used to go there and join in. We went until it was pulled down. Houses were put there. Jenkinson's had a big nursery there and we went up and ran around the gardens and nurseries.

THE WAR YEARS

During the war we had Lord and Lady Kildare parked on us for a short time. The troops were billeted at Keele. I felt as if I was in a hotel. They just sort of took over the house and I felt a stranger in my own home. We didn't have them for long, fortunately.

The Reading Room was taken over by an Officers' Mess and they came across to the Villa for baths. They used to pop in and have musical evenings with us. It was very interesting. We met all kinds of nationalities who used to come in from the camp. Americans and Cypriots were based at Keele. My children used to go and have a chat with them. They were given lots of sweets and chocolate that we couldn't get. They enjoyed that. We didn't see much of the POWs. I didn't meet any of them.

The Misses Harrisons from Maer Hall opened a canteen for the troops in the Assembly Rooms. Some of us went to help behind the counter. Miss Harrison was very strict and she would say ' You must not mix with the troops'. We had to stay that side of the counter. We sold cigarettes and tea. One soldier came and asked if we had any 'Pliars'. I didn't know what he meant. It was Players cigarettes.

We had concert parties during the war in the Assembly Rooms. We did Cinderella. Mr Glover was one of the Ugly sisters. My sister and I were in it. Janet Locker was Buttons. All the villagers came. Perhaps some troops came, I can't remember. The WI made masses of jam and we had a knitting circle for the troops and so on.

I remember Evelyn Laye. She would walk around the village looking very attractive.

My husband was in charge of the Special Constables at Audley so he had to go out quite often in the evenings. We had cellars in the Villa with bunks so we went down there when there was a warning. I would rather have stayed in bed up here but I had to go down because of the children. What worried me more than the bombs was the frog in the cellar!

There was bombing along Keele Road, to a row of houses along the the top. I don't know if it was a direct hit, but someone was killed.

My sister worked in the basement of Keele Hall as a volunteer, making something, I don't know what. Women had to do something during the War. You were exempted if you had a family. People from the village did go to fight.

THE WAY WE WERE

In the 1930s the village was so peaceful. Not much traffic. Both my children were born by lamplight. We had no gas or electricity at Brooklands. Towards the end we had a motor fixed up in the shed in the garden to make electricity for the house. We couldn't have a Hoover or anything, just light. We had coal fires everywhere. It was cold but we didn't mind. It was beautiful there, all open at the back until they built the tile works. We used Aladdin lamps but if you left them on too long they would smoke. Brooklands had a bathroom downstairs, four bedrooms and a box room.

There was only a little shop at Keele and a post office where the Middle House is now. You would ring a bell and the post mistress would come from the back to serve you. Newcastle was quiet and peaceful too. You could go to town and meet everybody who knew you.

I was a founder member of the WI. The only one who is still a member. I took over from Mrs Hollinshead, the first President in 1938. We started in the school and held our first meeting sitting in the children's desks. We had all kinds of classes and parties for the children. The subscription was five shillings. We had good fun and we did lots of good work during the War. I was President until 1952.

At first, we thought the University coming was a good idea. We didn't know what would become of the Estate, but a University sounded a good idea at the time. We never thought it would grow and come into the village as it has. We felt that if it hadn't got into the Hawthorns it wouldn't have come into the village so much. There wasn't much protest over the Hawthorns - not as much as over the Conference Centre!

It has found work for lots of people.

Courtesy H Lafford

The glamourous Evelyn Laye

Interlude: THE KEELE WI

The WI was started in Canada in 1897 by Adelaide Fudless after the death of one of her children, she felt, largely, through her own ignorance. It started in a pub in the Toronto area. I have been to the very village and had refreshments in the very place! The first WI in the UK was formed in 1915.

In 1932 the first WI meeting at Keele was held and Mrs Hollinshead was elected President. Mrs Hollinshead was always interested in Keele because of her father, Michael Brown, who was the tenant of Bush Farm, Silverdale, which belonged to the Sneyd Estate. Through her father she met Daniel Hollinshead. He was Director of the mine. He was also organist at Keele Parish Church and he also used to organise music at Keele Hall during the stay of the Grand Duke Michael of Russia. Edward VII was among the guests who were entertained.

I joined the WI just before 1950 when Doris Bates was President. Mabel Richards was President in 1953 and Mrs Lindsay was Secretary. Anybody could join, you didn't have to be married. We were proposed and seconded in order to join. Keele had about 30 members at the time. It did go up to about 60 once but it was usually kept at 40/50. It's at about 45 just now.

We started off with a business meeting which we tried to keep as short as possible. In those days we had a newsletter from Stafford. We then had a speaker and refreshments. Then and only until the last few years we had a social half hour and a competition. The social half hour has gone into abeyance because people got tired of playing games. People didn't always take part and there was no time. We still have a competition. We finished at about nine o'clock. The village was dark then, there were no lights.

The first committee meeting was held in the school room and attended by Mrs Strachan, the County Secretary, Mrs Bates, Mrs Bloor, Mrs Hollinshead, Mrs Bennett, Mrs Lawton, Mrs Sutherton, Miss Tomkins, Miss Grimwood, Miss Johnson, Miss Keeny was Secretary. 'Mrs Sneyd (she was there) owing to being away from the village a great deal would probably not be able to attend many meetings ... Mrs Strachan went on to explain the duties of the committee and gave the name of several lecturers ... the lectures to be held on the first Wednesday of each month at seven o'clock in the evening. Miss Tennant the Headmistress from the school was co-opted onto the committee.'

A list of speakers was sent from Stafford each year. We asked members for ideas and suggestions and then we'd hunt around for speakers. The Committee arranged the programme and got the speaker. I think we're a bit more ambitious now. In the past it was more cake icing, sewing, more village activities. Now we have lectures on nuclear energy, badger protection, water divining, drug abuse and bells and bell-ringing. We're not supposed to be political or sectarian. We have tried to keep apace of modern times.

We still sing Jerusalem at the beginning of every meeting. We should sing 'The Queen' at the end. A lot of WIs still do, but we found that a lot of people started slipping away.

We had a choir and practised in the village hall. We took part in the music section - there was a WI section - and we came second with 'All in the April Evening'. We sang for the blind once, at Fenton. Janet Locker and I were the smallest so we stood in the front. I watched the audience. I can feel it now, on their faces, they were singing it!

For the first few years we gave the children a Christmas party in the Reading Room. This little room was very popular. There was a gas ring and a loo at the bottom of the garden. There was just a bowl to wash up in. Those were the days!

The AGM of the WI was held in the Albert Hall every year. We would be asked for resolutions beforehand. Once a resolution is passed it goes to the various government departments to be followed up. We're assured of that.

I went to the Albert Hall as a delegate. I took the seven o'clock train from Crewe and another train to the Albert Hall. Had a wonderful time, came out of the Albert Hall, caught the train back to Stoke. A friend was on the train and gave me a lift back to Keele. I arrived home, put my things down and as it was a Wednesday went to the WI meeting and gave my report to the members, straight off the cuff. Now, can you beat that?

The choir won a shield. We came second in Road Safety and in 1937 we were awarded the first class certificate for crochet. Mrs Bedson had a gorgeous nightie. She showed this nightie at every show. Mrs Bailey was mostly the cook but Mrs Bedson was most certainly crochet and handicrafts.

The WI was partly educational. One of their main aims was the further education of country women in homecraft. Now it's geared to recording and passing on information for the Archives. The most recent survey is the Staffordshire Village Book (recently published). Some villages had two pages, Keele had just a paragraph - with a picture of Ipstones above it! I went to the County meeting and I said 'I'll be blowed!' The publisher was there and he said all the material was good but he had to bear in mind the cost. The yew tree would have looked good at the head of our paragraph.

In 1982 we did the Churchyard Survey. It was done for a competition, but it was done all over the country - and before the churchyard was tidied up too! We had a big base map provided by Mr Hemmings who was an architect, and we divided it up into eight divisions. In twos and threes we covered each section. We actually recorded the tomb stones as they stood. There were some gorgeous inscriptions.

We did a lot of jam making during the war. We still do it. There was a canning machine in the Reading Room. It was part of the war effort, I think. We did knitting. I remember presenting my husband with a long pair of socks. There was tree planting. The WI had a show with vegetables and flowers. Mrs A and I took the most gorgeous peas and broad beans. 'Have you grown these yourself?' they said. 'No', we replied. 'Oh! Then you're disqualified!' Mrs Bates had a garden meeting and we had country dancing.

The Yoga, dressmaking and floral art/arranging are all WI inspired. Years ago we had lamp shade and rug making. I made a stool and there was basket making and raffia. The first class I remember was glove making.

When Mrs Mary Stewart was President (1959 - 1974) that was the heyday for the WI.

Past Presidents:

1932 - 1939	Mrs D E Hollinshead
1939 - 1946	Mrs C P Bates
1946 - 1948	Miss J H Ramsbottam
1948 - 1953	Mrs C P Bates
1953 - 1956	Mrs M Richards
1956 - 1959	Mrs A McPhail
1959 - 1974	Mrs Mary Stewart
1974 - 1988	Mrs M Jackson
1988 -	Mrs J Jervis

Below stairs - servants at work in the vast kitchens of Keele Hall

Keele University Library Archives

CHAPTER NINE
IN SERVICE

I was born in 1924 at Paddocks Farm. I lived in the Botheys. Father worked in the gardens for Keele Estate and then came to live in the village. We used to go to live-in at the Clock House - father, mother and myself. Colonel Sneyd lived in a place called Codford - the Grange. He used to come up several times in the year to wind up the Estate business. We used to go to live-in for a week or however long he stayed, because mum used to cook for them. That was a regular thing. My father would come home and say, 'The Colonel's coming'. And we used to go up. We lived in the servants' quarters with the butler, the housemaid and the parlour maid.

She was a lovely cook, mum was. The Colonel used to have it done in the old-fashioned way - with the butler and the footman. The butler was a gentleman called Mr Sigmund. He had two daughters and they also lived at the Clock House. He would be on duty to take the food in. The Colonel used to come into the Clock House in the morning, into the servants' quarters into the back kitchen where there was a big black range to order dinner for the night. I was only young. He (Colonel Sneyd) used to pass around and I always remember him as a gentleman with a trilby and plus fours. His wife was much younger, but very nice. They were very happy. She was Doris Miller - a Harley Street specialist's daughter.

They would have pheasant and all this sort of thing caught on the estate, lovely vegetables, and thin sandwiches in the afternoon, cut for tea, cucumber sandwiches. Mum used to cook for all the guests who came, and then all the servants had to be fed as well. He did a lot of entertaining in those days. We didn't see the visitors who came. They'd be at the other end. The Hall was closed up except for Christmas time. Some people called Kerry lived there - they were the caretakers.

The last time we went to the Clock House was just before War broke out in 1939. Then Colonel Sneyd died, then his heir died. It made double death duties. That was when there was a big upheaval, when all his things were sold. Like my father, a lot of the estate men didn't know what would happen. A lot lost their jobs. Fortunately, father got a job working up at the college as ground staff. When Colonel Sneyd died everything was at sixes and sevens. The houses in the village were being sold and people wondered if they would be able to buy their homes. It was a big worry in those days. Everyone that could, bought them. People didn't want to leave Keele. I was glad we stayed on. We were living in this cottage and we were able to buy it after a while.

I went to Keele School from the Clock House. We had two teachers and about 100 children, in two class rooms. Our head teacher was a Miss Tennant from Newcastle and she used to bring children from Newcastle. The smallest children were in one room and the older ones in the other. We had an old-fashioned stove with coke in it. We had the cane - it had to come out occasionally, you know. We did English, reading, and sewing. School wasn't one of my favourite places.

We had to assemble and we had prayers and the register. If you were late you had a red mark. We went on nature walks and the Vicar used to come to see us. Colonel Sneyd and his wife came to see us at times.

THE WORLD OF WORK
Some who left school went on to higher education, but when you were 14 you left school and got yourself ready for work. You were expected to help out in the home.

I left school in 1939. I was fourteen. I didn't go to secondary school. I went to work in Enderley Mills. I got 6/6d a week. Jobs were hard to come by then. I'd go off at twenty-five past seven of a morning on the bus, go to the mills and come home just after six o'clock in the evening. The War had just started so the air-raid sirens would go off. It was a case of getting down into the cellar. It wasn't very nice.

My father was made redundant towards 1950 when the Estate finished. The College came in 1950 and my father worked in Lady Leonard-Jones' garden. Delightful couple! Father loved that, doing the Principal's garden. I worked at Enderley Mills until 1951. I would be 23 or 24. I started at the refectory at the college on 15 May 1951. It had been going for twelve months and there were just 150 students. I worked there until 1961 - exactly ten years. My father was taken very poorly so I decided to give up work to help mum. When dad died in the summer of that year, Miss Rolfe, who was the Head Bursar, asked Mrs A, who was the caretaker at the Hawthorns, what I was doing. She asked me if I'd take on Unit 2 and come back to the College to work. I started at the Hawthorns on 1 January 1962 and I worked there as a cleaner until 1982 when I retired.

The University coming was a shock. From just being a country village, suddenly there was going to be all those people around. And yet, it hasn't made that much of a difference. Some people didn't like the idea of the university, but I thought it was all right. It found us work near home instead of having to travel on the bus. I preferred it much more to Enderley Mills. As a country girl, the mill didn't appeal to me at all. But you couldn't be choosy at that time.

I was interviewed by Miss Rolfe, in Keele Hall, down in the basement. I started that afternoon. I got 1/9d an hour. We clocked in at half past two in the afternoon and we worked until nine at night. There was only one refectory then. We worked until much later if there was a dinner on - sometimes until midnight. Our supervisor, Miss Hawthorn, had this little old car and when I had to stay she used to drop me off in the village. She parked it by the pillar box, on the corner by the Chapel. To start it up she would get in and say to me, 'Push now, Molly', and I'd have to push it down the little embankment. She'd say, 'It's going now, and I'd have to dash to get in before it stopped again. She'd drop me in the village and I'd get out quick, and shut the door, so she could get off to Newcastle.

The following week we'd be on days - seven in the morning until 2.30 in the afternoon. Two evenings a week we'd have to go back for dinners. The work was general cleaning in the dining room area. We had to keep the floors swept and polished and the refectory tables clean. On days, we did breakfasts and lunches. There was a big dishwasher in the Brewhouse, but we had to wipe them. One week we were wiping silver, another we were cleaning trays and another serving on High Table. It was a different job every week. When we were on evenings a bus picked us up at the top of the village. There were two buses - one was driven by Mr Whieldon, who lived on the campus, and the other by Mr Watkins, who lived in the village. We were brought back to the top of the village at night.

On Sundays, Miss Hawthorn would pick me up at seven in the morning and we had to get the tables ready for breakfast. I put the marmalade and the cruets on the table. The other staff came in at eight o'clock. There was only one girl living in, an Irish girl. I used to go back on a Sunday evening for High Table. There would be about 22 eating. They would have a cold meal. I had to clear away afterwards and lay up ready for breakfast. We were paid a little bit extra for going back in the evenings. By the time I left I was getting nearly £4 a week, which was quite good in 1961. We had our food and our overalls free. We had white overalls and turbans, but for special dinners in the evening we wore black.

It was full time work. We had to wait on 24 tables. I'd never done it before in my life and on the first night we were short staffed, so I had to start. I took all the soup around, then all the vegetables. I remember one night, a friend and me were doing High Table and we got into an awful muddle. I accidentally lifted the wrong tureen off and instead of giving them soup, we were giving them gravy. I said, 'Edith, whatever shall we do? We're giving them all gravy!' She said, 'We've started so we shall have to go on. I hope Miss Rolfe doesn't find out!' We got away with it. They didn't notice they were eating gravy. The only thing was, we had to get rid of the soup before the chefs found out. We put it down the sink to hide our guilt!

Miss Rolfe lived right up in the Hall, in a wing on her own. I remember this big bedroom and this big kitchenette. If it was breakfast, you'd get right to the top and think, 'For goodness' sake, I haven't put the marmalade on!' And down again you went. I'd knock on her door and say, 'Good Morning'. She was so pleased. She was a single lady and always worrying about everyone else. She hadn't been retired five minutes before she died.

We had a lady, come to help Miss Rolfe. She didn't half give us the works. You'd be on the hot plates at ten past seven of a morning, imagine how you were feeling, and just as we'd finished Miss C would come in and say, 'Who's idle?' and we'd all have to pretend to be doing something - but you didn't know what to do! I remember thinking, 'I hope she doesn't ask me to make those horrible butter curl things'. I used to hate it!

Sir John and Lady Leonard-Jones used to do a lot of entertaining in the Clock House. I went along to help. We used to get ten shillings. It was an awful lot of money. She was very appreciative of us doing it and she would write us (thank you) notes. If she didn't see you afterwards, she would bring it down to the refectory.

I liked it best when I was serving the food to the students. The first students were lovely. They were quite young. You could have a quick word with them. Once I was caught. For dessert, they usually had an apple, a pear or an orange. I didn't realise the supervisor was behind me. This student said, 'Can I have a pear as well?' I said, 'Be careful, get it quick and I won't be looking'. The supervisor came up and touched my shoulder and said, 'You know better than that. They're only to have one piece of fruit. Don't ever do that again!'

They had soup and a good meal at lunchtime and a good hot meal at night. I agreed with them when they said there was a lot of stodge. I think they would have preferred a high tea in the evening. We wouldn't dream of having two hot meals a day. They used to have a lot of this roly-poly pudding.

The students had their gowns on for the evening meal. The staff ate with them at the High Table. I was amazed at the size of it, it was huge. They used to eat a lot of this jugged hare. The students would have pie or something. There was wine.

We used to do the afternoon teas in the Senior Common Room. There were cakes, little sandwiches and tea. The lecturers and professors came in at 2.30 and we served them. It wasn't free, I'd have to go up with the cash box.

We had the all-night Balls when Princess Margaret came. We went on at ten in the evening and worked through until six the next morning, because we had to do the breakfasts. Graduation was another busy time.

I waited on Princess Margaret, one time. I felt very honoured. I was very nervous. Two of us were picked who had been there the longest. Sitting with Princess Margaret was the Reverend Horwood - a very nice old gentleman. She really put you at your ease. You just had to serve her and call her ma'am. She was no trouble at all. We were given special instructions and by Jove, we had to be very much on the ball.

One time we had her for tea in Keele Hall refectory. It was a very big occasion. They put all this lovely food on and do you know what she asked for? A match to light her cigarette. She has tea without milk, lemon tea. She was really very nice. I always felt a bit sad for her.

RECREATION

The concert parties were mostly held here - where the Arts Umbrella used to be, through the back doors on Quarry Bank Road. My uncle and Percy Jackson did a lot of work on the electrics.

They were both electricians in the pit.

The concert parties were just like a social evening. One year we did Little Red Riding Hood. Mrs Challinor as the Grandmother, and I was Little Red Riding Hood. We won a little dish for that. I've still got it. Mr Glover was involved. He was a good turn. He did a bit of singing. The young and the old used to take part.

Mrs Jackson did plays there. I remember tap dancing. I was in my early teens and I was in a tap-dancing group. I remember wearing this short dress and these tap shoes. We thought we were the bees knees. We had dances there during the War. I'd be 16 or 17. Mr Bewes would come from Burslem with his radiogram. The troops were invited and it was 6d. They had whist drives too. Lots of village people used to go.

Every year we had a Show at Keele on the fields near Holly Lodge. It was the highlight of the year, Keele Show. Big marquees were put up and it was all open. It was always held on the first Tuesday in August. I don't know why. I was in the Rose Queen retinue. We had these white dresses with red sashes, and we walked in the procession carrying her train. Dad entered a lot of stuff out of his garden. We had a big garden. He won the silver cup for the best garden. He worked very hard on it, it was his life. On the cup it says, 'The Coronation Cup, Keele Show 1937. Presented by Colonel Sneyd ......for the most productive garden'. There was a lot of competition. I'm so proud of that cup.

Mum and Dad were always up for the whole night before the Show getting everything ready - vegetables, flowers. The peas had to be snipped off so that they weren't marked. We had to put the pansies in boxes. Our sitting room was full of stuff. We ate it all afterwards.

THE WAR YEARS

The Hall was used by the troops. They were billeted there. They used to march them up the road and you could hear the steady beat of them walking. We had Americans, and German prisoners of war. They were stationed all around. A lot went to the Digness Tileries (the German POWs). There were look-out points from the Dunge Wood and our soldiers had to keep an eye on them. There were big ovens there, you know, where they baked the tiles. There was a big upset when they came because, naturally, they thought they were going to be put in those ovens as they had done (to the Jews) in Germany!

You didn't see a lot of the troops, only when they were marching up and down. At one time there were some Cypriots here. One came around selling his shoes to make some money. It was a bit disturbing in those days. He was trying to make us understand what he wanted, but we couldn't.

Life wasn't the same. People from school were going out and getting killed. There were the air raids and bombers coming over. There were some nights when it was very frightening. We used to assemble in the cellar of the Smithy with my grandmother who was blind and we stayed there until the all-clear.

Someone was murdered in Gallowstree Lane - it was only a lane along there with woods and trees. It was very disturbing. People were very worried and upset about it. It was a woman from Newcastle area that was murdered. I thought it was a Cypriot soldier that was murdered.

THE WAY WE WERE

Keele was extremely quiet, mostly horses and carts. Then the odd car started coming out. We used to play hop-scotch in the road and there was no trouble being there. I was working (1939) and the buses had already started - Crosville. It cost 2d to go into Newcastle. It was a bumpy ride. There were big potholes and cobbles. They've improved the roads since then. But no-one seemed to bother. There were quite a lot of bicycles, people rode horses and there were a lot of horses and carts.

When we came to this cottage, gas had come out but the gentleman who lived here wouldn't have it in because he would have had to have the garden path up. So we had oil lamps. We had gas later, but we didn't have electricity until the late 1960s.

The Middle House used to be the old post office and my auntie and uncle kept it - Mr and Mrs Askey. You went in through the porch where there was a big, high counter. The room that goes into the garden (on the right hand side of the house) was the Reading Room. My father used to go there to read. We had little functions in there. I had my 21st birthday party in there. The WI met in there, all sorts of things.

The Hall drive I remember very well. There was just road enough for a horse and cart, with a row of trees on either side. Where the university buildings are now was all open fields. Very quiet.

Mr Goodwin the Estate Agent used to live in Keele Lodge. My auntie and uncle lived in Drive Lodge - Mr and Mrs Podmore. He was the blacksmith, you know. The blacksmith's shop was under the flat in Highway Lane. That's where my uncle would shoe the horses. He had a young man from Silverdale who helped him. It was a full time job with all them horses.

When the Hawthorns Block went up (in the village) some people thought it was terrible. In fact, I miss the students when they go (on vacation). It's nice to have these young people about and they don't make a nuisance the way they do in towns. I think we've been very lucky. They all speak to you and they come to church. We had a party with them last week.

There were a lot of tramps. They used to come and knock on the door, bring an old can and perhaps ask for water and a bit of bread. We had gypsies that went down the lane in their old fashioned caravans. A lot of gypsies. They stayed down in Dunge Wood. We never had any fear of them. They didn't frighten the children or anything.

There was the old workhouse on Keele Road (where the home for old people is now at Thistleberry) and some of the tramps used to stay there. They would stop off at night and then walk on the next day.

Keele University Library Archives

Keele Hall servants above stairs.

Off the Record

Princess Margaret, watched by
Detective Alf Robbins, seen in
the centre background

Courtesy Mr A Robbins

Keele University Library Archives

The view down Lime Avenue - said to be a favourite of Princess Margaret's, seen from her
bedroom window when staying at Keele

CHAPTER TEN
A POLICEMAN'S LOT

BEGINNINGS

I was born in 1912. I'm a Black Countryman from Wolverhampton and proud of it. I was from a working class family and I had to work hard until I was 21. Unemployment was worse than it is today. I applied to join the Police Force. I didn't think I was cut out to be a policeman, but I applied along with many other jobs. I turned out to be successful and at 21 I left the Black Country and came up to North Staffordshire as a young constable. I remained up here ever since. I was stationed in the Leek Moorlands for the first part of my career. I got into the CID and I moved on when I was promoted to Sergeant at Stone.

It was whilst I was at Stone in 1950 that I first became associated with Keele. When the University College of North Staffordshire first came into being I was told that I had to go up there and look around - for security purposes. Although it was a long way off, Keele came under Stone. The Superintendent at Stone - Mr Crook, not a very good name for a policeman - told me I had to go up to Keele and find out all about it. I continued my connection with Keele until I retired.

THE WORLD OF WORK

My duties were to look at security. Lord Lindsay of Birker was the first Principal. He was a very forthright gentleman. Then Princess Margaret came on the scene. I went up in 1951 when the Queen Mother planted the tree near to the Hall, not far from where the fountain is today. It was a very pleasant occasion. Although it was open to the public it was mainly village people that went. There weren't many there. My boss came with me and we worked together.

I was the arm of the police intelligence. The Head Porter kept his ear to the ground. If he heard anything, I would be the first to know. He would contact me straightaway. If there was any doubt about anyone, we could find out, in a secret manner, about them - not that there were any. I would go to the Hawthorns and the Sneyd Arms. I would have a drink with some of the members of staff. We confided in each other over a drink and that's how we used to go on.

When Princess Margaret came, security of the Royal Party was a very important job. The Princess would stay in the Clock House. She had a room on the first floor which overlooked the Avenue down towards the lodge. Beautiful old trees. She loved it. She chose that room and she had that room. Our job was to make sure that the property was secure and that there were no items of an offensive nature hidden in cars or anything like that. We used to go through the buildings to make sure that everything was all right before she entered upon it. Whilst she was there, a policeman was on duty day and night until she left. Anyone could have entered on the grounds at that time.

We had to service the Hall itself and the Senior Common Room and such places where they had the Ball, before she arrived. On one occasion, much to our surprise, we found in a wall cupboard, in the Senior Common Room, a double-barrelled shot-gun. There was no ulterior motive. It was quite innocent and belonged to someone in the University. It was promptly removed to a safer place. I don't know if it was loaded. But, there again, there might have been some connection with some ill intent, so we did the right thing and removed it. That's the sort of check we had to make.

I liaised with Chief Inspector F G Crocker - he was the personal detective of Princess Margaret. He had accommodation in Kensington Palace and a private flat in London. He was a single man and I think he was chosen for her. He was a very smart gentleman. He was with her for a long time. He was a tall, dark and handsome gentleman and I got on very well with him.

The Evening Sentinel

When Princess Margaret was not fulfilling her official duties at Keele, she had fun in the neighbourhood

Keele University Library Archives

By now, student cars were appearing on campus, occasioning traffic calming measures on campus roads. Whilst many of the Nissen huts remained, the building of more concrete structures continued. The Library can be seen under construction in the background

He used to keep us informed. But the Princess didn't always tell him what was happening. When the degree ceremonies and functions were over she had a social side and I believe she had friends in North Staffordshire whom she liked to visit. She didn't always tell Mr Crocker where she was going. Suddenly, he would find that she wasn't anywhere. There was a bit of dashing about trying to find her. It happened occasionally, but it caused a bit of concern. These were her personal friends and she wanted a bit of a private life, so we understood.

On one occasion Princess Margaret, Lord Snowdon and Party were at the Clock House for Degree Day. Sergeant Silvester was in the Police Post which was across the yard from the Clock House. Just outside there were two Rolls Royce cars which were loaned from the Rolls Royce Company in Crewe, to the University, to transport the Royal Party around. The keys were in the ignition. The two drivers were at the back of the Stoke City greenhouses talking to Les Downing. I was on patrol in the Keele Hall area. Chief Inspector Crocker was having a nap upstairs near the police post. Princess Margaret, Lord Snowdon and members of her Party were then seen coming out of the Clock House. They got into one of the cars and left, with Lord Snowdon at the wheel. Sergeant Silvester alerted everyone. Chief Inspector Crocker certainly was in a panic, especially when Sergeant Silvester told him that he had overheard them saying that they were going to have 'a run down' the newly constructed motorway nearby. They returned later, safely, having taken a turn around the Keele campus.

There'd be a big marquee on the lawn for tea after the degree ceremony and the Princess would go with her party and we'd have a nice afternoon. She had a beautiful robe especially made by a well-known London tailor. His assistant used to come up from London on the train for every degree ceremony, with a suitcase with the regalia in it. He went to the Conference Hall (the Walter Moberly Hall) and he would dress the Princess making sure that it was all perfectly fitting. At the end of the ceremony the man would be waiting in the room. He would replace the regalia in the suitcase and nip back to Stoke Station and back to London.

I don't know who was responsible for her jewellery. I don't think Mr Crocker was in charge of that. She had, of course, her ladies-in-waiting who would probably take charge of it and produce it on request. I think they always stayed in the Clock House with her.

The Princess used to attend the Ball in the evening. She had her own dance-band leaders whom she favoured. Johnny Dankworth was one - he was there regularly and often Cleo Lane was with him. If not, it was Joe Loss. I saw him there on two or three occasions. She chose her band leaders. The University paid. She danced and she had a gin and she smoked a cigarette in a long holder. There weren't a great number at the dance - mostly her friends and senior people at the University. The Student Union President was there and people like that. It was by invitation only.

I would be on duty in the Great Hall outside the Senior Common Room when the Ball was in progress. On one occasion there was a student who had too much to drink. He wanted to get into the Ball. A commotion started and he had to be man-handled down the stairs and put outside. There was quite a hullaballoo. Mr Crocker disappeared all of a sudden and I suppose he went to the Princess. This didn't happen very often.

There was once a proposal to introduce a sheep into the Ball Room as a bit of a stunt. It never took place to my knowledge. It was just talk amongst the students, probably after a few glasses of Miss Rolfe's punch. The tricks were usually good humoured. Nothing really went off the rails.

Miss Rolfe was in charge of catering at the time - a nice capable woman. She looked after the refectory and she used to put the food on for special parties. She made a regular punch - a big bowl in the middle of the room and it was very potent indeed. I don't know what she put in it - all kinds of wines and spirits. I must admit, I used to partake of it. I enjoyed it but I had to be very careful. There were one or two that got a bit under the weather, but nothing serious.

CAMPUS CRIME

There was very little crime on campus and from the security point of view there was none at all. The Head Porter, Charles Wainwright, was an ex-policeman. He took over the old lodge on Keele Road. I worked closely with him. We kept in touch if there were any problems.

There was a crime in the Physics Department. This would be in 1963. I recorded it in my notebook. Someone was stealing cash, nipping into the office, that sort of thing. Eventually the man was caught. Professor Ingram's secretary saw a man walking down the stairs one morning. She went straight to her desk and found the cash box was missing. She'd missed the cash box before, so she was on the alert. Looking through the window, she got the number of the car going up the driveway.

She got on to CW immediately. He got in touch with me and we circulated the details. The man was stopped by the Police in Cheshire. He was entirely innocent, so he said. He was a genuine businessman and he knew nothing about the case, whatsoever. He was taken to the police station in Alsager and from there I took him to the Newcastle Police Station where we held an identification parade and the lady picked him out as the one going down the stairs. Lo and behold, the cash box was found in a lane, in a hedge, in Madeley. The lady in the house nearby found the cash box. She had heard the noise of it being thrown and she had seen the vehicle drive away. Her description corresponded with the vehicle that the Secretary had seen at the Physics Department.

All this was put together and put to this gentleman. He said he was innocent. I charged him with theft. His fingerprints were taken and sent to Scotland Yard. Two days later, his records came back. He'd got a previous conviction of theft at some other university. He denied the charge and the case went to the Quarter Sessions in Stafford. Stephen Brown was the QC and Chairman of the Quarter sessions. The man was convicted by a Jury and was imprisoned. He was a traveller and did visit universities in the course of his business. The one job helped the other, that sort of thing. There was a report in the Evening Sentinel:

Prison for Keele University Theft
A sales engineer who stole a cash box and two shillings from Keele University was jailed for 18 months at Staffordshire Quarter Sessions yesterday. Prosecuting, Mr John Lee told the jury that the cash box was taken from an office on the first floor of the Physics block at the University and was later found abandoned. The secretary saw .... leaving the building and Professor David Ingram chased the car up the drive. ..... said he had visited the Physics block in connection with his job but he had not gone onto the first floor and had not stolen the box.

Occasionally we would get a student for theft. The then Registrar, John Hodgkinson, was very concerned if the student was involved in a crime because, after all, they were the 'guardians' of these young men and women at the University, at the time. A student was involved with stealing a motor car and damage, and one thing and another. He was arrested and the University came straight away. They were most concerned about it. In those days crime was very rare. There was very little security. But times have changed and it's amazing what has happened since I left the Force.

The students were a bit resentful of police on the campus, if it affected them personally. They were a bit sensitive then.

A MYSTERY SOLVED - THE GALLOWSTREE MURDER

The Hall had been taken over by the Government, mainly to billet foreign soldiers. Accommodation was very scarce in those days.

The incident in question concerned a Mr D and his wife. They lived in the Thistleberry area somewhere. They hadn't got a house to live in. She was in digs so they used to leave at night and come up to Gallowstree Lane, which was a footpath at the bottom of Sneyd Avenue. They used to go into the woods at Keele to make love there. Someone must have been aware of their activities because they stalked them one evening. Mr D was shot dead and she was raped. Scotland Yard was called in and special detectives. They never got down to the brass tacks of who had done the murder.

Probably twelve months or a little longer afterwards, a Cypriot at Keele Hall committed suicide with a hand gun. The gun was examined and the ballistics expert was of the opinion that the bullet that killed Mr D was fired from the same hand gun. But, who fired the gun? We shall never know.

In 1968 we went to live in Gallowstree Lane and I worked it out that our house was probably built on the exact spot where the murder took place. It's funny how things turn out.

The Clock House

**The Coat of Arms
of the University of Keele**

Part Two: THE GREAT

Interlude: THE UNIVERSITY COMES

The idea of North Staffordshire having a University of its own had been proposed from 1890 onwards. Mountford (1972) states that the University Extension Movement played an important part in fostering this idea. Added to this was the strength of the Workers' Education Association (WEA) which was especially active in the Stoke-on-Trent area, particularly amongst the mining and pottery communities. Alderman Reverend Thomas Horwood, who believed passionately that Stoke-on-Trent needed and should have its own University, was an important driving force behind the local wave of activity in the 1940s. As a clergyman and a politician he was a potent force, although there is some suggestion that his role in the matter was somewhat over-emphasised.

This new push for a university came at a time when public morale was low, unemployment was high, the current government was running out of ideas and had come virtually to a dead end and when men were returning from the War with nothing for them to do. In the post war years, Britain was not a fit place for returning heroes. The time seemed right for an initiative that would not bankrupt the Exchequer and would take people's minds off rationing and other pressing problems. A new university was just the thing to spearhead new thinking. However, to justify its existence, it would have to be different from the rest - who were ready to expand after the War, and who needed extra finance to do so.

On 11th March 1944 the *Evening Sentinel* reported that it 'strongly advocated and supported a new university', giving its 'wholehearted and glad support and cooperation to any practicable and well-founded plan'. The very idea opened the flood-gates to parochial interests and wrangles ensued between those who thought it should be located here rather than there, or that it should or should not grow from an existing further education institution, and if so which one, and, of course, who should run it. Much energy was diverted from the task in hand - to found a university - to the point where the project looked to be in jeopardy. A letter published in the *Evening Sentinel* on 27th May 1946, in response to one printed previously by the Reverend T Horwood, gives a nicely garbled account of the behind-the-scenes power play:

> *'None but the socialist need apply. All you bloated middle-class people have had your day and education and your children and your children's children shall be denied admittance to the new socialist-minded University. The Reverend Gentleman derides all achievement of the past and spurns all help and cooperation for the future.'*

Whilst the meaning is somewhat obscure, the fear that this would be a 'socialist university', is clear. The general public seemed of the opinion that because the project was supported by some members of the Stoke City Council, a Labour stronghold, the new University would turn into a hot-bed for Socialism - anathema at the time.

Despite local and national wrangling, events accelerated, although not necessarily in the preferred direction. On 3rd November 1946 the *Evening Sentinel* covered a report which had been presented to the Chancellor of the Exchequer and the Lord President of the Council by the Parliamentary and Scientific Committee which recommended 'a decision on the upgrading of four Technical Colleges, including Stoke (the North Staffordshire Technical College) and calling for a large-scale expansion of existing universities involving the capital expenditure of a possible £100,000,000 in the next 10 years'. It continued, 'The Committee express the view that it would be preferable to build on existing institutions rather than to form other University Colleges'. On 9th November 1946 the *Evening Sentinel* came out in full support of upgrading the Technical College to University status:

> *'consonant with the representation of the British Manufacturers Federation and the Pottery Working Party and with our own continuing advocacy there is reasonable prospect of the Technical College being upgraded and accorded University College status. That is exactly what we need here. The parochial kind of Committee dominated by the Stoke-on-Trent socialists with a trailing unenthusiastic addendum of delegates from some other Authorities was not the organisation to found a University'.*

No doubt the *Evening Sentinel* and its supporters felt that they would be better suited to the task. In the same article Meaford Hall site near Stone is first proposed publicly as being suitable for a university. By 12th November 1946 the *Evening Sentinel* regards 'a university college, as distinct from a university, is practicable', especially as, at the time, the University Grants Committee (UGC) was advocating an expanded higher education sector, and probably at no extra cost to the Exchequer!

Enter Lord Lindsay. *The Manchester Guardian* on 15th May 1947 reports a speech made by Lord Lindsay in which he quoted 1934 figures for those attending university: '1:1015 (in England) went to University compared with Scotland where the figure was 1:473 and in Wales 1:741'. He asked, 'Can we suppose that the standard of intelligence of the English is so low compared with the standard of intelligence of other countries? In America the figures were 1:125'. He went on to urge that an 'enquiry be made into how far we ought to have, beside our own academic universities, something like the American Model'. (And indeed, that appears to be the line that has been pursued ever since with regard to Higher Education institutions.)

Between November 1946 and May 1947, it seems that much discursive persuasion had been going on behind the scenes and that education in a new form was emerging, no doubt, to save Britain from a continuing downward spiral. *The Guardian* article continued; 'with the recognition that the prosperity of industry-demanded research depended on the numbers of trained students the university could supply, more and more businesses were asking the universities for training in management and for courses which did not lead to a degree'. This added yet another dimension to notions of what a university education should provide.

On 17th September 1947 Keele Hall was proposed as a possible site for this new university college. The Estate was being sold quickly to recover death duties so it was offered cheaply. By 23rd September 1947 Lord Lindsay had been invited to become the first principal at a salary reported to be £2000 a year rising to £2500, with an entertainment allowance and a 'tied' cottage. The project was sewn up by February 1948 and it was reported that the UGC meeting in London had decided that 'the proposed University College for North Staffordshire is in the interests of university education' and that they would 'recommend that the Exchequer provided the necessary financial assistance'. It did, and by August 1950 the Keele Estate was preparing to be transformed into the University College of North Staffordshire.

The *Evening Sentinel* reported that 'as well as detailing academic accommodation in the Hall and the building of a new refectory, staff housing which would be financed by a Treasury Loan would be as follows: comparatively large houses for Professors and independent Heads of Study; somewhat smaller houses for lecturers and bungalows made by the conversion of the brick and concrete buildings which formed part of the American Army Camp built in the grounds during the war (ie the Nissen huts).

The first members of staff to arrive on the campus in an official capacity were said to be the Librarian Mr Stanley O Stewart and the first academic member of staff, Mr Bruce Williams MA,

Professor of Economics. The University College opened to students on 18th October 1950. Lord Lindsay addressed the first students thus:

> *'Most people who go to College go into a going concern with Captains of football and cricket, Presidents of the Union and so on, but you will have to do all that from now on and how you do it will make an enormous difference. For me it has been an exciting job and for you, I am sure, it will be great fun'.*

On 17th April 1951 Queen Elizabeth (The Queen Mother) officially opened the new University College. The rest might be considered history!

SOME LANDMARKS

13th January 1951: Horwood Hall is opened by Alderman, Reverend T Horwood.

26th January 1951: 'Whispering attack' on the College for left wing bias. Lord Lindsay replied to his critics, 'I think any political bias out of place in a University, altogether'.

7th December 1951: Professor Stanley Beaver of the Geography Department, sets up the weather station (which exists today).

16th February 1952: Henry IV Part One is performed by the student Drama Group in the courtyard of Keele Hall.

18th March 1952: Lord Lindsay dies. In the Manchester Guardian an obituary says of him, 'He was once described as being dangerous'.

27th March 1952: Professor Arthur Vick is elected to be Acting Principal (Daily Telegraph).

25th April 1952: Hopes for a Medical Faculty at Keele are expressed.

24th October 1952: Parts of four new buildings open: Biology, Chemistry, Physics and Geography.

21st November 1952: Sir John Lennard-Jones is appointed Principal

6th January 1953: Dr Walter Allen Jenkins resigns as Registrar to change post to Director of Studies.

16th March 1953: The first game on the new playing field takes place in brilliant sunshine. It is a hockey match between Professors and the Women's Hockey Club. The Professors win 3-2. From 1953 onwards, conferences are held regularly at Keele.

29th July 1953: Sir Lennard-Jones asks permission to erect signs in Newcastle to the College.

5th September 1953: Five hundred and twenty five students are registered.

7th November 1953: New Physics Laboratories are opened by Sir John Cockroft, Director of the Atomic Energy Research Establishment at Harwell.

15th February 1954: The swan leaves the University College lake, but returns safely on 19 February.

6th May 1954: 'As You Like It' is performed in the grounds of Keele Hall. It is described as 'the best student production'. The youngest Professor of Philosophy is appointed - A G N Flew - he is 31 years of age.

14th June 1954: Sir Lennard-Jones is admitted to hospital and is unable to participate in the first Degree Ceremony.

3rd July 1954: Alderman, Reverend T Horwood is awarded an Honorary MA degree.

8th September 1954: The Financial Times reports, in an article on education, that there is a need for 'applying science to industry in that there is a need for technical direction in universities'.

24th September 1954: Sir Lennard-Jones undergoes another operation.

1st November 1954: Sir Lennard-Jones dies in hospital. His memorial service is held at Keele. So many are present at the service that it is relayed to more than 300 student rooms adjacent to the Chapel. He was 60 years of age.

1st December 1954: The first play by the staff and their wives, the Keele Players is performed, entitled 'You Can't Take it With You', by Moss Hart and George S Kaufmann. It is produced by Dorothy Hodgkinson. It was reported that Roma Williams, wife of Professor Bruce Williams is the Stage Manager and that 'she has previously had experience in Australia'.

7th January 1955: Keele's new Village Hall is opened by Acting Principal Professor J W Blake. He says, 'I regard this building as a happy omen for the future relations of the people of the Parish and the

University. Many of the staff, their wives, children and above all students, have contributed towards the building'. Two hundred pounds was raised by them towards the fund.

20th May 1955: The University buildings are described as 'hideous' by the Times Higher Education Supplement which suggests that the University was 'developing without a Master Plan'.

2nd June 1955: Work on the Conference Hall, which later becomes the Walter Moberley Hall, with a capacity for over 500, commences.

12th September 1955: Board fees for students increase by £10 to £125 per year.

1st November 1955: Sir George Barnes quits the BBC to become Principal of the College in Sept. 1956.

24th November 1955: The College plans for 1000 students.

14th June 1956: Sir George Barnes thinks that the use of television is limited. He did not think that short circuit TV was necessary at Keele. In 1957 schools radio broadcasts would begin. He was opposed to the idea that TV could be used for the instruction of students at Universities and Colleges.

28th June 1956: First Development Plan is approved. Princess Margaret is installed as the first President of the University College. She is described thus by the *Evening Sentinel*:

> *'The Princess is famed for her innate sense of fun and for organising her activities with a minimum degree of formality, but in the last few years a more mature and positive personality has evolved. As a Sea Ranger she learned other accomplishments not usually associated with a Princess - cooking and washing up as well as boat sailing'* (7th March 1956).

11th September 1956: The Conference Hall is completed and opened.

4th October 1956: The Barnes Appeal Fund for the University College is launched to speed development. The target is £250,000.

1955-1956: The annual income for special research to the University College from the UGC is cut for the first time.

19th November 1956: Princess Margaret attends the Students' Union Ball in Keele Hall.

1962: The University College of North Staffordshire becomes the fully fledged University of Keele.

Bequests

In 1950-1951 endowments and donations to the University College amount to £25. The Exchequer grant (UGC) accounted for 64.1 per cent of the total income. Local Authority grants accounted for 26.4 per cent.

2nd November 1950: The Tunstall firm Alfred Meakin Ltd donates £1000 to the University College.

14th December 1950: Dr Barnett-Stross MP donates a collection of 60 pictures and an Epstein bronze to the College.

7th March 1951: The University College appeals for donations and endowments to meet a variety of needs of University life which are not covered by the State and Local Authority assistance. The recurrent Government Grant in £48,500, with £20,000 coming from the three Local Authorities - Stoke-on-Trent City Council, Staffordshire County Council and Burton-on-Trent.

2nd May 1951: Josiah Wedgwood Company donates £200; Richard Tiles Ltd £75, W T Copeland and Sons Ltd £50 annually for seven years.

19th January 1952: the Electricity Authority donates 5000 guineas for the purpose of study and research. Much controversy surrounds this bequest.

20th December 1952: A portrait of Lord Lindsay by Robin Goodwin is presented to the Senior Common Room.

21st July 1953: Two large swans are given to the College by Queen Elizabeth. Their likely names are Peter and Paul.

9th July 1954: A Ceremonial Chair is presented to the College at the first Degree Ceremony.

4th October 1956: The Newcastle-under-Lyme Borough Council presents a silver mace to the College.

Keele University Library Archives

The first on-site shop and the University bank were housed in Nissen huts

Keele University Library Archives

Portrait of Lord Lindsay, the first Principal of the new University College of North Staffordshire

Stanley Stewart, the first Librarian and said to be the first person to step onto the new campus site. he continued to work in the library on a voluntary basis until his death in 1995

Keele University Library Archives

Colonel Sneyd (centre) with the movers and shakers who oversaw the development of Keele from country estate to campus. The Reverend Thomas Horwood is on the right

CHAPTER ELEVEN
HERE WE GO

BEGINNINGS

At Queen's University, Belfast, I had created a course in Economic Institutions which was, in part, a course on comparative Economic Systems and in part a course on Economic Sociology, in which I had become interested. I had created the course because I thought that academic economics was becoming too remote from real life problems. The external examiner of the course was J G Smith, Vice Principal of the University of Birmingham, and one of the two Birmingham members of the Keele Academic Board. He informed me of 'the Keele Experiment' and persuaded me to apply for the Chair of Economics. I did so rather reluctantly. I was very young, I did not think that I had done enough to justify a Chair and the nature of the Keele Experiment was not at all clear. However, I did think that undergraduate education was becoming too narrow and I was a great admirer of A.D. Lindsay. I had read most of what he had written, had been strongly influenced by his analysis of the relations between ethics, politics and economics and impressed by his speeches during the by-election in Oxford when he had stood against Quintin Hogg.

The first time I met Lindsay was at my interview at the Stoke Town Hall. It was a very curious interview. J G Smith asked me to outline the course that I was giving at Queens and I was asked what I meant by an 'institution'. One of the interviewers disputed my concept of an institution and after I had replied that I had adopted Durkheim's definition, a great argument developed between the panel of interviewers. The interview ended when Lindsay told me that I had the capacity to create controversy. At the end of the interview Lindsay informed me that 'they' wanted me. I learned later that Lindsay wanted Hugh Jones, who succeeded me.

Keele would not have existed without the sponsoring universities. The representatives of the sponsoring universities (two from each university) were not always helpful although always essential. The University of Manchester two were, at first, hostile to the Keele Experiment but became enthusiastic supporters. It is not easy for those not involved at the time to realise that the general academic view was that Keele was either a joke and would not last, or a threat to the established university system. A former teacher of mine wrote from Cambridge to implore me not to ruin a promising career by accepting the Chair at Keele. Even after I had accepted the appointment he advised me to resign before it was too late. We also suffered from hostile criticism from subject colleagues in other universities, but the fact that we were sponsored by Oxford, Birmingham and Manchester and that the Academic Board appointed external examiners was a very important source of strength.

FIRST IMPRESSIONS

The first impressions of the campus were that it was a wonderful site and that it would be so if it could be made ready in time. The grime on the windward side of the trees indicated that there was a pollution problem and the winds made us wonder whether we would be able to keep warm in winter. The villagers were not slow to tell us that no one from the Romans on had been foolish enough to put houses on the high ground until the University folk came. I think the village and local people were a bit suspicious of us at first but soon became cooperative. The latter were inclined to mistrust Horwood as Labour Boss of Stoke-on-Trent Council and Lindsay as a Labour Peer, but they soon decided that they were not dangerous. I did not get to know Horwood very well although I soon discovered that his accounts of the creation of Keele and his part in it were not always impeccable.

My wife accompanied me on one or two of those week-end meetings. I well remember the look on her face when the train came into and through the Potteries. Had she made the journey before I accepted the Chair, I doubt that I would have done so. Fortunately she was impressed by Keele Hall and its location and she took to both the Lindsays. When we came into residence we lived in one of the brick huts - which in army times had been the latrines. Gum boots were essential as were good supplies of hot water and soap to prevent children's clothes from turning red-brown. Our youngest child had a passion for mud pies. The accommodation in the huts was quite good and we were not unduly upset by the delays in getting the houses built.

The design of the houses, the rent to be paid and the question of whether, for tax benefits, we were required to live on campus, were all matters that encouraged frequent and at times, acrimonious discussions with Lord Lindsay and the Registrar. The wife of one of the professors was adamant that the design of the houses had to be changed because the lavatory seat in the downstairs WC was directly opposite the door and one could, therefore, be seen sitting there if the door was opened! The architect gave way, the floor of the WC was lowered so that the lavatory bowl could be sited around the corner under the stairs and, as a consequence, there was a rather dangerous step down, which visitors could not see until after they had opened the door inwards. I must confess we were rather a difficult lot, both as a gathering of professors and as a gathering of professors' wives.

The first professors were appointed almost a year before students were admitted. Our universities allowed us to spend part of our time on planning courses and we met for weekends of discussion, I suppose, on half a dozen occasions. It was far from clear what the shape of the University was to be except that students were to receive a broad education, that they would attend lectures given by the 12 professors, get some idea of relations between the disciplines and maintain work in the humanities, social sciences and laboratory sciences after the first year. Each professor outlined what he thought it was important for students to grasp in the first year and what students would need to do in the remaining three years if they were to be regarded as competent in a particular discipline. (The issue of professional recognition by, for example, the Institutes of Chemistry and Physics was raised quite early.) During these discussions Lindsay got to know 'his professors' and the professors to know him and each other but, when we broke for examining in our various universities, we were a long way from agreeing on a Foundation Year. We had made more progress on years two, three and four. The concept of a joint Honours Degree, of critical importance for a more general education, was known to us all and the idea of principal and subsidiary subjects was also familiar.

GETTING STARTED

Lindsay was an ideas man, not an administrator. He had been an excellent Master at Oxford because the Registrar, Sir Douglas Veale, was, in my view, an excellent administrator. He was less successful as Principal of Keele because the Registrar at Keele, Walter Jenkins, was not, in my view, an excellent, nor seen as a good, administrator. I was the first Professor to come into residence at Keele. I did not like the idea of 12 separate sets of professorial lectures as the basis for the Foundation Year, and whilst I was confined to bed at Keel on Achill Island (off the west coast of Ireland) before we travelled to Keele, Staffordshire, I got the idea of a main topic for each term which would involve all 12 'apostles'. After I arrived at Keele I committed this to paper. It was, in fact, very close to what became the Foundation Year lectures. Lindsay, who was recovering from a mild stroke, liked the idea and sent it out over his own signature. When the other professors came into residence I worked with them on the sections of the lecture course that most affected them, and we soon reached agreement on the FY course. That left the issue of tutorials.

There was ready agreement on having tutors from each group to conduct tutorials on the lecture course, but not ready agreement on the subject 'tutorials'. Some of the professors - most notably in languages - were keen to maintain the skills of those with A Levels and to provide opportunities for others to get up to A Level standard in Year One. Others were more concerned with the overall student experience of Year One and suspected that the other professors were trying to entice a good supply of 'majors' in Years Two to Four. The possibility of providing opportunities for students to decide on Year One what subjects to take later was taken seriously. One unforeseen problem was that lectures tailored for the FY might not give a good guide to the nature of subjects as part of joint Honours courses. It was, for example, very easy to give lectures in Economics that would persuade students to choose Economics and then find that they didn't like the later year courses or that they wouldn't be able to cope with them. I had to find ways of building warnings into the FY lectures without destroying their interest and usefulness to those who were not contemplating Economics as a major. By the Third Year I think I had got it right.

The allocation of staff was a major issue and produced considerable ill-feeling. Professors in the potentially less popular subjects had an incentive to recruit during the first year and that added to the friction between people during the early months. As Chairman of the Board of Social Sciences I took it on myself to discuss the staff needs of all the professors and I managed to produce a staffing formula that was generally acceptable. (John Lawler referred to this in his citation when I was awarded an Honorary D Litt. many years later.) Neither Lindsay nor Jenkins were at all good at coping with that sort of problem.

The choice of academic staff was handled by each professor with the aid of professors from related disciplines. Appointments had to be approved by the Academic Board but unlike procedures for appointments to Chairs, they let the professors choose their own staff and only checked paper qualifications. All staff appointed in economics in my time went on to get a Chair - two in England, two in USA and one in Australia. We were a young professorate faced with problems that normally first-time professors would not have to solve. Usually, first-time professors would join a going concern that was familiar to them. We did not have such support so it was not surprising that we often showed signs of strain and suffered from anxieties. That we were all thrown together within the walls of Keele did not help. Years later when I was a member of the Academic Board that created Lancaster University I emphasised from my Keele experience the importance of including in the first professorate some who were already professors, of achieving a much wider age range than had existed at Keele and of not providing residence on campus for more than one-third of staff.

The Academic Board lasted longer at Keele than at any of the other new universities of the 1960s, in part because Keele started off as a University College. However, the success of Keele made it possible for the UGC to make provision for new universities and not simply University Colleges with power only to give first degrees. The Academic Board at Keele lasted long enough for staff to think that it was past the time to abolish it; earlier there had been annoyance at times with particular decisions they had made. One thing that gave an important boost to our confidence was our appointment as external examiners in established universities.

Quite early Lindsay imported Mary Glover to develop a course in Social Work. Mary worked in Sammy Finer's Department, as did, later on, Mary Bell Cairns who laid the foundations for the development of Legal Studies. Monica Cole, who had worked before with Stanley Beaver came in the first round of sub-professorial appointments. Four other women played important parts in the early days at Keele: Mrs Morton, the Principal's Secretary, Marion Bailey, the Registrar's Secretary, Mrs Morgan in charge of the general housekeeping arrangements and Denise Lindsay, who was in charge of catering. They were all able women who knew that they, as well as academics, had important jobs to do and they often annoyed, but coped well with, academics who tended to suffer from a curious type of snobbery.

The recruitment of students was managed by preparing and broadcasting material on 'the Keele Experiment' and by putting on conferences for Headmasters and other Masters and Mistresses. Arthur Vick came in for some ribbing when it was learned that he had meetings with Assistant Mistresses. All students were interviewed to choose students most likely to make good use of the education Keele offered and to advise students who seemed unlikely to appreciate what was on offer to apply elsewhere. Some staff were good at identifying the former and some not, but by and large the selection processes worked well although they were expensive in terms of time.

THE LINDSAYS

I got to know Lindsay very well in the months before we came into residence, partly because we enjoyed discussing issues and problems, but mainly because at the end of our week-end meetings I stayed longer than the others because my train from Crewe to connect with the Belfast boat was not until mid-evening, so I had a meal in the Clock House kitchen with Lord Lindsay and Mrs Lindsay. (Mrs Lindsay had issued a notice in The Times when Lindsay was 'peered' that she was still to be addressed as plain Mrs Lindsay).

There were some delightful evenings when Sandy and I joined in singing the funniest hymns and Sunday School songs that we could remember. We were both sons of parsons - he Presbyterian and I Methodist - and between us we developed a good repertoire. It was then that Mrs Lindsay developed the habit of reading me her latest poems. Later when I was at the Clock House with Sandy and she came in he would always say, 'Well, Mrs Lindsay, have you written another poem for him?' - although that wasn't always the reason for her visits. She and my wife became very friendly and both Mrs Lindsay and Sandy took great interest in our children.

I had a great admiration for Lindsay before I came to Keele and this deepened as I got to know him. That did not stop me from dissenting strongly from some of his proposals and actions - he could be very imperious at times. (I once heard him say to Walter Jenkins, 'Find out what that woman wants and tell her she can't have it!') However, it was an indication of his stature that my sharp and, now I think about it, abrasive criticism did not affect his friendship for me.

EVER ONWARD

It was, of course, a great blow when Lindsay died. The Acting Principal, Arthur Vick, did a very good job. However, the professors did not handle the issue of succession at all well. Our lack of experience and sense of insecurity led us into going for really outstanding scientists or humanists and turning down lesser mortals who would have been good principals. Sir John Lennard-Jones was an outstanding scientist and his reputation was good for Keele and reassuring for the staff. His period was tragically short, however. John Blake kept the place running well as Acting Principal. Sir George Barnes, who had made a reputation as creator of the Third Programme was a considerable step down from Lindsay, in my view. However, he was good with people and he was an effective administrator. I used to meet George Barnes later, when I was at Manchester, and although I did not regard him as an outstanding Principal I did enjoy his company and conversation very much.

I do not recall that the question of nursery provision was raised in preliminary discussions. The only organised provision for children was Mary Glover's Sunday School. All children of primary school age went to the village school, I think, and later by the University bus to St Lucy's or to the High School. The first generation of children still talk about the good times they had.

If Keele ceased to be unique it was after my time. However, during my time I became worried by the extent to which original or early appointed staff tried to prevent change. One example was the size of the University College. We started with the limit of 600 and there was opposition to going beyond our 'ideal number'. In fact, Lindsay had wanted to have 1000 but the UGC would only support 600. It became clear to me that 600 was too small if we were to get full University status and recruit graduate students. 'But surely Horwood and Lindsay Halls were of critical importance to the success of Keele and going beyond 300 each would reduce their effectiveness', it was argued. In response a few of us came up with the idea that we could grow without the threat to quality of education by creating another Hall and later another and another. That idea took some selling but it did lead to the creation of another 300 or so at Hawthorns. I went to Southampton to examine what they had done to provide places much more cheaply than the Lindsay and Horwood buildings. We used this experience to design places much less expensively (in effect by adopting council house designs) at the Hawthorns, in order to get funds from the UGC.

I was disturbed also by the reluctance to do more than tinker with the FY programme on the grounds that it would be contrary to the ideas of our 'Great Founder', which did not impress me.

When it was announced that I was leaving Keele to go to Manchester, I was summoned to the Royal Presence to explain myself. I told her that Keele might be happy with my contribution up to that time (1959) but I wondered whether such happiness would last if I stayed until my year of retirement in 1984. She thought that was a good enough answer for us to get on with, and enjoy, our meal.

Keele University Library Archives

Lord Lindsay shows the Queen Mother the great wealth of books - reputedly purchased by the van load from a collector in Edinburgh by Stanley Stewart - in the 'new' University College Library

Keele University Library Archives

Tree planting - a regular occurrence at Keele. Lord Lindsay and Mrs Lindsay are standing on the right

Keele University Library Archives

Lord Lindsay accompanies the Queen Mother on her first visit to Keele

CHAPTER TWELVE
A FRESH START

BEGINNINGS

I was twenty when I came to Keele, and we were amongst the first intake of students. I'd left school at the end of 1948 and I did my National Service in the Royal Army Ordnance Corps. I was demobbed in 1950. Just before I was demobbed I saw an advertisement, at least, an article in *the Birmingham Gazette* and there was a picture of Lord Lindsay and the first Registrar, Walter Jenkins. I thought, 'That's interesting!' I'd got a provisional place for 1951 at Nottingham but Keele sounded better. The article contained stuff about the Foundation Year (FY), so I sent for an application form.

About a month after I was demobbed I received an invitation to go for an interview. I was interviewed by Lord Lindsay and the Registrar in the huts that used to stand close to Keele Hall (then the Registry). Lindsay noted that I was keen on sport. Then he said, 'We haven't got a place for you at the moment, but we'll put you down on the reserve list'. Time was marching on and I'd got a job with the local parks department as a labourer. At the end of September 1950, I received a post card from my Headmaster. I had met him and he'd asked me what I was doing. I told him I had applied to the University College of North Staffordshire. He said, 'I'll write to them!' That's exactly what he did. He had written a letter to Keele saying that I ought to be admitted. The postcard to me said, 'I've written strongly to North Staffs today and I think it might come off'.

I got an invitation for another interview about a week before the University College opened. I was interviewed by Campbell-Stewart. He said, 'We'll let you know', even at that late stage. About 48 hours later, I received a letter saying I could start on the 15th October. So that was it. I don't know if we were handpicked. There are suggestions that Lindsay looked for other skills, not just academic potential. I know that one of my friends who was President of the Union hadn't done much work and at the Handshaking his Tutor, who was also present, was making all kinds of excuses for him. Lord Lindsay said, 'Now go and do some work!' My friend ended up as the Director of Shell. We used to like to think that we were handpicked. I don't know that there is any hard evidence to prove it.

It needs to be said that it was Stoke-on-Trent that took the initiative for the new University College. It wasn't the County and it definitely wasn't Newcastle Borough. The fact that Newcastle began to benefit economically from Keele's presence was forgotten.

GETTING STARTED

I intended to read History and Geography. As a result of the Foundation Year, and also because I was friendly with one or two members of staff who influenced me in one way or another, especially Paul Rollo, who said, 'Why don't you do Politics with History?' I thought that was a good idea, so I did.

When I arrived the campus looked like a big building site. The playing fields weren't ready, the top soil had been taken off so there were mounds of soil everywhere and the huts weren't quite ready either. I think they were laying linoleum until the half hour before we moved in on that particular Monday. Keele Hall courtyard looked like a builder's yard - they were trying to improve the area where Horwood Refectory is now. That was being rebuilt and refurbished. Right from the beginning Keele Hall was used for lectures. The Foundation Year lectures were held in the Salvin Room. The first ever lecture was given by Lord Lindsay himself. That would be on 16th October 1950. The then Chairman of the University Council was Alderman Tommy

Horwood and I can remember him all passionate, eyes closed saying, 'I want you all to have a go. Get stuck into this new venture'.

Towards the end of the first term we moved to the Chapel for our lectures. The Chapel was one of the three big Nissen huts, roughly where the Chapel is today.

I lived in Hut 3 for four years. There was almost double the number of men to women. Very early on there were demarcation lines for the men and women. Everyone had to be on their particular side of the campus by 11.00 pm. The opposite sex had to be out by 7.00 pm and you couldn't be in the room of some one of the opposite sex before one or two in the afternoon. There was a confrontation because someone had complained to the Warden about couples saying good night and embracing on the demarcation line at 11.00 pm. You could see this every night. The Warden was very embarrassed at having to tell us off. The rules had been broken, there was no question, and everyone knew it. People did get into trouble for being out after hours. I was hauled up myself in 1953!

In the first term 37 different societies were founded within three months. I was interested in sport and because our grounds weren't ready we had to play all our matches away. We went all over the place. I went to play football in Birmingham once and the students there were talking about this 'new place'. Suddenly one of them shouted to his pals across the room, 'Hey! Here's a bloke that knows a professor!' There were 13 professors and two readers in those days and we did know everybody. There was babysitting so you got to know people.

RECREATION

There is this myth about everybody entertaining each other. Some did. I was thinking about this very recently. There were some staff who were most conscientious and regularly asked people to their homes. Others, who might have been very pleasant in tutorials, didn't interact. A lot didn't turn up at the Union, a few turned up to the dances. Others would retreat into their own homes. Staff were friendly, they knew everyone by name. That couldn't happen now. We were aware of this friendliness, but as for students and staff entertaining regularly, that didn't happen.

I went to concerts regularly in the Victoria Hall. We'd get up a coach party to go. There was an effective drama group. The first open air production was 'Twelfth Night', which was performed at Church Mansions in Nantwich. It was a restaurant and the proprietor decided he would put up the group for a week and they would perform in the garden in the evenings. It was the end of the Summer term. I came up from Walsall to see them and half way through the Second Act it rained and rained so we had to go home. In 1952 they did Henry IV Part I in the Courtyard of Keele Hall.

In the first year there were only two or three cars on campus. Gradually the odd motor bike appeared. There was a dance and a film on alternate Saturdays. We went home twice a term. We tended to stay. We used the Crosville bus to get in and out of town. The fare was tuppence half-penny. There was a College bus which was free. We also used to hitch lifts into town.

I played in the first ever cricket match on the campus in 1953 - when the first cricket pitch was completed. I was the first President of the Athletics Union in 1951. The duties weren't very onerous. The remarkable feat was that although there were so few students we competed successfully with other Universities and Colleges. We lost more games than we won but the enthusiasm was there. It was very easy to raise teams. The girls played hockey.

THE LINDSAYS

Lord Lindsay was a big, tall, shambling man. He wasn't well and he had probably been told that he had a few years to live when he left Balliol. He died on 18th March 1952. He was born in 1879. He and Mrs Lindsay were married in 1907 so they must have been quite old. He had been

The Evening Sentinel

Lord Lindsay greets the first of the students upon their arrival at Keele

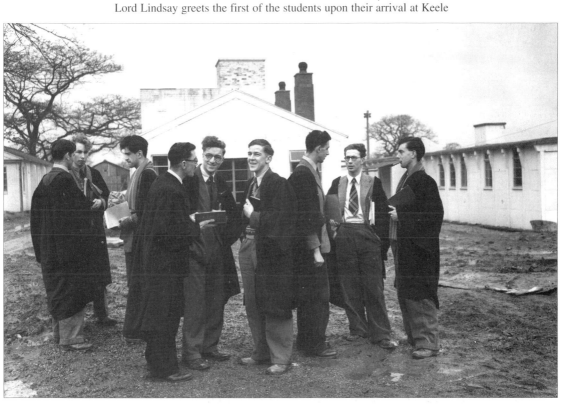

Keele University Library Archives

The fact that they were inhabiting a building site clearly did not bother the first students unduly. They were, after all, 'young pioneers'

Keele University Library Archives

A Tutorial Group - only wealthy institutions such as the Oxbridge colleges could afford to keep such a system going in the modern age of increased numbers of students and reduced numbers of staff

Keele University Library Archives

A Discussion Group - also a casualty of cost-cutting exercises

Keele University Library Archives

One of the first lectures to be held in a Nissen Hut. Despite the unconventional setting everyone wore gowns, jackets, shirts and ties

Keele University Library Archives

'Tree and tea, Ma'am! Lord Lindsay looks on as the Queen Mother plants one of the first trees

Keele University Library Archives

Student fare - the first refectory

The Queen Mother inspects the catering facilities on a visit to the Keele kitchens

Master of Balliol for 25 years. He had also been connected with Stoke-on-Trent via the Extra-mural Delegacy and he had been to Stoke to lecture. There must have been a big gap between the very young Professors - their average age was about 37 years. The oldest Professor was 50 and the youngest 27 or 28.

Lord Lindsay came to the first lecture in the Salvin Room. He also came into the Nissen huts which were used for lectures. The powers that be decided that there ought to be an exam at the end of the (first) year. He said, 'We've got to have a silly exam because Manchester, Oxford and Birmingham say we need to have one. But I don't want you to worry about it at all'. He was full of stories, so he went on, 'I want you to think about the story of the Scottish Presbyterian Minister who was about to give his first sermon. He was very nervous. An older and more experienced Minister tried to help him and said, 'I want you to get in there and talk as if you didn't give a damn for any of them.'' He said, 'That's how I want you to treat this first exam!'

We had the Oxford system of Handshaking at the end of term. We had to go and see Lord Lindsay to see how we were getting on. He would say whether we were progressing or not. To us, the students, this was the common touch. We felt someone was interested in us.

Mrs Lindsay, I thought, was slightly eccentric. We went to tea at the Clock House. She was a tiny woman. We talked about the sound of falling rain in Beethoven's Pastoral Symphony. When the Queen (now the Queen Mother) came to open Keele on 17 April 1951, the detectives had to walk about to see if there were any hidden fire arms. The rumour was that a shot gun had fallen out of one of the Registrar's cupboards. The other was that they went into the Clock House and there was a double bass case in the corner. ' You don't want to look in there. Nothing in there', said Mrs Lindsay. The police opened it and it was full of dirty washing.

THE SYSTEM

In the Foundation Year we had 300 lectures, two each morning. We started with the Geography of the Ancient World. The first was by Stanley Beaver. Lectures were an hour long and some were much better than others. I was totally baffled by mathematics. The maths lecturer admitted that he didn't know how to teach. He covered the blackboard in hieroglyphics and mathematical formulae then he turned to a girl who was reading maths and said, 'Margaret, when you've got your education diploma, would you come and tell me how to put this over?'

We were fortunate to have the tutorial system. There were about four in a group. As far as I was concerned it was the tutorial system that was important. You read your essays out and they were discussed by staff and the other tutors. It was only when I talked to students from other universities that I realised how lucky we were. It did help to train you to think and look at what you were writing. This was very much the Oxbridge tradition. One tutor used to light his pipe behind his desk and make an enormous smoke screen between his desk and us. The discussion groups started after I'd graduated. When I was there we just had lectures and tutorials. There was an end of year exam and one or two fell by the wayside and had to leave. We even lost a few at the beginning of the final year.

The system of grants was very eccentric and depended entirely on the Local Authority. There was, therefore, tremendous variation in the amounts that people received. Walsall gave me a Borough Scholarship. It paid my tuition fees, residential fees and left me with about £20 spending money per term. I had about £187. Stoke students had about £250. That was very generous compared to others. No parental contribution was expected then. Our needs were fewer. To give some idea of inflation, the Professor of Politics, Sammy Finer, called a meeting for his students and said, 'I think you'll need to buy my brother's book. It's rather expensive but it's a very good book'. This book cost £2 10s 0d (1951). We thought it an enormous price to pay. Books were a big problem. The library, I suppose, was inadequate. We were probably not too aware of this at the time. There weren't funds or time to build a Library before the college opened. A lot of FY books were on reference so we didn't have to buy the core texts. The Library then was in the Great Hall and the Old Library, which gives you an idea of its size. It wasn't extensive. I suppose some departments loaned out books. There was a History Library.

OUTSIDE-IN

Before I came, I read about people's worries concerning this new University College. Lord Lindsay was a Labour Peer and a life-long socialist. As a student there were one or two funny things. We'd be on the bus coming back to Keele and the bus conductor would say as he took the fare, 'Kremlin?' which we thought was quite idiotic. The proprietor of one of the bookshops (no longer there) in Newcastle said to us once, 'You at the College? You realise it was founded on political bias don't you?'

I always thought that relations between town and gown were friendly enough. I used to go into the Red Lion, in Newcastle, if ever I had to wait for a bus. The Landlord was one of the Burgesses of the town and he was pro-Keele - perhaps because he was getting our custom!

There were also suggestions that people with Conservative opinions were not well regarded at Keele. This led to the Chair of the Conservative Association writing to the Daily Telegraph to say that he had been in Keele for a year or so and that he had never been aware of any bias against him whatsoever. In the second year I had supper with a family who had a daughter at Keele. A few of us went to her house in Newcastle. Her mother said, 'Are there any Socialists here because that's all I hear about the place'. Well, we were getting a pretty good supper so nobody admitted to it. It was a Labour creation and some people were very suspicious of the place because it was new, but in time that changed.

It took a long time for Keele to get established. When a University for the area was mooted, there was a suggestion that it should be a University College geared to the pottery industry. That didn't happen. If local industry had put some money into Keele then, possibly, there would have been some practical courses. The first University Appeal was in 1956 and £100 was donated by one firm. When you think of what Boots gave to Nottingham and Sainsbury gave to East Anglia! I suppose it was because the pottery industry wasn't a wealthy one.

It was said that employers liked Keele graduates because they were thought to be more mature. There were 35 ex-Servicemen in my year. We benefited from having them around and they contributed a great deal to Keele. Many of the first intake of men were successful in business on the management side. We lived on a campus of a small University so we had opportunities to socialise and develop in a way we wouldn't have if we'd have gone to one of the provincial universities. Some of my friends at Birmingham University had to live at home.

THE OTHER HALF

As women we were encouraged to go into teaching, I suppose. There was a female warden but there wasn't a female appointment to the academic staff until a few years later. We weren't conscious of feminism at all. There were few female lecturers so we had no role models. When we left school, for girls there was Training College, University, the Bank or the Civil Service. There was a General election in 1951 and although I was always fascinated by politics I couldn't have cared less what was happening on the outside world at the time. We couldn't afford a television and some of us couldn't afford newspapers. We might not have wanted to change the world, but I think the nature of some of the courses opened our eyes a little wider. It might have made us more accepting of new ideas. We must have been influenced by those opportunities that were there, even if we were slightly slow in taking advantage of them.

THE WAY WE WERE

I was interested in Keele's pub, the Sneyd Arms. For the first few years there were more locals. I found it difficult, at first, to understand the local dialect. Professor Beaver of the Geography Department talked about the local area and took a field trip around the Potteries.

There was a shop on campus run by Mrs Dale, so we used that. It was in a Nissen hut and is roughly where the Chapel is now. There were still some shops in the town which had above their door, 'By Appointment to the Grand Duke Michael'. We were rather intrigued by that.

There was a boycott of refectory food when I was in my final year, but on the whole it wasn't bad. We were very conscious of the state the place was in. We came to tutorials in Keele Hall and we had to take off our wellingtons and leave them outside. I can see them now, all in a row. We were never uncomfortable. The huts may not always have been economical to run but I can never remember being cold there. We didn't feel a sense of privation at all. We didn't know what to expect, for a start. We were pioneers.

Keele University Library Archives

The Department of Geography, now transmogrified into the Department of Environmental and Social Sciences

Keele University Library Archives

Keele University Library Archives

The male staff hockey team detailed to play the female students' team. Youth, beauty and mean bullying-off
ensured victory for the women's team

CHAPTER 13
HEALTHY MINDS IN HEALTHY BODIES

BEGINNINGS

I was 30 and really a mathematician. I did PT in the army. The PE degree at Birmingham appealed to me and there was also a recreation scheme whereby every first year student did some exercise. I was lecturing at Birmingham University when Lord Lindsay came down to give us a talk about this funny new University College at Keele. He saw what we were doing in the way of PE and he asked my boss if any of us would be interested.

I was interested for two reasons. One, I didn't like Birmingham or the thought of my children growing up as 'Brummies'. Two, a university in the country appealed to me very much. Indeed, I liked the sound of what was being proposed. In the first year of its existence, I came up to the College one day a week. We were doing the very first PE degree in the country at Birmingham and there was no-one else there to do what I was doing so I had to stay.

To start with I helped found all the sports clubs at Keele. I arranged for students to go swimming at the local swimming pool, and organised coaching instructors. There were no sporting facilities here whatsoever except for a half completed playing field and a sea of mud and rather a silly plan of pitches that were to be put in. I soon put that right! I arranged for the tennis club to play at the Westlands and for hockey to take place at a local school in the Westlands. The only place where we could do anything indoors was in about one-third of a Nissen hut - the other part was a furniture store. We had a curtain put in and flooring. One of the porters told me that there was a load of lino in store, so we carried it in my car and laid it. I had an office - a single room - and a lady, Vera Baxter, came up to teach ballroom dancing there. Someone else did weight training.

GETTING STARTED

When I came full-time in the following year I began to do a lot of coaching myself - tennis outside, etc. By then we had stoves to keep the place warm and the lady who did ballroom dancing also did yoga. (She gave up in 1993)). The roof leaked so we had to swab out before classes. I had to push a bit at first, but I think the students got a lot out of these activities.

In the first December before I came up, I put some of my proposals to Senate suggesting that some activities be compulsory. Some members of Senate threw their hands up in horror. Lindsay agreed that sports activities should be compulsory, like lectures. I had to modify things a bit too: 'all students are encouraged to take part in some form of physical activity and first years, in particular, are normally required to ... etc'. I got away with that. With such poor facilities I really couldn't offer what I would have liked. I quickly realised that with such small numbers of students and staff and a whole lot of subjects that we had to teach, there was no point in thinking of PE as a discipline. As we only had a half of a playing field and half of a Nissen hut, I had to be quite inventive. I managed to find a basket-ball court in Longton which meant a mini-bus ride.

Eventually, I moved down to an out-building outside Keele Hall that was waterproof and centrally heated. It was about the size of a single badminton court. By this time even the snow was getting into the Nissen hut and I can remember Vera taking her last ballroom dancing class up there, in her fur coat and boots. That night a storm blew up and the hut just disappeared. Only the arches were left. That was the end of my first Sports Centre.

I thought the whole Keele thing was very good. I attended some of the FY lectures myself. I taught a certain amount of maths for about one-and-a-half years and I was involved with the discussion groups. I also did some work in the Education Department.

Building a sports hall and a gymnasium, when there wasn't even a proper library, wasn't worth contemplating. The Sports Centre came on the bottom of the list, but by about 1959, money was granted for it. We had carried on without a Sports Centre for about 16 years. We had acquired a couple of tennis courts and it was two or three years before the sports fields were ready. These were built on clay so a tremendous amount of drainage had to go on. The tennis and netball courts came in about the third year. The running track, which was once a corn field, came much later.

I got reasonable support in Senate although the Sports Hall development plan was on the bottom of the list along with the Students' Union. There was £200,000 available between the two of us and Senate allocated £120,000 to the Students' Union. I was furious. I went to see the Vice-Chancellor, Sir George Barnes, and he said, 'Prepare a plan and costing'. I went home and it was on his desk by 10.00 am the next day. It took a long time to design and the final cost was £230,000. By now new universities had come along, but there was some money to spare at the end of the year. The Registrar shoved my plan in and we got the go ahead for Stage I so long as the first brick was laid by the new year. That was 1963. We did. Stage I included the Sports Hall, dance studios, changing rooms, tea room and offices. The rest came later. We didn't get the swimming pool. That was Stage III on the plan but the money ran out. Stage II was the gymnasium, team changing rooms and the squash courts.

We decided to raise our own money for the swimming pool, so we set up a swimming pool committee. The plan went in in 1966 and the estimated cost was £130,000. I made enquiries and found that we could probably do it for £80,000-£100,000; it would have been built on the car park and joined onto the boilerhouse. We struggled doing all kinds of fund-raising activities but really, I don't think the University was behind it. It would cost too much to run. It was a long and disappointing story for those on the outside who were supporting it. It was very short-sighted of the University. I had all kinds of plans for its commercial use, too. The fund reached just over £20,000 at the time. By then the cost would have been £180,000 - £200,000. The University estimated the cost at £300,000. I thought that that was just an off-putting statement, but that was the sort of thing that was going on. We could have done it.

Here was the big new building going up behind a paling fence. When the students went down in June that's what they saw. When they returned in the Autumn (1963) there were all these splendid facilities. Walter Winterbottom opened the new Sports Centre - he was one-time Manager of the England football team. Princess Margaret paid us a very informal visit. Usually after degree day she would go and visit the latest building that was almost ready. I was down there pottering about and I heard a little knock on the door and there she was with the Vice-Chancellor and her Lady-in-Waiting. I welcomed her in and when she went into the Sports Hall she said, 'Oh! Isn't this lovely!' and she started to dance around it. In due course she paid more formal visits.

As soon as the Sports Centre was ready I wrote to all the local sports clubs saying they could make use of our facilities, especially during the vacations. I could offer 20 different sports. I had given myself five years to build up this interest in sport and it worked. I had been on my own for 14/15 years. It was jolly hard. In 1963 when we moved to the new Sports Centre I had a female assistant. Later a male assistant was appointed and we had a sports manager. He ran things and started volley ball, five-a-side and football leagues.

RECREATION

When we first came to Keele my daughter was four and my son was three-and-a-half years of age. My wife used to come and help me with the skiing trips in Scotland. We knew almost all the students. We lived in Holly Lodge before moving into a house in Church Plantation. For two children to be brought into a university environment in the country, in rather a nice village, it worked like a dream. We took the two children with us on skiing trips and the students used to come and babysit. They all had a whale of a time. They gained a lot from the students. We've loved every minute of being in this community.

Minor entertainments were going on. For special reviews we used Horwood refectory. Within the first four years the students had so many ideas. So many songs had been written about the legend of Keele - the ghost of Lady Sneyd. After the evening meal they'd carry out all the chairs and tables and start the do about nine at night. It would go on until about one in the morning. There was a staff group called the Keele Players. I was an Income Tax Inspector in one of their plays.

In the Summer the students performed around the lakes and we used to sell everyone midge cream. One year we went to see 'The Tempest' and just as the play started there was a great thunderstorm. It was an ideal setting.

The Sneyd Arms was quite a club in the early days where staff and students mixed. It was a bit difficult around exam time. The students wanted to know if they'd done well!

Relations were soured when the students revolted. It started on the Continent and spread over here. The students occupied the Registry at one point. They wanted to design their own courses, be represented on Senate, that kind of thing. We had a vigilante arrangement with staff and people on top of the Geography building with field glasses keeping an eye on things. It was a sign of the times.

Keele University Library Archives
Accompanied by director Harold Haley and Sports Centre manager Gus Nabney, Princess Margaret inspects the new sports facilities

CHAPTER FOURTEEN
DIGGING DEEPER

BEGINNINGS

I first visited Keele Hall during the 1939-45 War, shortly after it was vacated by the Dutch Army. There in the basement I met a group of ladies who were making grommets for the navy.

I followed the discussion reported in the press concerning the establishment of a University College in North Staffordshire. It was a long time before its location at Keele was seriously considered. One day in 1949, I saw an advert for a geologist to set up a department in the new University College at Keele. It was a condition of appointment that all academic staff should live on the campus. This was just the opportunity I was looking for - a post in an area which I knew like the back of my hand, together with the chance to introduce my subject to young people and the opportunity to continue my research. I was also in full agreement with the main part of the so-called Keele 'experiment' - to give scientists the opportunity of studying arts and social science subjects, and arts people an introduction to the sciences. They could then better communicate across the frontiers and no longer perpetuate the over-specialisation leading to the two discreet worlds of CP Snow. The prospect of building up a department from scratch was both challenging and awesome.

GETTING STARTED

We moved to Keele in September 1950. A houseful of furniture and personal effects had to be crammed into an army hut, sited roughly where the Geology car park now stands, on the edge of the wood. The hut had been well converted into a bungalow. It was all electric, light and airy and comprised a hall, kitchen, dining room, bathroom, cloakroom and three bedrooms. There was a small garden area but no garage. I converted an unwanted army hut in the wood close by into a garage and made a road to it. This arrangement lasted until late 1951 when the building of the Church Plantation houses was completed. Apart from the main drive from the Hall to Keele village and to Newcastle, there were no main roads. In the winter of 1950/51 we lived in a sea of red mud and we all moved about in wellington boots. We had many parties and it was commonplace to see a mass of wellington boots outside a lighted front door of the bungalow, at night. There were no road lights so at night you moved around at your peril.

In the autumn of 1950, with the first intake of students in residence, administrative and organisational work was hard and long. Senate Committees proliferated and informal Senate meetings were held in between. The science departments faced a difficult time finding accommodation for laboratory work. I took over an army hut outside Keele Hall for Geology. For some months I coped single-handed doing lectures, fieldwork, lab work and tutorials. I was eventually able to appoint a technician and about half-way through the year two assistant lecturers were appointed.

The first undergraduates arrived in October 1950. They were a mixed bunch of around 150. The ratio was roughly 2:1 men to women. For entry the required minimum was two reasonable A Level passes and all were interviewed before they were accepted. In those days they read two principal or Honours subjects to cover a wide spectrum of knowledge. All academic staff wore gowns. We didn't use Christian names. Students were addressed as Miss or Mister. The second intake of students served to consolidate the so-called Keele 'experiment'. Tutorials were improved and the Foundation Year lectures were modified. All this imposed a heavy burden on the academic staff. I don't recall experiencing any real financial stress. One day I said that we needed 50 petrological microscopes - expensive items even in 1950. Approval for their purchase came without delay.

In the early years the Professors were left with little time to pursue research. But in spite of the fact that many of them had quite lengthy lists of publications to their names, most continued to carry out original work. The more junior staff were busily occupied in designing their courses but there was always emphasis and encouragement to publish the results of their research. I think that largely through its residential nature Keele was a friendly and invigorating place. I always found it so.

At the end of their first year, some students neatly painted the words 'Freshers' Gate' on the sandstone gatepost between the footway and the carriageway to the entrance of Keele Hall courtyard. At a meeting of the Building and Development Committee the architect asked what action should be taken to remove the 'graffiti'. I urged that any physical or chemical treatment would damage the stonework and that as the printing had been done so neatly it should be allowed to stay. This was agreed and it remains to this day.

At the bottom of the Ironmarket in Newcastle there is a statue of Queen Victoria in a seated position. A hundred yards or so away were the public lavatories. One night in 1955 some wags from Keele carefully painted white footprints from the statue to the lavatories and back.

THE LINDSAY ERA

Lord Lindsay took a keen interest in all that was going on. He was a genial grandfatherly figure usually seen around the campus with his wife, who insisted on being called Mrs Lindsay. Lindsay's knowledge of science was abysmal and he boasted that he could not read a plan or a map. He had no time for fools, neither did he stand on ceremony. He told the consultant architect that we needed a High Table in the refectory. The day arrived for it to be unveiled in Lindsay's presence. The table legs were about six feet high. Lindsay took one look at it and with a grimace and smile said, 'Pooh! Pooh!'. When Queen Elizabeth formally opened the University College in April 1951, she got a little behind with a tight schedule. Suddenly Lindsay walked into the laboratory and called out, 'Your Majesty, tree and tea!' The Queen duly planted a tree on the slope below the Clock House. The poor thing (the tree) died the following winter and had to be replaced.

Lindsay inaugurated formal 'Dinners' which were attended by students and staff, and were a success. He was genuinely interested in the progress and welfare of the undergraduates. He even gave a Handshake to each student at the end of term. But, with a fresh intake of around 200 or so students in 1951 such niceties soon became a physical impossibility.

He took a personal interest in the planning of the Foundation Year courses. All staff cooperated and subscribed to this Year. The Keele 'experiment' was successful, especially when measured by the general acceptance and success of the first crop of graduates in 1954, who were in competition with graduates from other universities. However, the 'experiment' could not be expected to continue. After 1954 there were some minor changes in the conduct of tutorials, the FY lecture course, and there was a reduction in the number of subsidiary subjects read by students, from three to two.

REVOLTING STUDENTS

The undergraduates began to lose their gowns and turned up to tutorials without them. Lindsay had died and so had the 'Dinners'. Student activists became more militant over such things as increased residential rents and confidential files. In the late 1960s and early 1970s a vociferous fraction of students joined a nation-wide fight against any form of discipline. At one stage we had to guard our department through the night. Some events were criminal and quite disgraceful.

In my view, university administrators were lamentably weak in the face of all this. One

Wednesday afternoon, when all members of the Senate, gowned, went to the Walter Moberley Hall for a Senate Meeting, it was pouring with rain and the door was locked against us. A student holding the key said that we would not be allowed in unless we voted in a certain way on some item on the Agenda. Had I been the Vice Chancellor I would have sent the student down immediately - but doubtless there would have been some ugly repercussions. Not a single university in Britain had the courage to stand up to this nonsense.

Over the years things tended to become sloppy. Some members of staff ceased to wear gowns or even ties when they gave FY lectures. Christian names were bandied about everywhere and the woman Vice President of the Students' Union circulated all Heads of Department saying that in future you will address all women students as Ms. My copy immediately found repose in my waste-paper basket.

The student unrest coincided with the period when graduates had no difficulty in funding well-paid posts. Within ten years of graduating one of my students was Head of a large Australian mining company and had his own 'plane. He had just scraped a Third Class in his finals. As jobs for new graduates became more difficult to obtain, students worked noticeably harder and staff-student relations improved. With the lowering of the age of majority from 21 to 18, the University ceased to be 'in loco parentis'. Halls of residence became autonomous and any discipline was that laid down by the student residents. Cohabitation ceased to be extraordinary.

RECREATION

There must have been 20 to 30 school-age children of academic staff on campus. They were taken to school in Newcastle in the College bus. Not everyone had a car then. The children had a wonderful time playing in the woods. We rarely saw them between meal times. These children, now grown up, say that they were all raised in ideal surroundings.

Academic staff had little free time. Some did get in a game of golf or tennis. When the professorial houses were finished on Church Plantation in 1951, we nearly all took to making gardens of what had been a birch wood. I constructed a wide footpath - with a roundabout, for toy cars and cycles which ran the whole length of the garden - from large paving slabs (around 50) that had been left in the woods by the army.

When students suggested a game of football on Sunday afternoon, Tom Ball, a local man who was the first Finance Officer, said there would be strong local opposition to such an event.

INSIDE-OUT

From the beginning, the University attracted immense local interest from business people, especially from the heads of firms such as Wedgwood, Copeland etc. We quickly got on good terms with the general public of Newcastle and Stoke-on-Trent. There was initial criticism that there were no courses being run which were specifically designed to help local industry. That was more clearly the aim of the Stoke-on-Trent Technical College.

CHAPTER 15
A BIRD'S EYE VIEW: The First Eye

BEGINNINGS

We had seen the campus once before, in July, when R came to be interviewed. Because the whole Estate had been taken over by the army during the war it was still in a state of disrepair and very rough. The grounds had been neglected. Keele Hall was very impressive and we could see that it had been a wonderful place.

The University College opened in September 1950 so my husband's appointment dated from then. But the University where he was employed insisted that he work out his full contract, until the end of December. During that first term he came to Keele once a fortnight for departmental meetings. The department consisted of Professor Gemmell, the secretary and one technician. We came in January. It was wonderful! The whole place was covered in snow. It looked beautifully clean and there were wonderful trees. We came from Southampton to Keele on the train to Crewe and from Crewe to Keele by bus. It took about two-and-a-half hours in this lovely snow. We were then taken on foot - there weren't many cars in 1956 - to Keele Hall. We were very junior and R was one of the three non-professorial people appointed. Everyone was very young. We were the youngest and we had no family.

We met the Principal, Lord Lindsay, who lived in what is now called Keele Lodge, with his daughter-in-law. She was in charge of all the domestic side of the University College. Later on these jobs became separated and other people took charge. Here he lived with his wife, who insisted on being called Mrs Lindsay because he was a socialist Peer and she felt that she had done nothing at all to contribute to his success. She was never called Lady Lindsay.

THE KEELE EXPERIMENT

My husband was quickly involved in organising courses with his professor, Alan Gemmell, who was already quite a distinguished botanist and broadcaster. In fact, he was one of the very early members of *Gardeners' Question Time* from Manchester. He insisted on his full title because he wanted to put Keele on the map. People began to come and visit Keele, apart from academics. The national press was very interested and 'The Keele Experiment' was a phrase coined. I was once on my way home from holiday in Devon, by train, and I was reaching for my suitcase and a gentleman kindly offered to help me. When he saw Keele on the suitcase label he said, 'The Keele Experiment! What is it?' It was talked about in the press and on the radio. There wasn't much television in 1951.

The Keele Experiment was a very expensive idea for local authorities and for parents who had to pay, because they had to fork out for a four year course. I think it was a very good thing. Lord Lindsay, and people like him, decided there were far too many specialists - people who knew more and more about less and less. They tried terribly hard to produce Arts graduates who would have a smattering of Sciences from the Foundation Year, and vice versa. With the Oxford system on which it was based - the tutorial system - there was a lot of discussion and in the tutorials there would be a member of staff who ran the tutorial and with him, sitting in, would be, if you were a scientist, two Arts people. They would join in the discussion and there would be an interchange of views between the Arts and Sciences. This made for a very long working day.

In the first seven years there was this constant working out of courses. Every year there would be a slight change. This meant discussions, committee meetings, Senate meetings, sub-committee meetings. The whole programme was overseen by 'sponsors', as they were called, from the Universities of Oxford, London, Birmingham and Manchester. These were the senior professors who came and studied examination results and courses to see whether or not they were good enough and up to standard.

There was a first year course called the Foundation Year and students were expected to take every possible subject on offer. Many subjects were not taught in schools in those days, for example philosophy, psychology, astronomy. Many students changed their minds after the Foundation Year and graduated with very good results in a different subject. When R gave the first Foundation Year lecture in Biology entitled 'Reproduction', Professor Gemmell insisted that he wore a mortar board and gown!

It was eventually decided that this little place, the Keele Experiment, had worked and in 1962 it attained full University status, with a Vice Chancellor instead of a Principal. Lord Lindsay having died within the first three years, we had various Acting Principals and Vice Principals in the meantime.

Sir George Barnes was one of the Principals. He had founded Radio 3 and was very interested in the Arts. He was a very cultivated man. We have down below Keele Hall a little bluebell wood. His idea of relaxation was to go down and tidy up that wood. You'd find him down there with a great axe, chopping. Single-handed, he tidied up the little stream. It became a favourite spot for children on the campus to go paddling in and have a picnic around. When he died, it became the Sir George Barnes Memorial Garden. I don't know if it still is. It had been known as Bluebell Wood because it was the best place for bluebells.

The students were not completely hand-picked, but locally, word went around to schools saying that this new University College was to be opened up and they were invited to send their most suitable sixth formers. In the first year or so it was left to the head teachers to pick suitable pupils, I think, for this experimental University College. There were to be two principal subjects at finals level - a new thing completely. It was a four year course and very hefty to do, particularly if you were doing a teacher training course or field work for the social sciences or sciences. There was practical work for that, so there was an enormous amount of work compared with a traditional University with a three year course. It was really very tough and students had to work jolly hard.

Some who had been in the War came to do a degree. They were given scholarships by the Ministry of Defence. So, there was an enormous age range - some undergraduates were older than we were - who had had experience of travelling around the world and doing different things. The first students were very conformist. Some were mature, they had done national service, they were good sportsmen. Others wanted to come to Keele because it was new. Because the staff were young and because there were few students, we knew everyone's name for the first intakes. Those that we got to know we kept in touch with. Quite a few made their mark in public life and industry.

RECREATION

We had to make our own entertainment. There was something happening every night. Because food was still rationed we pooled our food and had marvellous parties in the Nissen huts which were still up then. There was an exchange of views from the young academic staff, plus the technicians who had come with them from other universities, and the mature students. There were, I think, 145 students in the first year. There were no facilities for them. There was just Keele Hall still in a state of repair after the occupation by various troops and a range of huts left by the army. The big huts were used for the Students' Union, the refectory and the Chapel.

The students did a review, very amusing, about the ghost of Lady Sneyd who was supposed to wander around the top of Keele Hall with her hands chopped off - in Keele Church there is a tomb with no hands on the effigy. The students wrote the words. They also performed Gilbert and Sullivan operas and members of staff played different instruments. Quite a considerable amount of talent emerged. There was an orchestra made up of anyone who could play anything. There were concerts and quite a few well-known people came to give recitals. I remember Joan Sutherland came in 1951/2 and sang ballads accompanied by Richard Bonynge whom she later married. She wasn't famous then, just someone Professor Lawler had met at Oxford. The Professor of Mathematics was also keen on music so between them they managed to round up quite a few famous musicians. A famous Greek pianist came once and gave a concert because the Professor of Classics had met him on a Greek tour and invited him to Keele. Later, an established concert programme was set up.

Some staff wives joined the Women's Institute. The lady who ran the shop, and eventually the post office, was a keen member of the WI so whenever wives went into the shop or post office they were invited to join. The first person to entertain us was Mrs Bates who lived in the Villa. She invited us to a tennis party. There were about 30 of us and we had a traditional tea on the lawn and it was very enjoyable. We were the second people to have television on the campus and that was in 1952. I had had an operation and I was ordered to take four weeks bed rest. R couldn't see me staying in bed for that long so, when I got home I found this 'thing' in the house. The first programme I saw was lessons on how to become a ballet dancer. Right from the word go I thought TV was a silly thing. I still do.

THE LINDSAYS

The Lindsays would often take a walk around the campus and in those days there were no decent roads. It was either a sea of mud or churned-up red earth. Lord Lindsay was not very well. He had retired as master of Balliol and was hoping his working life had come to an end and that he could relax. Instead, he had to take up this mammoth task of running a new University College. So they would take an afternoon walk. When he was feeling a little under the weather they would drop in, literally, to the nearest front door. And when you were washing or changing the baby or making lunch, these two would arrive and sit and talk and have a cup of tea and he would say, 'Do you mind if I come in and rest my weary heart?' And she would say, 'Do you mind if I bring Sandy in to rest his weary heart?'

On one glorious occasion, it must have been the winter after we came in 1952, we were living in a hut which was very warm and comfortable. On this one cold day I was in the middle of washing - we had no washing machine - with a lot of water and mess around. The front door opened and the unmistakable voice of Mrs Lindsay said, 'May we come in and rest poor Sandy's heart? He's so cold and suffering from such a cold'. They teetered down to the sitting room and flopped down. He obviously had a temperature. She was wrapped up in her usual black wrap. I said to her, 'Mrs Lindsay, I feel the Master (she always called him the Master) is not at all well. We should ring up somebody who has a car to get him home'. ' No dear, he'll be all right. It's just the fresh air. He needs a cup of tea'. I told her I had a good old fashioned Welsh remedy for colds. It was my grandmother's elderberry wine - very thick and potent. Mrs Lindsay and I had a cup of tea and I gave the master a big breakfast cup full of elderberry wine which he knocked back and immediately fell fast asleep. We rang Mrs Gallie, whose husband had come from Balliol and was a great friend of theirs, and she came in the car and took him home where he sweated it off. I think it did him the world of good, actually.

The first Royal occasion was the opening of the University College. This was held in the Salvin Room, at Keele Hall. Various dignitaries came - the Chief Constable, the Bishop of Lichfield and his wife, etc. Mrs Lindsay couldn't care whether you were the coalman, the milkman or the Queen Mother. She treated everybody exactly the same. She would start off by quoting a bit of Coleridge who was constantly on her mind and then she would say, 'Now, who are you dear?' She was about four foot eleven inches and Lord Lindsay was six foot two. On this occasion Mrs Lindsay was meeting everyone at the Clock House door. They were entertaining everyone to lunch. A very tall man approached her and she said, 'Oh my goodness! You're late! Now who are you?' He was the Chief Constable of Staffordshire and he was being very self-effacing when he replied, 'I'm just a policeman'. 'Well', she said, 'you go off into the kitchen with my housekeeper'. He was about to wander off into the kitchen when somebody rescued him and found him his proper place at one of the tables. It just didn't matter to her, and Lord Lindsay was just the same.

ONE'S PLACE

The University didn't give wives an official role at all. We didn't have a family, so it was assumed that I had nothing to do. So, various people found odd jobs for me. Fortunately, I had a bicycle. I was young and energetic and it started off with Alan Gemmell, the Professor of Biology, saying, 'We need to start up a collection in this Department. We don't have the money to buy everything we need'. Daily, Professor Gemmell used to call in on his way to the Department, which was one room in Keele Hall, and say, 'Will you go around the lanes on your bicycle and take with you these matchboxes and glass phials?' I would stick a basket on the front and on the back and go off and bring back anything that moved or had been described to me. When I returned the whole Biology Department - Professor Gemmell the Botanist, R the Zoologist and the Secretary Paula Jenkins and me - would set to, writing labels to put on anything that they could identify. The specimens were still there in 1970! I used to go and look at them fondly, remembering the times that I had got lost around Butterton.

Then the Professor of Geology discovered I was doing this so he would say, 'When you're going along here, will you look to see whether that range of hills can be seen from the left or right?' So, I was the roving messenger. I would be given jobs to do in the Library. I happened to mention to Professor Charlton (Classics) that I was about to go off on my bicycle tour. He said, 'If you've got an afternoon free, do you think you could have a look in the Library for various things?' The Library was on the first floor of Keele Hall on the landing. It had newspapers going back a long time. I was very excited on one occasion because I found the original report on the Battle of Waterloo. At the time we lived on the top floor of Keele Hall so I could pop down and have a 'recky'.

The other wives were busy with small children and trying to get their houses in order. We also had to entertain anybody coming to the University to give lectures because there was no hospitality arrangements and definitely no hospitality expenses. In fact, years later someone complained, because not only did you have to entertain the VIP, you also had to have various other members of the department in and it became very expensive. The first payment we got was one guinea a night (1960) for providing dinner, bed and breakfast, laundering the sheets, etc. The Villa wasn't used then for putting up guests.

ENTER ROYALTY

Princess Margaret became the first Chancellor of the University. The academic staff decided that they must have a member of the Royal Family to be their Chancellor - someone a bit jollier than the Queen, so they chose her younger sister who was delighted to come, and who was an absolute joy. She continued to do this for 25 years, faithfully. She came even when she was suffering from her chronic bronchitis. She came to graduation ceremonies, balls and twice a year when we began awarding higher degrees. When she retired she sent a message to the University saying that she had enjoyed coming so much that she would like to entertain as many of the remaining staff as could be rounded up. She gave a tremendous party for senior members of staff in the

House of Lords in 1986.

People would wangle invitations to come to be presented to Princess Margaret. She was incredible because she did seem to remember from year to year people she had met before. The Queen Mother came to open the University College in 1951. There was another occasion, the Tenth Anniversary of the founding of the University in 1961. The Library in Keele Hall has a Gallery. We were asked to assemble there for a sherry reception at 7.30 pm. The Queen Mother and Princess Margaret came through a secret door and as if by magic appeared between the rows of books on this Gallery. We all 'Ooohed' and 'Aahed' because we had never seen them like this. There was Lord Snowdon in his own-designed evening dress, very smart, but the ladies were quite breath-takingly glamorous. It was every child's idea of a fairy tale princess with all the jewellery and off-the-shoulder gowns - all the shinies and special gloves and shoes and hair-does. We all thought we were pretty hardened to royal visits by then, but it was all rather breath-taking. Then they went out of the secret door and appeared on the same floor as we were and just moved about and talked.

Princess Margaret brought her own detective and one year R had the marvellous job of being in charge of 'the Royal Detective'. He was a splendid chap. We looked after him when she didn't need him, which seemed to be most of the evening. This was a Royal Commemorative Ball held in the Walter Moberly Hall. In those days it was called the Conference Hall. Once we had seen her onto the premises and once she had been photographed by the press and everybody else, the Princess, in those days, removed her precious jewellery and tiara, necklace and ear-rings, etc and would dance with the President of the Union and anyone else who had been lined up. Sometimes she would actually ask members of staff to dance. That was the thing to do. The men had to catch 'the Royal Eye' and decipher whether or not the Princess was saying, 'Ask me to dance'. Without her jewellery it was difficult to tell who the Princess was. So there she was, young, vivacious, obviously enjoying herself. She always stayed much longer than she was expected to. People used to say, 'It will be all right after 1.00 am when the Princess has gone, we can let our hair down'. But not a bit of it. The Princess was still there enjoying herself and it was up to the Vice Chancellor or whoever was in charge to politely suggest to her that perhaps she was tired. Usually, if she left at the proper time the Vice Chancellor would invite various members of staff and their wives back to the Clock House with the Princess, and the party continued.

We were lucky enough to be asked back on one occasion. It was at the time when the hula-hoop was in vogue. Bea Lilley had been on the stage in one of the West End theatres and she used a long rope of pearls to set whizzing around her waist. This evening at the Clock House the Princess did a marvellous take off of Bea Lilley using a rope of real pearls whizzing them around her neck and waist. I think if she was not the person she is, she would have made a very good actress or a variety performer. She was a very good pianist, took Noel Coward off beautifully. She smoked non-stop through a long cigarette holder and played Sir George Barnes' grand piano and sang. She did a wonderful interpretation of 'Mad Dogs and Englishmen' with this clipped accent. She was quite a good mimic and she had quite a good cabaret voice.

The most amusing part of all these Royal Occasions were all the unofficial rehearsals that went on. We all had to learn how to curtsy. One of the wive's (Mrs Finer) mother was Lady McFadeyan - so she came up and taught us how to curtsy right down to the ground not taking our eyes off the Royal Face. These were all the instructions we were given. Can you imagine? We had been warned, too, that we were never to forget to address her as 'Ma'am' and the first time you spoke to her it was 'Your Royal Highness'. Apparently, someone got over-familiar and actually called her Margaret during one of these Royal Occasions, and at a very informal moment when you would have thought she would have been off her guard. But not a bit of it. Immediately she snapped back and I forget the exact words, but she did ask him to remember that

Courtesy of Mrs Mairwen Evans

The annual presentation of the Dr Ron Evans trophy, 'Herbert', by his wife, Mrs Mairwen Evans, to the winners of the annual raft race held on Keele Lakes each year to mark the end of University life - examination results!

Keele University Library Archives

Children at play group on campus. Those brought up on campus had a wonderful time

she was her father's daughter - implying that she was the King's daughter.

The preparations for the Queen Mother's visit in 1951 caused great amusement. We had meetings of wives - all twelve of us (that didn't include Mrs Lindsay). It sounds stupid these days, but we met because an edict was issued telling us what to wear and what not to wear. We were not to wear anything in the colour red or purple because those were the prerogative colours of the Royals visiting and they might be wearing these colours. We were all asked to wear white gloves for shaking hands, and hats. I didn't even have a hat for my wedding! We had great fun going off in the 'wives shopping' bus which took us into Newcastle every Friday at 10.15 am. We spent two hours looking for suitable hats and gloves to wear. My husband's gown was burgundy and gold. I decided I would have a burgundy suit with a gold silk shirt, hoping that burgundy would not be classed as either red or purple. Nobody arrested me!

REVOLTING STUDENTS

Security became tight in the mid-1960s when students started to get a bit anti-royalist. In about 1967 and 68 a few students wrote in the student newspaper, *The Cygnet*, that they did not want to receive their degrees from a member of the Royal Family. It was all part of an international thing which started at the Sorbonne in Paris. Some of our students got cross because they weren't allowed to look at their academic records. This started things off at Keele. They discovered that all the undergraduate records were kept in the Registrar's Office. That was a very temporary pre-fabricated building and some students broke in and set fire to the place. It was a very stupid thing to do. I think they were quite frightened by what they had achieved that night. A few confessed that it had got out of hand. They then decided they would exercise witchcraft on the Vice Chancellor who, at the time, was Professor Campbell Stewart, who had become the first Professor of Education. The students surrounded the Clock House, where he lived, and tried to levitate it. Mrs Campbell Stewart, who was a very down-to-earth, practical and charming lady, appeared on the doorstep and said, 'I don't know what you think you are doing, but would you please go home to your beds. The Vice Chancellor is fast asleep and needs his rest!' The students quietly went away mumbling and the thing fizzled out.

It was from these times that security for Royal visits began to be thought important. So, on Royal Occasions, you would find policemen hiding in the rhododendrons with whistles. Even people living on campus had to have passes. I thought it was all rather sad.

OUTSIDE-IN

People didn't quite know what to make of us. Professional people saw the University as an oasis, but the man in the street whose rates had gone up to pay for the place regarded us with some suspicion, I think. The doors were open to the local people. There was an annual garden party just after the end of the academic year, when the whole of the Estate was thrown open to the public. Quite a lot of people came from the village. There were side shows and stalls and auctions. As time went on and proper buildings went up, people came to see where the students worked. The garden parties were held on the lower terrace. There would be a buffet in a marquee and people went for walks along the lakes. It gave people a chance to see what went on inside the walls. The bus route, then, went outside the walls. I think some came to see how the money was spent. But, on the whole, I think people approved.

THE WAY WE WERE

When we first came the post office was an extraordinary place. It was in the Middle House as it is now called. It moved across the road in the late 1950s. You stood outside the window and pressed the bell. The window was pushed up and a head appeared. It was Mrs Askey, the post-mistress. She gave you your stamps and if you were lucky you got them on your letter before they got soaking wet. It was all outside. The Post Office moved over to Juniper Cottage before it came to the present building.

The shop on campus came after the Students' Union was built. Then came the banks. There was always a shop on campus. It was a little hut. The huts had five small rooms and one very big room at the end of a long corridor, which ran down the whole length of the hut. One of these huts was taken over as a shop and was a popular meeting place. The supermarket came later, run by Mr Wood. It was run by the Students' Union at first.

Lord Lindsay said he wanted this to be a place for families. So, he would say to wives, 'When you've finished your shopping bring them to the Senior Common Room for tea'. Can you imagine this happening now? But it did then.

The Second Eye

BEGINNINGS
After the professors were appointed we came down to stay at weekends at the North Staffordshire Hotel - husbands and wives - to discuss with Lord Lindsay the kinds of houses we wanted, what the houses were going to be like and the general set-up of the place. All the numbers of the houses were put into Lord Lindsay's top hat and that's how we chose. The houses were not built but they were plotted out in Church Plantation.

When we arrived on 15th September 1950 we were in bungalows. Some were better than others. There were lots because they put us up and all the undergraduates. Ours was a former ablution block, which meant it was better built. The others were long things with rooms in rows. They were very warm and very comfortable and had been well converted.

The undergraduates came in the middle of October. It was quite nice weather then. The girls were in bungalows close to us so we got to know them. Occasionally the hot water didn't work so they came to have baths in our bungalow. The men and women were segregated. The men were on one side of the main road and the women were on the other. All the bungalows were situated roughly between where the Chapel and the Chemistry Building are today.

We (as wives) had no official role but we took our role as wives of professors seriously and generally entertained for our department and undergraduates. The wardens looked after the students very carefully. There was a health centre of sorts and a visiting doctor. It wasn't long before Dr Scott came. There was always a nurse or sister about for family emergencies.

GETTING STARTED
When the idea of the place was mooted all the schools were contacted - send us a boy or girl whom you think would be a good person to start in the University. We were all pioneers so we were all in it together. They were all hand-picked, the first lot, pretty well, anyway. Some had done their military service. In the first intake there was only one man who didn't wear a tie. They wore shirts and gowns. My husband walked around in gum boots. He wasn't known for his good dressing. The students worked hard; the lights were on in the labs nearly all night. They played hard too.

The students had their rooms in the huts. There were no playing fields. The Chapel was a slightly larger hut. Another was the Union. There were no departmental buildings, of course. The first Chemistry Department was a room in Keele Hall. There was just my husband and his secretary and his laboratory steward to start with. It was mud, mud, mud. Professor Williams used to carry his children from the bungalows to the school bus because they were too small to go through the mud. We all wore gum boots.

There were two buses, one to the College which took the children to school and brought the cleaners in and out, and one for shopping. There was a hard-standing for the bus stop, where the Geology Department is now. Church Plantation was finished after about two years. The army had been all over the gardens and we dug up old helmets and tins of oil. The gas men found about eight leaks in the gas pipes after the gas was laid on! This was somewhat dangerous given that we were burning off the undergrowth in our gardens at the time.

When we arrived they hadn't got Keele Hall quite right. The floors were not completely finished and the electricity wasn't right. In fact it was a miracle that it was finished as it was for the beginning of term. How the tapestries remained, I can't think! Various inhabitants during the War had burned the roof off and dug up the floors. The ceilings were completely redone and painted. The grounds had been neglected during the War. The landing craft were trained on the lawns. It was quite a job to get it all put right.

We were glad to be out of the bungalows. The rent for Church Plantation houses was higher so it was assumed that those higher up the ladder would be able to afford it. The idea of Springpool was started off by staff who wished to stay after they retired. We tried to keep it like an Estate and keep away from 'campus', but it was no good, it just took over. The Estate then became just like a housing estate rather than an Estate in the traditional manner.

RECREATION

The staff and students socialised continuously. We had them all to parties and they had us to their rooms. There was a country dance class that we all went to. There were film societies and almost as many societies as there were students. The Walter Moberly Hall was used for concerts and general get-togethers. The interest in the Arts was quite strong. Everyone was interested in everything. We had a Fine Art Society and we got various people to come and lecture. We had some very good people come to give concerts. There was no Music Department then. There were Art Exhibitions usually in Keele Hall, and a picture lending club where we could borrow pictures for the year. I went to some Foundation Year lectures. There was also music in Hanley and more cinemas, and the students put on Gilbert and Sullivan and various plays. There was also bingo and the Theatre Royal.

The Keele Players was then all staff. There was a student Drama Society and I was very involved with that. I saw the first production in the Clock House courtyard - it was Henry IV Part I. I said, 'Those costumes are dreadful!' and I complained to the Professor of English who looked after it and helped them. So he said, 'Why don't you do it?' So I did. I set to and got them made for two or three years. The Dell was sometimes used for small productions and on the slopes just in front of the lakes we sometimes held drama productions. Dorothy Hodgkinson was the leading light, certainly of the Keele Players. She acted and she produced. The productions were held in the refectory.

The Senior Common Room was for academic staff and registry. The other staff had their own Common Room in the Brewhouse. The non-academic staff Christmas Party was started by Mrs Morgan. When she died it lapsed. When my husband became the Deputy Principal I said, 'Let's start it again'. So we did. The staff and their wives ran it. It used to be hilarious fun. We had dances and games and the academic staff worked behind the bar.

When we did get the sports field going many people turned up to watch games. I was very much involved with the rugger club. My husband was the President and I held a party for them every year. The girls challenged the professors to a game of hockey each year. At first it was played at the Westlands.

Baby-sitting was a good way to get to know students. We took one on holiday with us. We got to know the local medics very quickly through the GP in Madeley, who looked after us. They'd have parties and they'd invite us to meet other people who were consultants, so we had quite a large circle of friends that way. There were garden parties in summer for the locals. I don't remember when they started. The Senior Common Room also put on a Neighbours' Dinner, where they invited local farmers and people to come. I don't know if it was an all male event. I never went. We also had a party after finals, just before the results came out. I remember a boy sitting in the corner crying the whole time!

A lot of campus activities died out as people got much more interested in thinking that they had to get a degree rather than be educated.

We didn't bother about nurseries or play groups. We looked after our own children and the children were in and out of each other's houses all day. They played happily together. I think some went to the village school and into Newcastle. After the 11-plus some went to Wolstanton High, Newcastle School or boarding school. They had a wonderful time. We were all young so the children would be aged from between two and 14. The students adored them. They organised bonfires for them and everyone knew everyone else.

By the time Princess Margaret came all the mud had gone. I remember it mostly when Sir George Barnes was here and my husband was the Deputy Principal. When Princess Margaret first came she brought a much larger entourage - footmen and everybody else. At the end it was just a Lady-in-Waiting and an Equerry. She was extremely good fun and extremely intelligent. Preparations for her visits were very elaborate and I remember policemen in every bush. Security was very strict. We were taught how to curtsy and directives would come up from the Palace. We couldn't talk politics with her but otherwise it was perfectly easy - like talking to friends. The first 'Royal' Balls were held in the Conference Hall (now the Modern Languages Building - once the Walter Moberly Hall), Keele Hall and the Students' Union.

REVOLTING STUDENTS

These were nasty times. Paint was thrown through the Registrar's window. I was away when the very worst happened. I am sure there was a reason. Since then, students have become quieter. There were more innocent pranks. There is a big chandelier in the Great Hall. One night that was found in the woods - lit. How it got there and how it got lit, I've no idea. In the first few terms it was just high spirits. When the Clock House was being refurbished someone built a wall right across. After a few years the pioneering spirit died, of course. At first we were all in it together. We had a special feeling for the first lot because they were not much younger than we were.

INSIDE-OUT

Because Lord Lindsay was a Labour Peer, I think people thought that we were teaching all these children to become communists. The local people called us 'The Kremlin'. I think people in the village rather thought that we would be like the Grand Duke Michael and have garden parties for them; but we were poor academics. We got to know Mr and Mrs Jackson in the village shop well. Some members of staff went on to the Parish Council so they probably got to know them better. Goods were delivered from the town - Brassingtons, Bodleys and Capener the butcher - delivered. We didn't have to bring bread back. Indeed, the butcher would decide himself what we might want and he would leave it on the doorstep. This happened twice a week!

The grounds were better then. The Covert was a covert and there were partridges in it. Barnes' Dell, in the woods, was very nice - until it was 'landscaped'. It was full of bluebells with a stream at the bottom - between the second and third lake.

The Third Eye

We came in August 1954 to Larchwood. We moved straight into a house and I think we were the first to do so on appointment. All the grass was mud, no grass had grown. The houses hadn't been built that long. The garden was a field really and the patch in the front of our houses was mud. It was a very special kind of mud, a very red mud, a very staining mud. We were conscious of the fact that we could make pots out of it. The children were rolling in it and you couldn't get the washing clean. We all went around in gum boots. If you were there from the beginning you were the golden gum boots. I think we just missed being the bronze gum boots. It was my husband's first job and we didn't have children.

The houses at Larchwood had no fitted kitchens. We had a dresser and a kitchen cabinet, that kind of thing. Nobody had a fridge. We had one in 1968 and my husband marked O and A Level papers all summer to buy one. We took our things to wash, to the launderette in Newcastle, on the wives' bus. I went on the bus for many years until we bought a car. I think rationing finished by 1954. We weren't back to normal. Things were much shorter after the War than during. Bread was rationed after the War; it wasn't rationed during. We didn't have dinner parties, we invited people around for coffee and lemon meringue pie, that sort of thing.

A WOMAN'S PLACE

As wives we mucked in as best we could. It was an enjoyable and exciting time. We had a hand in our husband's job because we weren't stuck miles away. The University was very happy that wives were there to make the amalgam of staff and students work. We did a lot of entertaining of students. Tutors had their groups around for buffet meals at least once a term. There was a time during my first year when I knew every student's face. There were about 800 then. It didn't happen to us but it happened to others that students would arrive at the front door and say, 'The water isn't running, could we use your bathroom?' Late one night, one of my husband's students arrived holding a girl by the hand saying, 'This is Cyn'. We kept our faces straight because he was a very serious young man. Cynthia, who was the daughter of a clergyman, had arrived unexpectedly to spend the week-end with him and 'She couldn't possibly stay in my room', so could we 'possibly give her a bed for the week-end?' So we took in Cyn.

KIDS ON CAMPUS

Children were coming along at a fair rate. At that time we could have children at home and the District Nurse in her little black Austin 8 would come. We would see this car parked outside someone's house and you'd think, 'Ah! She must be pregnant'. In the fullness of time another child would arrive. In the late 1960s I'd open my back door and the boys would charge out and there would be about 30 other children playing on the grass in the middle. We'd just keep an eye on everyone else's children; we'd pick them up and dust them down, that sort of thing.

Life on the Larchwood was very entertaining. There was a visiting American Professor who was a scientist and on this particular afternoon he decided he would make a hot-air balloon for the children. He made it out of tissue paper with a platform beneath on which he put straw and lit it so the hot air filled the balloon. It was all rather daft now I come to think about it. The balloon took off and we watched it as it headed off towards the farmer's haystack yard with everybody chasing after it.

The children used to muck in together to play. Occasionally, in the summer, they would combine all their toys. Once they got all their train sets and linked them together so that they joined from one end of Larchwood to the other, with sidings and so on. It was a life, I think, we couldn't have experienced anywhere else. Then we made a wool house. They stuck bamboo canes into the green and borrowed, stole, gained, balls of wool from their mothers and they wove this house around the sticks. It was about six foot across.

The village school was, when we first arrived, the old village school. It had two rooms with a big iron stove in each. The floors were extremely rough and worn. There were two teachers - one very elderly. My son spent two or three days there at the end of one term and when the new term began he started at the new school. Parents on campus decided early that they would

Keele University Library Archives

Staff progress to the Degree Day ceremony. It was on one such occasion that the Extraordinary General Meeting was called to decide upon the representation of the Keele Nursery on the Residents Association

Keele University Library Archives

The wardrobe mistress at work - Jean Springall, Dorothy Hodgkinson and Mairwen Evans doing their bit for the Keele Players

support the village school and make it bigger and better and lobby for a new school because the old one couldn't cope. I think the teachers at the new village school might have had a pretty rough time because the fathers, most were academics, were very interested, particularly those on the Education side, to know what was happening at the school and they kept a pretty close eye on things which might have made teachers' lives a bit difficult. A lot of the children were rather bright and had a lot of opportunities at home. By making the school develop it benefited everyone. There were 6 and 17 in a class then.

When our second child was three he joined the campus nursery. Inge Miller lived in 16 Church Plantation and I think she had had training as a nursery school teacher and she wanted to start up a nursery school. She was asking which children would be interested and so on. I went along and helped. She turned the sitting room into the nursery and she had built on to the house a little conservatory for the sand-and-water-and-splashing-about area. I think we must have paid something but I can't remember what. We helped out because we wanted it to work. My son would have been the youngest and he went three half days per week. There would have been 15 to 20 other children. The Principal at the time had just died - that was Lennard-Jones and we were waiting for another, who was Sir George Barnes.

The nursery school was, as far as I know, private. It was so independent that the wives felt that they needed a voice on the Residents' Association. We felt that anything that concerned the residents, certainly concerned our nursery school. The Residents' Association was for those employed by the University and that didn't include (many) women. There was quite a big fight, I might say. It started off with us thinking that the nursery school needed a voice, so we applied to go onto the Residents' Association. I believe the application was turned down. This led to us feeling that wives should also have a say. We were told that our views would be there in the shape of our husband's. We said 'yes, but our husbands don't always share our views'. (At that time we were told what colour our front doors had to be. There was a choice of two colours and we were told the colour to paint our walls.) We were beginning to get a bit stroppy, shall we say. We didn't ask for a vote, we simply asked that the wives be able to attend the association meeting and, when it was appropriate, express our views. This was denied us. There were one or two husbands who understood our view and who were anxious to help. But there were one or two who were adamant that we should not be represented on the Residents' Association. We were asked to talk to our husbands and try to persuade them to vote in favour. One wife spoke to her husband and his views were rather negative to say the least. Her husband was quite a character. Anyway, there was something of an exchange of words and he was quite firm in the matter. They were eating spaghetti at the time and there was a tureen on the table. She said, 'I simply got up and inverted the tureen of spaghetti over his head and walked out!'

The only way we could get anything done was to get a quorum of the whole membership of the Residents' Association, which was difficult because they were never together, to hold an Extraordinary General Meeting. The menfolk in favour decided they would spring an EGM when they were queuing up for Degree Day, in their robes. When they were all gathered in the Hall courtyard, waiting to process, suddenly, they had this EGM, voted, and we got on. I'm not sure that we exercised our right very much but at least Inge could go and represent the Nursery. It was the Nursery that had sparked it all off.

When Inge left, the Nursery had to move and I think it went to the huts before it got taken over as a more professional nursery school.

DRAMA AT KEELE

In 1954 I got involved with the Keele Players. I think it had just started. The very first play was produced by Dorothy Hodgkinson - 'You Can't Take it With You'. All the plays were done in what is now Horwood Refectory. In those days we had the hall downstairs with the stage. It was purpose built for performances. The Walter Moberly Hall wasn't built then. We did one or two plays a year. The performances were, at first, for three nights then it went to a week. We did 'The Father' in 1958. Mary Glover who played the lead fell ill, so Dorothy had to take over at the last minute. This play had a certain amount of drama and in one part the father throws an oil lamp at his wife. As this happens the curtain closes so the audience doesn't know whether it hits her or not. We did it rather well. At one performance, there were nurses and a blood transfusion unit downstairs, which had been there all day; this caused quite a frisson amongst the audience in the interval. I based my part on a woman I knew. The play was about a battle for control within a marriage. My husband was in the audience and during the interval he overheard someone say, 'By Golly! I can't believe that that's acting. I bet she's type cast. I bet she's absolute hell to live with!' My husband came home chortling.

Sammy Finer and Mike Paffard were in The Players and in one particular production they played FBI Agents or something. Sammy looked marvellous in slouched hat and with cigarette dangling from his lip. My husband and he had two lines to say between them and Sammy got so worked up, he was pacing up and down and rehearsing both lines in the wings so that when he came on he said them both. The audience, which was mostly students, enjoyed watching the staff make fools of themselves, at the very least. The hall was always packed. We enjoyed it and we did quite well. We decided amongst ourselves what we should perform. We put on our review, at one time, in the Salvin Room. It was wives, in particular, who started the Keele Players for their own entertainment. There were others who did musical things.

THE ROYAL 'OUI'

I remember Princess Margaret coming. I was introduced to the Queen Mother when my husband was Deputy Vice Chancellor. There were lots of functions and the Vice Chancellor would have to look after his guests, so the Deputy Vice Chancellor looked after the wives of the Honorary Graduands. There would be a lunch, very often at a different location to the one Princess Margaret was at. We would 'sheep-dog' those that were introduced to her. I am sure there were instructions to the University on what the Princess would like to eat, what she would like to happen. There were instructions about curtsying and there were practice sessions. I think John Hodgkinson, the Registrar, taught the undergraduates how to curtsy. I'm sure he did it beautifully!

I remember once that I had five wives of Honorary Graduands that I had to 'sheep-dog'. I lost one. She just disappeared. She had decided that she didn't fancy going to the Degree Ceremony so she went off to see a friend without telling anyone. I went to one Ball on the occasion of the Twenty-First Anniversary of the University at the King's Hall, Stoke. There were under plates of such magnificence! It all belonged to Stoke City Council.

Princess Margaret's favourite band was, I think, Johnny Dankworth. She enjoyed dancing to them and she always requested that there be such a band. It was very expensive, I think. She danced with the most handsome young men that we could find. Of course they had to be brought along and introduced to her first. I remember my husband and I were told to go and find so-and-so. He would be with his wife, so my job was to keep the wife company whilst he was off dancing with the Princess, and it might be a little while before he came back. She enjoyed dancing and she enjoyed balls and often stayed much later than scheduled.

The Queen Mother came two or three times. On the Twenty-First Anniversary, they both came. On one occasion, when the non-academic staff were gathered at the Hawthorns, the Queen Mother and Princess Margaret were brought along to be introduced. They were all lining the walls of this room and the arrangement was that the Queen Mother would go down one side and the Princess down the other and they would cross over at the bottom and proceed until they had

Professor Alan Gemmell, a *'Gardener's Question Time'* favourite

Sir George Barnes, conservator of Bluebell Wood. Digging and delving in the Keele undergrowth was a relaxation for him

The Queen Mother receiving her Honarary Degree from the President of the University College, Princess Margaret. In her acceptance speech she said, 'Madam President and dear daughter'

Keele University Library Archives

The Keele Players in action in 'You Can't Take It With You'. Professor Sammy Finer stands in the doorway (middle). The cast hold their breath - will he get his one line right this time?

Author's collection

The Larchwood, Keele University

gone right around the room and chatted to everybody. We got them there and hung around whilst they did their gavotte, as it were, and came back to us. Princess Margaret had gone down one side and was half way up the other before the Queen Mother had got half way down one side. The Queen Mother gave the appearance of enjoying talking to people. Princess Margaret tended to be more rapid and efficient. She would pick the ones she stopped to speak to, which would be all of the young men. The Queen Mother made everybody's day.

On that occasion I was 'parked' with the Queen Mother and I was introduced to her and I began to talk to her. The Lady-in-Waiting said, 'Just talk to her and don't leave her until we come back'. I had a nice conversation with her. Her eyesight seemed to be unfocussed. The conversation went on and we talked of this and that for really a long time. I felt uneasy, but the Queen Mother was so relaxed, laid back and warm. Talking to Princess Margaret was rather different. You were very conscious of protocol and her status.

On one occasion when she came, we were in the Great Hall having sherry and very self-consciously talking to one another, conscious of the fact that 'THEY' were there and moving around. I looked across at the Princess and noted that she was really quite slight. She had the most beautiful and vivid violet eyes. I think Elizabeth Taylor was seen in a film with eyes of such a colour. I think I was looking across at her and suddenly she turned around and looked at me. She'd known that I had been looking. She fixed her eye on me in a most autocratic way as if to say, 'Stop staring'. I felt the full presence of her personality on that occasion. Lord Snowdon was a little ill-at-ease I felt.

We were usually in charge of the 'second tier' - local councillors, and their wives. We had to stack them up and keep them entertained until things were ready. It was a very efficient and smooth operation. The Ladies-in-Waiting would be there - two if the Queen Mother was present - and an Equerry, at least one who made sure that we did everything smoothly. So we had this flight path of people who were waiting to be introduced and have this little conversation and we would keep them, I won't say entertained, because they were really quite nervous.

REVOLTING STUDENTS

The students began to feel their feet just as, I suppose, we the wives began to flex our muscles to be on the Residents' Association. They began to feel that they wanted their say in what happened. Maybe the University was a bit slow in complying. However it started, the people of 'rent a crowd' began to come in. It turned nasty in that our students were not in the forefront of the troubles. They were egged on by the more professional agitators that came in. I say this with some certainty. The police were there and my husband would go around the campus at night keeping an eye on things and he would say to the police, 'I don't recognise these people'. The police officer would say, 'That's so-and-so'. The agitators would just move around from one university to another.

There was a summer in 1968 when it was particularly bad. I remember them surrounding the Clock House and chanting. There were suggestions or worries that the students would burn something down. There had been a fire at the Registry. My husband used to go out at night to see what was happening to make sure that the Library was secure. One night some students were spotted on the Library roof. The police were called and they surrounded the building. Eventually two figures abseiled down. They were arrested and when they were asked what they were doing, it turned out that they were two climbers who night climbed. The police didn't believe them. But, when they went to their rooms the police found books on climbing so they believed them in the end.

At another time the students made a protest by taking all their clothes off. In front of the Students' Union, in those days, there was a large area of grass and against this the buses used to draw up to take the cleaning staff home. The students had got there in a fair number and took their clothes off. Luckily it was a sunny day. The cleaning staff were half amused and half taken aback. We were sunbathing in our back garden and the first thing we knew about it was when my son's friend came rushing up saying, 'The students have got all their clothes off down at the Union!' They got on their bikes and cycled off and got into a line around these students and made comments on what they could see, the size of what they could see and the various merits of what they could see. This crumpled the students and they dispersed. The national press was out in force. They would be there within a quarter-of-an-hour of anything happening. Either someone had rung them when things happened or they were informed before hand.

Up until this time we'd had a close, friendly relationship with the students. Perhaps they had had enough of this. Perhaps we were too close and, just like a family, the children were growing up and felt that they needed some distance between themselves and us. Also the numbers were growing. Certain things began to happen. A pot of paint was thrown through the window of the Registrar's house, across a valued family treasure, frightening their very elderly mother. This was seen as beyond what was acceptable. Our house had flour bombs thrown at it. It didn't worry us unduly but it agitated the children.

It all died down. There was genuine concern at the time because unpleasant things had happened in France and London. We valued the relationship we had with our students so we thought it all a shame. I think our own students were fond enough of us not to take the extreme measures that might have been taken elsewhere. Looking back, for a revolution, the Keele Revolt was a mild one. Whilst it was all going on the students were coming around campus singing Christmas Carols and we had them in for mince pies and punch and they would stay and chatter. The worst events happened, probably, in two terms. The disagreements, the protests, the sit-ins, stand-ins, letters etc. went on for much longer - about three years. It was 1968 to 1971 - something like that. It was all over by 1971.

Things changed after that. Numbers grew. Things weren't as close as they had been, yet I don't think the relationship between staff and students ever broke down. These events confirmed the worst fears of the town to some extent. But, you see, we had got used to living amongst students. We didn't take them at face value. We knew how they dressed and that their appearance was a necessary part of their removal from home. We took very little notice of it. Some of the most ragged, long-haired, bare-footed students would be the most polite, interesting and interested and we had conversations with them that we enjoyed.

INSIDE-OUT
We couldn't live off campus so we were a bit hesitant about joining in village things. We couldn't live there but we were very interested in what happened in the village. Our children went to the village school. I think we were a bit hesitant about swamping the villagers' opinions. We were aware that we were a vocal lot.

The Potteries people might have felt resentful that this University had been tacked on to the edge of them because they had tried, in the past, to get a University in their area but the proposal had been turned down. Also, the Potteries is a very close-knit society. It is a stable community. This means that they don't have the same needs as you to make friends. They have no need of your friendship in the way that you are grasping for theirs. We, on the campus, therefore, clung to each other. We only had the bus to link us to the outside world.

CHAPTER 16
FROM ANOTHER COUNTRY

BEGINNINGS

The first time I set eyes on the place was May 1951. I had just come back from France for an interview. It was a beautiful Spring evening. I was a bit late arriving by train, but I was just in time to catch dinner in Horwood which was attended by the first batch of around 150 students. The staff also attended and everyone wore gowns. The first wave of staff had been appointed a year earlier to begin in 1950. I was appointed during the second wave. I was struck by the rural atmosphere, just having come through Stoke. There was a lot of building going on. There were many huts and it was much like an army camp. The first houses were being built at the top of the hill, Church Plantation, and there were the beginnings of some science blocks.

What is now the Senior Common Room Bar, was the home then, for six assistant lecturers in the humanities. We had a desk each and that was the sum total of the accommodation. There were about 15 students in one year, another person and myself.

The students were recruited by the senior academic staff. It was a peculiar situation because the staff were divided between senior professors and assistant lecturers, with little in between. Most of the administration was done by the senior professors. There were, of course, committees. Grades for the first students were, I think, important, but I think to begin with, they were looking for something else. There were certainly a lot of mature students. My first preoccupations were setting up a course in French. There were only two of us to do that and there was a lot of French literature to be taught. For the first 2 to 3 years we were in Keele Hall. We were then moved to the Tawney Building which was then the General Arts Building.

THE FOUNDATION YEAR SYSTEM

The Foundation Year (FY) was an attempt to get away from what was deemed dangerous - specialisation. The novelty has, I think, been a little overplayed. It was inspired, in some respects, by the Scottish education system, but it had to be different in order to justify setting up a new university. The original programme for this FY, as I understand it, was put together by about three people who were original professorial appointments. They did the donkey work, and in a great hurry as well. If you look at the first prospectus it says, *'during the first year course, the exact nature of the requirements has not yet been decided but it will not involve external examiners, and students who fail the first test (in June) will be allowed to retake the test before the next session'*.

All the students had to take three subsidiary subjects, and not just two principal subjects. Some took the Certificate in Education. It was therefore a considerable undertaking, which explains, perhaps, why one of the subsidiaries was dropped in later years. The students took the FY seriously and there was a general feeling of enthusiasm amongst the students. It was new, it was different. At first, local authorities questioned the extra year. When it was explained they became sold on the idea and thought it a good one.

During the FY the students could change their minds re their specialism. They could shop around. At the time the standard idea of a university was to specialise in a single Honours subject and it was specifically to contest this idea of single Honours that the joint Honours system at Keele was established. As a teacher here I found that I was forced to look at my own subject in a wider context. I'm not sure this would have happened had I been teaching in another university.

Students were allocated to a member of staff who was 'the Tutor' - the moral Tutor. I don't know what they did, but they were responsible for a particular group of students. In my day, when you got to college you were on your own. Now, if you were in trouble you went to your

Tutor. But you'd better not be in trouble!

The 'Discussion Groups' were a feature of the FY - a later innovation. Each group had three members of staff representing the three Boards of Study - Arts, Science and Humanities. One would be chairman or 'in charge' of about eight to ten students. We would all discuss a topic. Certain group topics were suggested in the handbook and these topics related to the lecture courses. It was a showcase. In my day, European Literature was flavour of the month. I must confess that it was a bit of a chore. The success of the Discussion Group depended entirely on the group and some chairpersons were better than others. Some groups visited local mines and various places. The professors gave lectures. Although it wasn't intended as such, it was a selling point for a department or subject. Eventually, everyone did the lecturing. In the end the Discussion Groups were got rid of.

The idea was that Keele would have 600 students maximum. Masses of money was poured into the newer universities in the 1960s and left Keele behind. Now, in the last ten years there has been another change. Lord Lindsay was a Philosopher, 'sociologically oriented' as he put it, but a Labour Peer and a well-known figure who had won a famous by-election. He was interested in the Social Sciences. The Reverend Tommy Horwood, the Vicar of Etruria and a well-known local figure, may have been instrumental in getting things off the ground.

The religious thing was another feature of the Keele landscape. It was intended that there would be a moral and spiritual content. Historical Theology was a topic of the FY programme. Two Professors of Philosophy were appointed. Lord Lindsay had a Scottish and Oxbridge background, so Keele was modelling itself around these. There were very, very strict regulations - just as there were in Oxford - about men and women liaising after dinner. They had to be on one side or the other of the 'spine' road according to their sex, after 7.30 pm. The porters used to patrol. The students accepted this, or got round it if they could. The naivete of authority to think that nothing could happen until it was dark! The fact that there were public standards and that these were accepted as such was important - not that they were adhered to.

The original people who came here tended to be idealists. It was a bit of a dream, a bit Utopian. A lot of work had been done on the FY so some couldn't let go to make it more acceptable. When it came to our 20 year celebration I thought that this would have been a good time to take stock. People outside wanted to understand what we were doing. At the same time there seemed to be very little discourse between the University and the Potteries and we didn't do anything to attract them. Keele never attracted money from local industry as Nottingham did (Boots) and East Anglia has done (Sainsbury). Little was done to 'sell' the place. Now, sponsorship is taken for granted. My wife became involved in this side of things at Keele, as she will tell you.

The original professors were as young as the assistant lecturers. As a research fellow in Paris we earned more money than here. Students paid about £100 per session to stay at Keele, at that time. We had had many changes of address, so as accommodation was offered, Keele was attractive to us. In the 1950s houses were difficult to come by. People didn't buy homes as much. I had finished in Paris so I had to find a job. I could have gone back to Nottingham to teach at a school there.

A Woman's Place

As a 'wife' I was invited up for the weekend. I sat there on the terrace - echoes of Edwardian grandeur - having tea. The reality was different. We lived in a concrete, prefabricated hut situated near to the Geography Department, next to the site of the Walter Moberly Hall. There was a static water tank at the bottom and Molly Badcock used to fish in it with a net for various things to do with her research interests.

We had one child at the time who was not quite equipped for Keele and the mud, in her little white coat and boots. Most wives had small children and were involved in that. Some did part-time teaching. Some were more outgoing and more socially minded than others. We had a fair amount of getting together with the students. We were also visited by members of other institutions. There weren't many foreign students then so we used to have them in for Christmas lunch if they weren't going home.

Some of the mature students were as old as us and would have been working really hard. However, they did quite a lot for the children. They did Christmas pantomimes, there was a rag, and bonfires, and the Brownies. Children had a very good time. Very few of the professors had cars. We had young children so we tended to stay on the campus. There was the weekly 'housewives' bus which accommodated about 14 people. It was used to take the domestic staff onto the campus but it ran free on Friday mornings, and that was 'the great escape'!

There were lots of babysitters so we went off to Scottish dancing, dinners and parties. We were mixed together; students, staff and staff from other departments. There were occasional film shows and the usual student societies. Most of the subjects had their own societies. There were free concerts in Keele Hall.

REVOLTING STUDENTS

There was a genuine student movement in the late 1960s. There was this problem about confidentiality of files so there were these sit-ins, break-ins, half-hearted arson and nudism. Every university had it. It was the fashion and there were some rather unpleasant episodes. There were fears at Graduation ceremonies so there were policemen with dogs, and a nasty atmosphere. The Vice Chancellor did keep the lid on things. The students wanted access to everything. They wanted representation and consultation. Then they had no representation on Senate. The staff united in an unofficial way to keep watch on Keele Hall to make sure it didn't come to harm. The Registry was set on fire.

It was the age of protest and it suddenly blew up. It was part of a movement that started in Paris. Then there was Vietnam. It did change the whole atmosphere and things were never quite the same again. It was mainly aimed at the administration, although students also wanted a say in the curriculum. When identity cards were introduced there was the ritual burning.

The single thing which did the most damage to Keele was when the students stripped their clothes off and walked into the campus shop. It was a hot day. They had probably contacted the press beforehand. That lingered for a year. It was more than a student prank. They intended damage - the national press was there. These were not like the pranks of the early days when they put a bike on top of a building. You can still see the graffiti from the early days on the refectory wall on the left as you enter Keele Hall courtyard. There are traces of paint which says 'Good Luck Lads'. That was put there on the eve of the first degree examinations. It's still visible. The other prank was, someone shinned up the tower of the Chemistry building and daubed 'frying tonight' on the chimney.

OUTSIDE-IN

The 1960s was the age of the young person. In the 1970s things began to get tight. Jobs were harder to come by so people seemed to take life more seriously. There was a purpose.

We didn't talk about the media in those days, but the newspapers wrote a lot about Keele. *The Times* did a regional spread in 1951, just before I came here, on 'The New Development'. We were referred to as 'Stoke'. This was not so much about the University as a geographical location. *The Sentinel* did regular reports. There was certainly an upsurge of interest when Princess Margaret became Chancellor. That did change the standing of the place with local people.

There was a mixture of curiosity and suspicion, I suppose. We were an ongoing interest to the education establishment because we were a new university. We were later overtaken by other, newer universities - Sussex, Lancaster and so on.

The original extra-mural thing was not done at Keele, but by Oxford. This might have been a factor mitigating against Keele's involvement in the locality. One thing that could have provided a link, which didn't, was that the University had nothing to do with ceramics and therefore nothing to do with the Potteries. This was one of the errors. Some universities developed on the basis of local industry. That never quite happened with Keele. The idea of a local education establishment got snarled up with the precepts and educational idealism associated with Lindsay, and the two things didn't quite produce what people wanted to see.

In the 1970s the Students Union were thinking of installing a contraceptive machine in the Union. There was a terrific brouhaha about that in the press and that came at a time when the University was appealing for money via their Expansion Appeal and they did lose money as a result. Then there were people thinking that the University was a hot-bed of sex and whatever, which simply wasn't true. It was just a practical suggestion, but at the wrong time, and it outraged public opinion.

THE WAY WE WERE

When I first came the Salvin Room was the Reading Room. The Library went into the Old Library. Everywhere else in the Hall was being used for practical purposes. The spine road was once a main road and we'd see the students walking up and down in their gowns. All the students wore gowns to tutorials. The Chapel was a Nissen hut and there was a Sunday School for the children run by Mary Glover.

The semi-family atmosphere has gone now. We used to remember students' names and faces and we knew all our academic colleagues. The atmosphere now is more commercial and the emphasis is on making a buck - be it fast or slow!

In 1953 a pair of swans was presented to Keele by the Queen Mother. This one, which cruises the Keele Lakes, is probably descended from the original pair. Photograph by Peter Kirby

Keele University Library Archives

Interlude: DOGGED ADMINISTRATORS, REVOLTING STUDENTS

By the 1960s change was in the air. After the Robbins Report more students were being admitted into higher education, jobs were still readily available for eighteen year olds and graduates and although there was a general feeling of security there was also a prevalent feeling of restlessness. Inflation crept upwards as the Wilson government outstayed its welcome. Economies, the pundits said, had to be made but economising was never the expected role of a labour government. Education, health and the nationalised industries were obvious targets but few politicians had the courage and, possibly, the imagination, to make monumental changes.

A small revolution had taken place in the infant and junior sectors of state education but change in secondary schools was held up by the universities, who were unwilling to change, fearing, partly, that standards would be adversely affected if Ordinary and Advanced Level examinations were to be abolished or tampered with. Universities were still, at the time, part of the 'old school tie' network and the type of education dispensed to students was based largely on the Oxbridge system, which in turn had its roots somewhere between classical Greece and ancient China. If innovation existed in this sector it was tolerated rather than warmly embraced. Much of the educational debate at the time centred around the need to undertake evangelical work amongst the working classes and many volumes were written on the how and the why of enticing working class children into higher education and the need to keep or abolish the eleven plus and grammar schools in favour of comprehensives. In retrospect it felt as if a large wooden spoon had begun to stir the contents of a somewhat stodgy pot, if only to see what would happen as a result.

The student movement of the late 1960s should have come, therefore, as no great surprise. Stage management of the system was no doubt happening then as it is more obviously happening now. Student revolt therefore, was possibly encouraged in order to force the hand of stubborn institutions which in the 20th century saw some cachet in continuing to operate 'behind the times'. Had it not been welcomed one can only wonder if the 'student revolution' would have taken off as quickly. Initially the students were not asking for anything extraordinary - representation on university governing bodies and a relaxation of some of the more paternalistic rules and regulations. The fact that university staff appeared unable to deal with such requests in a rational and adult way, amazes. The democratic principles enshrined in their University Charters were clearly empty words in reality and the only way that some universities knew how to deal with the conflict was to create a 'them' and 'us' syndrome and to treat the whole matter as a disciplinary problem.

The revolt on the Keele campus was harder to take since students and staff inhabited the same campus territory - they lived together and had done so reasonably amicably since Keele's inception, thus divorce, when it came, was harder to accept. However, it seemed that the relation was close provided the masters ruled and the students obeyed. The Keele Estate role of master had been assumed by the university and all was well, provided that everyone knew their place. But the 1960s saw a challenge to the old order and change, however small, was inevitable. Had the universities been more proactive and less defensive at the time, the student revolution would, no doubt, have petered out. As a result of this mismanagement the student revolution cost many institutions dearly in terms of grant aid and local investment. The aftermath lingered on until the 1980s, when a new regime was ushered in by a Conservative government.

The following events covering the period of 'the revolution' were reported by the *Evening* and *Weekly Sentinel* and the national newspapers. It is interesting to note that when speaking of the University of Keele none of the Keele villagers mentioned the student revolt which took place inside the walls, but on their doorstep, or remembered any of the events which were reported in national newspapers and which contributed to the national student movement at the time. All events unless otherwise stated were reported by *the Evening or Weekly Sentinel.*

OCTOBER/NOVEMBER 1969

7th October: Keele gets top marks in 'avoiding student unrest'.

7th October: Jack Straw, President elect of the National Union of Students, calls for student representation on university governing bodies (*Yorkshire Post*).

12th November: Two hundred Keele students marched in a non-violent demonstration in support of their claims for representation on the Senate, the University's Governing Body.

13th November: Keele students kept Senate in the rain. Students linked arms to prevent members of Senate through to their meeting. Eight of the student Senate representatives were present. The Vice Chancellor addressed the students using a loud hailer.

13th November: Two hundred and fifty Keele students were barred by porters from entering a Senate meeting. On a majority vote students eventually allowed Senate members in.

14th November: Keele students claim that Senate was completely ignoring their problems and discontent.

JANUARY/FEBRUARY 1970

29th January: The question was asked whether the £20,000 grant from the Stoke City Council should be continued to Keele University.

5th February: The Auditor General explained that universities were asked to estimate their accommodation needs. As a result of the exercise Keele was found to over provide for student non-residential accommodation. In 1968/69 Keele had 1800 students and an increase of 2050 was envisaged for 1971/72. The Auditor General estimated that the academic buildings provided for almost 2600 students, the Library and central administration and maintenance services were sufficient for more than 5000, dining and catering facilities for 4700 and social and recreational facilities for well over 3000.

10th February: Student flats at Hawthorn Hall were ready and students queued all night to be sure of a tenancy. There were 45 flats in five blocks, each three storeys high, at a rental of £2 per week (*The Manchester Guardian*).

11th February: More than 200 students were preparing placards and banners for their demonstration at Keele University before the Senate meeting. The demonstration would be 'non-disruptive' said the Union President. The protest is the latest move to have a minimum of eight representatives on Senate.

14th February: Thirty students boycott examinations and protest outside the examination hall.

24th February: Students at Keele are to set up a watchdog team to ensure that secret files are not made on anyone at the University. The move follows a recent claim that students at Warwick University have captured files made by the Special Branch. A small watchdog team of staff and students would be allowed access to all personal files. The plan would be considered at the next Union Meeting (*Wolverhampton Express and Star*).

24th February: Warwick University votes to drop militant action where a 'secret files' probe is underway (*Birmingham Evening Mail*).

24th February: Keele is chosen as one of the centres for the Open University when it begins in 1971.

MARCH 1970

3rd March: Nineteen hundred students at Keele, yesterday, gave their support to Manchester University students in the row over confidential files. Keele University Students' Union sent a telegram pledging full support to the Manchester students who are involved in a 'sit-in'. Mr John Taylor, the Student Union President at Keele said that he had been assured that no files with information of a critical nature were being kept at Keele (*Wolverhampton Express and Star*).

5th March: Sit-in at Glasgow, Sheffield and York Universities threatened to occupy the administrative blocks. There is a strike at the London School of Economics (*Manchester Daily Express*).

5th March: One hundred and fifty students marched on the Vice-Chancellor's office at Keele demanding that all files should be opened to students. He agreed to meet them.

11th March: A group of students broke into Keele Hall into the Vice Chancellor's office. They threw from

The Express and Star, Wolverhampton

Despite the student troubles, Royalty kept coming, although on occasions it was suggested that they should not

Keele University Library Archives

Princess Margaret with members of the Music Department following a concert put on for her in May 1981

a window papers to others waiting below who began to search for evidence to support their claims about political information being filed. One hundred and sixty students began their sit-in after talks lasting seven hours. One thousand students end their sit-in at Nottingham University (*Evening Telegraph*).

12th March: Students organised a whip round to pay for damage to a room where files are kept. They had entered Keele Hall by smashing a window and rifling through filing cabinets. Sit-ins were reported at Liverpool, Salford, Hornsey Art College, Exeter and University College London (*Manchester Daily Express*). Mr Fred Peart, Leader of the House of Commons, condemned the keeping of political files on students and staff at universities (*Morning Star*).

13th March: Eleven Oxford students ordered to appear at the Proctor's office to answer allegations resulting from a recent sit-in at the Clarendon Building, the University's Headquarters (*The Times*).

13th March: Disciplinary action is to be taken against students who broke into offices and ransacked files at Keele. The Vice- Chancellor and four members of his staff were pelted with flour bombs by the students who did not find any political files. Vice Chancellors in Leeds and Glasgow decided against punishing students who had forged letters about the political files issue (*Daily Telegraph*).

20th March: A dispassionate and down-to-earth interpretation of what the student revolt is really about is badly needed. But we are not likely to get it as long as many people in authority in universities look on the student movement as primarily a disciplinary matter (*The Times Education Supplement*).

MAY/JUNE 1970

3rd May: Fires at Keele are reported.

4th May: The Registry Office at Keele University is damaged and the matter is being treated as arson (*The Manchester Guardian*).

9th June: Four pots of paint were thrown at the home of the Registrar. Two smashed through the windows showering paint over a chair, carpet and piano.

11th June: University locks at Keele are filled with glue.

17th June: Police patrol the Keele campus.

19th June: Roof top watch over Keele students. Fifty members of staff are on call for the patrols which were first suggested by people living on the campus, anxious to save their homes from damage. Professor Roy Shaw described them as 'observer patrols' (*Evening Mail*).

20th June: Police were called as naked students go shopping ... a mixed band of thirty students peeled off their clothes and frolicked outside. A twenty year old male student said, 'Some of us fancied a sun-bathe so we took our clothes off. I don't really see what all the fuss is about' (*Sheffield Morning Telegraph*).

20th June: 'Phew! what a stir as thirty nudists go frolicking on campus.' (The incident is reported by *The South Wales Echo, The Liverpool Echo, The Dundee Courier, The Advertiser* and *The Guardian*).

21st June: 'How they kept their cool' (caption under a picture of two nude female students sunbathing - (*News of the World*).

21st June: 'Calls for dismissal of nude students.' (*Evening Mail*).

22nd June: Nudists may delay grants for Keele.' Staffordshire County Council said it wanted student discipline tightened before handing over its £20,000 grant (*The Star, Sheffield*).

23rd June: *The Guardian, Daily Telegraph* and *The Times* cited incidents of petrol bombs and glue in locks at Keele.

SEPTEMBER/OCTOBER 1970

17th September: Students appeal against penalties imposed for their part in the nude sunbathing incident.

21st September: Talks take place to restore the £20,000 grant withheld last June by Staffordshire County Council following a series of incidents involving students on the campus.

17th October: Tariq Ali talks to 200 students at Keele University.

18th October: Students to fight against a ruling made on nudes (on campus). Legal action may be taken against the University of Keele over its disciplinary proceedings in last terms's nude sunbathing incident. The students were each fined £10 and banned from living on the campus for one year (*The Observer*).

19th October: The University drops Princess Margaret from their social plans when 200 students voted to end their annual Royal Ball on the grounds that it was too expensive.

28/29 October: Forty students break into the Registry. Three hundred students marched to the Clock House, circled the house and began humming loudly in what they said was a move to levitate the building 300 feet off the ground. (Numbers at the sit-in varied from 100 to 500) (*The Daily Telegraph and The Evening Sentinel*).

NOVEMBER/DECEMBER 1970

11th November: Three year degree mooted at Keele.

14th November: Senate decided in a meeting last week to set up a General Purposes Committee consisting of the full University Senate augmented by 12 student members (*Birmingham Post, The Guardian*).

23rd November: Dons denounce violence. Twenty-two universities and colleges attack in a manifesto published today, student violence and intimidation, damage to property and sit-ins. The manifesto suggests that students sign a code of discipline before being admitted to university and that they should have no part in decision-making bodies (*The Daily Telegraph*).

2nd December: Students accept places offered to them on Senate (*The Times, The Daily Telegraph*).

5th December: 'Keele University students were unenthusiastic about a move to give them more say in university affairs. The University Council has decided to allow the Student Union President and Secretary to attend its meetings but the two students will not be allowed to vote and will be asked to leave when academic and staffing items are discussed. Bob Curry, Union Secretary commented, "It doesn't seem much help to us".' (*The Birmingham Post*).

MAY 1971

11th May: Keele's shattered trust on the mend once more.

Keele University Library Archives

Professor Campbell-Stewart, Vice Chancellor during the students' 'troubles'

CHAPTER 17
MANAGING A REVOLUTION
The Establishment View

BEGINNINGS

The place was up and running when I arrived in September 1953, with my wife and three children. There were no desperate problems. Most of the committee structures were already in place but things became modified, changed and developed over the years. There were 12 to 13 professors when I arrived, all living along Battleship Row (Church Plantation). The staff had not grown very big, but were growing - there were about 50. The laboratories were being built and they were the first permanent university buildings that got going. Geography, Geology, Biology, Chemistry and Physics were all starting. Keele Hall had the departments of English, Classics, History, Modern Languages and Philosophy. Geology was the Architect's hut in front of Keele Hall. Later this hut became the Estates Department. Today the fountain is where it was.

I think Lord Lindsay knew when he took this project up that it would be the last thing he did. I was interested in the 'Keele Experiment'. When I was at Birmingham a great deal was written about it, and I had organised a Common Room trip here and we spent the day looking around Keele. I had some idea of what I was coming to. I also knew Hank Hayley who had been on the staff at Birmingham and who was already at Keele.

My predecessor, Walter Jenkins, who went out to be the Vice Chancellor of Dhaka University, Bangladesh, was still employed by the University for a bit as Senior Tutor. He was still living in the Registrar's house at Firs Hill, so we couldn't move in until he went. The children went to school in Newcastle on the university bus - there were three buses driven by Mr Watkins, Mr Whieldon and George White. The school was at the end of Keele Road. It was a private school, St Lucy's. It's now an advertising firm. After the school went it was a church hall.

When we came everybody asked you to come and have coffee, so you got to know everyone. There was a lot going on socially. The inter-departmental friendships were strong.

I was appointed when Sir John Lennard-Jones was the Principal. I think he had taken over in April 1953 so the appointment of Registrar was one of his first tasks. Sir John was only in office for about a year when he developed cancer and died. This was sad because he really pulled the place together. Lindsay had been great as an inspiration but he was not, I understand, a born administrator. He had been head of an Oxford College for quite a long time and I think people coming from older universities couldn't quite understand how modern, provincial universities could be somewhat more democratic. It was a great tragedy that he died so soon. After Sir John died there was an Interregnum with an Acting Principal for two years whilst the search went on. Then Sir George Barnes was appointed. He was Principal for four years before he died of cancer, so, again, we were without a Principal for a year. Harold Taylor took over and was the first Vice Chancellor of the University - that was the year we got our University Charter.

The staff was small and pretty well united on the whole. There prevailed a unified view so I don't think we suffered all that much from this quick succession of Principals. I don't think the progress of the place was much retarded. It was going to be slow anyway - that was the nature of things at the time.

THE ROYAL PREROGATIVE

Princess Margaret was recruited by John Blake in the Interregnum. I think she came in as President in 1956. I think they chose her for publicity. She was very good, very faithful and efficient in carrying out her duties. The University Statutes laid down how she was to be appointed but it was a question of behind the scenes invitation and exploration. I knew what was going on, but it was John Blake who did it. It had to be approved by Senate and Council.

The Princess usually came twice a year and very often to the Students' dance at Christmas. Once the Union was built she attended balls there. The balls before this were held in either Keele Hall or the Conference Hall. They were very good, very well run and very formal. I was nearly detailed to dance with the Princess but it didn't come off.

Mary Glover suggested that some of the students should be coached on how to curtsy. When the Princess first came, some of us were a bit anxious about their curtsy, so I coached some of the girls, who had to curtsy when they received their degrees. The thing was, her hand was so low down that you couldn't use it to balance with.

There were lots of police of course. She usually stayed in the Clock House. There were her secretary, her lady's maid, her lady-in-waiting, her footman, who didn't always come, and her detective, of course. The secretary stayed with us in Firs Hill. The others stayed in the Clock House. A lady-in-waiting stayed with us once. We had to put her in the little room.

The Queen Mother came once when she was Queen, when she opened the University College. She also came on the Tenth Anniversary to receive an Honorary Degree from her daughter. In her address, she said, 'Madam President and dear daughter'. The Queen Mother was so nice and it wasn't a formal occasion at all.

The Princess came down for Degree Day at the end of that awful term - the term of the 'student troubles'. She insisted on coming. By that time we had our degree ceremonies in Stoke and we felt she oughtn't to come. She said, 'Of course I'm coming!' with the result that around our house there were so many police, you would see police helmets bobbing up out of the rhododendron bushes.

UP AGAINST THE SYSTEM

The university establishment viewed Keele with grave suspicion. They thought it was the most extraordinary idea and that it was bound to fail, and what on earth was the Department of Education doing wasting its money which could have been better used by them? There was very little sympathy, but the Grants Committee was sold on the idea, had put the place up and were going to back it. So although there were lots of murmurings, they had no effect on the development. That was determined by other factors. Had we sprung into existence in the 1960s we would have been much bigger, much faster. We suffered, if you could call it suffering, by insisting on and sticking to a large number of residences. We received a loan from the Treasury to build staff housing.

In 1953 there were around 500 students. We were taking in around 150 per year. I was Secretary of the Council and the Senate and I was under the Principal, and later the Vice Chancellor as the Chief Executive Officer of the University. There was a build-up of courses during the first years until we had four intakes. Once the four year course had been established it rolled over from year to year and there were no new subjects for a very long time. The Foundation Year was amended, although not substantially. The main alteration was the abolition of the third subsidiary course. Anyone could attend the FY lectures - we didn't have to pay then.

The Senior Common Room was flourishing because everyone met for morning coffee every day and that was a very efficient way of doing business. More was done in a half hour in the SCR than in the office over three hours.

There were great arguments about the curriculum and general matters on the organisation of the University. We were sponsored, in those days, by Manchester, Birmingham and Oxford Universities. It got us off the ground but it wasn't useful subsequently. No, they tended to be a damned nuisance. They had a majority on the Academic Council to which each of the three

Sponsors appointed two members. These met regularly with the representatives of the University Senate to ensure that academic standards were being maintained. They had to approve new courses and whilst in theory this sounds a jolly good idea, in practice it meant that the sponsoring universities came around to see who they could appoint for a trip to Stoke, and we had some members from the sponsoring universities who were less than enamoured with the sorts of things we were trying to do. They thought we didn't know what we were about. This wasn't what they had been accustomed to. They had been professors for 20 or 30 years and they thought that this was not the way to go on. Perhaps I am exaggerating the picture. So, I don't think it was a very helpful way of carrying on and perhaps something can be inferred from the fact that none of the other new universities underwent the same method of assessment.

The Foundation year got a bit of a blow at the time, when we talked about increasing the numbers to 1400 upwards. They couldn't all do four year courses. So some students started to come for three years.

REVOLTING TIMES
Revolution was in the air and we had our share of it. It spread through all the universities. Really, we didn't have anything terribly serious. There were rowdy nights, loud music playing, a fire bomb was thrown through the Senior Tutor's office window. It didn't do all that much damage. Paint was thrown through the Registrar's dining room window. That was very unpleasant. There were one or two individuals who had the finger put on them. Looking back, I came to the conclusion that things wouldn't have taken the course they had if any one of the four ring leaders had not been at Keele.

The general cry going up was that we were keeping secret files on certain students. It was so hysterical. A couple of filing cabinets were being sent to be repaired. They were brought out of Keele Hall and put on a lorry and it was rumoured that these files were being taken to the police. It was absolute nonsense. We had staff on night duty going around the campus and on top of Keele Hall with binoculars keeping their eye on things. Students took over the Registry but the Registry knew it was going to happen. The police didn't want to be involved any more than they had to be. They pointed out to us that if they were involved their action would be prompt and efficient, and maybe unpleasant.

The occupation was a total flop because we simply decamped to our houses and carried on from there. *The Evening Sentinel* rang up the Students Union one time and asked to speak to the Union President. They said, 'I'm sorry, no-one's here. They're having dinner with the Vice Chancellor'. Campbell-Stewart had invited the Union Committee to dinner.

At the end of that summer term two students decided to have a bit of fun, so they climbed onto the Library roof. They were hauled in by the police and found themselves in cells in Newcastle. That was an innocent prank. It was lovely weather that term. There was no lasting effect on relations generally. The ring leaders eventually left. The government insisted on our liberalising our constitutions and students were allowed on committees, that sort of thing.

RECREATION
There was a certain amount of sporting activity: a staff cricket team from quite early on. There was no hockey but the staff produced a team to play the women. There was tennis - a grass court in front of Keele Hall, just below the Mary Glover Garden. There was a staff and student orchestra and there were concerts, although there wasn't a Music Department in the early days.

As the Registrar's wife I took a keen interest in what was going on. In 1954 I discovered there was no staff drama so I insisted that there should be. We put on 'You Can't Take It With You'. Everyone who could speak was involved. We put it on in Keele Hall in the refectory. There was a small platform where the staff used to eat. We performed after dinner. The offices at the back were our dressing rooms. I had produced this play in London. We did it for one night and it was so successful we did it again the next night. We hired costumes from a Manchester firm. Mrs Springall was on costumes for our productions and for the student productions. Rehearsals were in the evenings.

The students had their own Drama Society and they had put on their first one in the Keele Hall courtyard. They had to turn off the men's urinals because no-one could hear. That was Henry IV Part I. They did two or three performances in the open air, down at the Lakes. 'The Tempest' was one. The first Clock House Courtyard production was 'Romeo and Juliet'.

There was a hut called the RAF Hut which was a free-for-all and I used to have my scenery down there. I used to go down and paint scenery like mad. Not all the plays were good. Staff and students came to watch and we did manage to sell all the tickets. Gradually it fizzled. The Keele Players eventually became the Keele Players Theatre Group. They didn't act, they went on theatre visits.

KIDS ON CAMPUS

All the children were growing up together so there was a great deal of interchange of families. Student babysitters were on the spot at about three shillings an evening. That was an enormous help. It helped us to get to know the students and they us. John Golding was one of our babysitters. Once, when the local hunt was meeting for the first time at Keele, in the courtyard, John Golding organised a drag hunt. He put a trail of aniseed down and spoiled the Meet. They didn't come back after that. My husband came running down the bank from Firs Hill to warn them not to start.

We had to put up Princess Margaret's footman once. The children said, 'The footman's staying. Can we look at him?' As he was coming down the stairs I said, 'I'm terribly sorry, but the children have never seen a Royal footman. Do you mind if they look at you?' They thought he would have a powdered wig and all that. He came downstairs in a lounge suit. My son looked at him and said, 'Well, he has a nice tie'.

We had a big house with a nursery and a big toy cupboard. People were complaining that they had to take their little ones shopping. There was the housewives bus on Fridays and it was an awful nuisance having to take children so Thelma Hunter, who was the wife of the Economics lecturer, and I, got together. I said, 'We've got this big nursery. Anybody who wants to leave their children there may, but I'm not going to run it. People are welcome to bring their children up on Fridays and I'll provide biscuits and drinks and children are welcome to play with the toys'. Thelma said she'd be liaison/Secretary. My children weren't too keen on it initially, but people came up and left their children. I think they paid tuppence or something for orange juice, but no fees.

Somebody got a bit officious about it and said, 'This is a nursery school, it should be registered and have the right number of potties...' and so on. I said it was my hospitality. There was a rota of mums, I certainly didn't look after the children, I didn't even organise it. That went on for some time. Then some thought it was a bit of a bind having to come up to Firs Hill from their houses before they went on the bus. One of the mums went to Thelma and told her this. Thelma said, 'My God woman, you want it with jam on don't you?' So, gradually, it faded out.

I'm not sure if there was a gap but Inge Miller, who was the wife of Terry Miller, had a conservatory built onto their house at Church Plantation and she used that for a nursery school. It was a pre-school nursery school for staff children (students didn't have children in those days) and mothers came and taught at it. It was more official and people paid. It had to be registered. That was at Number 16. When Inge left it was carried on in one of the huts. It was nothing to do with the University. It was Inge's idea and it was successful. There was also a coffee club that Margaret Millar started for wives and children. That was held in Lindsay Hall.

THE WAY WE WERE

When we first arrived we found the estate as it is now, except that the University didn't own any of the Home Farm site at that time. The purchase of Home Farm took place under John Blake who, with Harry Taylor (the Town Clerk of Stoke) was the moving spirit. Up until its purchase in 1955 it belonged to Charlie Heath. He had bought it when the Estate was sold. Harry Taylor persuaded the Council that for future expansion we had to have it. It must be about 300 acres. The University Grants Committee gave us an outright grant for the portion of Home Farm which looks down on the University and an interest-free loan to cover the remainder. Barnes Hall, and all the new Science Park buildings and car parks, are built on Home Farm land. Before this, the boundary of the University was the road. Cows and sheep came up to the fence.

The Estate was covered with the remaining army huts in which all the students were accommodated. There were no permanent buildings, although some had started. The first building for students was the womens' block at Lindsay Hall. The rest came slowly, partly because we weren't growing very fast because money was very tight. For many years single staff were accommodated on the top floor of Keele Hall in study bedrooms. Miss Rolfe, the catering chief, had her flat there. The Registry was moved from Keele Hall to a pre-fabricated hut just below the Walter Moberly Hall.

The Chapel was going right from the beginning. There were three parallel huts - one was the Chapel and the other two were the Students' Union. The Conference Hall was built before the Library. The main Library Reading Room was the Salvin Room and the Entrance Hall, the Great Hall, and all other rooms on the ground floor and basement. The Conference Hall was built as a general purpose hall - lectures, concerts, theatre performances, and as an adjunct to the Students' Union. They used it for all sorts of theatrical activities. My wife coached students, who came in to take a teaching diploma, in voice presentation.

In the town there was a theatre in the round at the Municipal Hall - where the Newcastle Library is now, opposite the old Post Office. It pre-dated the (old) Victoria Theatre. That started in the Municipal Hall under Stephen Joseph who had started in Scarborough. That was an interesting innovation and lots of people went to see productions. There were the Newcastle Players and the Rep.

A More Pragmatic Approach

BEGINNINGS

The previous Head Porter had retired in 1966, so we came in January 1967. I had been a Station Master until Dr Beeching. That year, 1967, was very peaceful. A lot of the original academic staff were still here - those who had come for idealistic reasons in the 1950s. Indeed probably 'the ideal' was still intact then.

When I first came there were two groups of porters; those in Keele Hall who manned the Hall around the clock and did the campus mail and the Chancellors Building porters who provided services within the building during the day. When I came the University had just begun to employ Securicor - two men per night. It was an experiment that didn't turn out to be satisfactory. By mid 1967 this was realised and the University decided to have its own patrolmen. Before I found my feet we had recruited patrolmen and they had to be trained. We recruited four, a senior patrolman and three 'foot soldiers'. My job was a matter of supervision and organisation. Our senior patrolman was an ex-Chief Prison Officer who was a very sensible, sound man with a lot of experience of human nature, which was helpful. We also had a Traffic Warden who was not directly under me, but we shared an office. He was an ex-Police Sergeant from Newcastle, so he had a lot of knowledge of police procedures. One of our duties was to cooperate with the police when problems arose on the campus. One of his major chores was to register all the cars on campus - staff and students. Each had a disc for the windscreen. He went around checking speeding, dealing with minor accidents, illegal parking etc. Staff transgressing the University procedures led to the first speed ramps on campus. The first were on Keele Drive, the invention of Sir Harold Clowes who was a Stoke-on-Trent councillor and a member of the University Council. They were a set of cobbles arranged in a rather uneven way. That was thought to be too savage so they were developed into, more or less, what there is today. The outside world has caught up with Keele. We were the first pioneers of traffic speed ramps! This was a much better approach than trying to report academic staff to their Heads of Department. It worked for every car, staff or student.

THE HONEYMOON ENDS

By the time we got the patrolmen reasonably well installed there came the development of the student troubles. There were troubles in Paris, the USA, the LSE - it was a disease that was spreading. The first time we had difficulties was on the 12th June 1968 when the students picketed Senate. That day the Senate meeting lasted nine hours. This set the pattern for using porters and patrolmen to hold the Senate doors closed. The next day there were various slogans painted on walls. Some you can still discern if you know where to look for them. Another night a red flag was hoisted on Keele Hall.

On 18th June the Registry was besieged. We tried to keep the doors closed but the staff were working and wanted to get in and out. There were also legitimate visitors going in so eventually the students forced their way in and stayed for about two days. The staff went home that night and didn't come back until the students had left. There was a very active minority and there was some suggestion of them going into the Senior Common Room, but I managed to persuade them that it was a private club. They took that and didn't persist. That week-end the Vice Chancellor addressed the students in the Union. It was the end of the Summer Term so some matters resolved themselves.

It went on until January 1969. On 21st January there was a Union meeting about direct action over confidential files. This had grown into a great issue. There was a suggestion of breaking in to where the files were kept and taking them away. The Union Committee resigned because they were not in favour of direct action. Ten days later there was another Union meeting. The students had written to the Vice Chancellor about trouble at the LSE and wanted him to support the LSE students. Presumably he responded unfavourably because they got up a petition which they delivered after a march to the Clock House.

On 3rd February came the first occupation of Keele Hall. The students forced their way in during the evening and camped out in the Senior Common Room for 24 hours. They were always willing to let people carry on doing their own work, except that they couldn't. Staff were apprehensive about what was going on. We tried to keep things low key, as far as we could.

The next disturbance came on 8th May. That concerned a student proposal to allow Gypsies to live on campus. Some of our students thought that the campus was an ideal place for them. There was a staff and student meeting in which the students asked the University to consider providing a gypsy site. On 29th May there was a Residents Association meeting which resolved otherwise. That seemed to be the extent of the troubles in 1969.

In October, when term resumed, there was a campaign for student representation on Senate. On 12th November there was another siege of Senate. Students would not let members of Senate attend unless their representatives could attend too. In the end the staff did attend but the students didn't. People were obviously cross, but they didn't know who to be cross with. They were cross with the things that were happening because it was upsetting the even tenor of Keele's ways. This was followed by a picket of Council. On 10th December there was going to be another picket.

On the morning of that day I got a message to say that there was a live piglet in Lindsay refectory. We secured this piglet and after a time we handed it over to the police as found property. The intention had been to introduce the piglet into the Senate Room to create a bit of havoc. It was the end of term so everything went quiet again.

The next cause célèbre was about meals. The arrangement up until then was that students paid fees for accommodation and meals - for 20 meals per week - every meal except Sunday dinner. You either took them or not. If you didn't, you still paid for them. The students wanted a pay-as-you-go system. Then there was more trouble over exams. I think they wanted continuous assessment. That led to a picket of Senate on 4th March.

DIVORCE PROCEEDINGS COMMENCE
There was a more serious break-in to Keele Hall. Students got hold of a long ladder and broke into the Vice Chancellor's office. They forced open an office door and stole files. They occupied the Registry yet again. The next week was a Senate Meeting. One of the problems about the occupations was how to end them without loss of face. On this occasion they did it by leaving Keele Hall and picketing Senate. On this occasion Senate didn't appear. I have a note here which says that either they met elsewhere or they didn't meet at all. Once the Senate met in the Rural District Council Offices in Sidmouth Avenue - they just went off campus not to be disturbed.

It was probably then that things began to get serious. It resulted in four or five students being disciplined for breaking in. There was a reluctance to call the police in. Primarily the University thought it could deal with these matters itself, but it had never had to deal with such matters before. One student was fined £25, two were suspended for a term and one for a year. The Disciplinary Committee was held on 15th-16th March and then it was Easter.

When the punishments were announced at the start of the Summer Term there was a midnight march on Clock House. This was the night before Open Day, so obviously we feared the worst. During the night various obscene paintings appeared around the campus but we were able to get rid of these before the public came in. Trouble developed during the day. The students had a a very noisy pop group outside the Union. The Deputy Warden tried to stop it and there was some unpleasantness. About three or four in the morning I had a 'phone call to say that the Registry was on fire. I contacted the police and the fire brigade and they tackled it. The Registry was a wooden building next to the Chapel. Whilst they were dealing with that we had another message to say that Horwood General Block was on fire. That was beyond University discipline and the police were asked to take things in hand. They used the female Warden's house which was vacant and set up a police post. I don't think they found out who did it.

On 5th May there was a peaceful picket of Council. Council was discussing appeals of those students who were being disciplined. The following day the students had a pop group on the sports field and we thought that that would be a source of trouble. But the trouble occurred in the Union. The group moved there when it started to rain. They handed out cans of paint so everyone had a happy time spraying the Union Ballroom. This caused £1000 worth of damage. Two weeks later the Registrar's house was sprayed with paint. On 7th June cans of paint were thrown into the Architects office at Keele Hall. There was a lot of smoke damage. This escalation of events got people properly alarmed. There was a meeting of staff in the Old Library to arrange a fire-watching scheme during the night whereby Heads of Departments would guard their own buildings. I would act as coordinator at Keele and take reports of whatever was seen and deal with whatever needed to be dealt with. The police continued to have a presence on the campus.

RAKING OVER THE EMBERS
I think the nature of students had changed. A year or two before they were ladies and gentlemen.

Some of those coming in now were obviously bright but undisciplined. They were a lively lot and full of ideas. In 1969 there was a large intake of students and Keele wasn't geared to checking on them during the year. They just had a year-end exam and nothing in between. Some knew they were going to fail and they tended to be the ring leaders. Windows were broken in Horwood refectory and in the Library. There was a nudist episode. I was asleep at the time as I had been working nights.

The Registry was viewed as the seat of power. The Vice Chancellor was more remote. The students were asking for things which don't sound terribly unreasonable now but then it was quite new and asked for the University Authorities to change some of their arrangements. Things flared up and down from 1968. The peak was the fires and the nudist affair in 1970. There were well-attended Student Union meetings but a majority of students didn't take part. They kept their heads down and got on with getting a degree. Some of the trouble-makers were very clever students. Occasionally coaches would take students to London to demonstrate. Keele was so self-contained and so isolated that activities here didn't have much of an impact, although the nudist incident did make the national newspapers. It was small beer really. The City, I think, withdrew their discretionary grant and the County reduced its grant. Local wrath was heaped upon us.

The Vice Chancellor disciplined the nudists by taking Vacation Powers. Whatever he did was obviously wrong because as soon as term started there was a student occupation of the Walter Moberly Hall. On this occasion students went off to levitate the Clock House. They joined hands around the Clock House and by wish fulfilment attempted to raise it off the ground. It was the time of levitation. After this they broke into the Registry once again. Things calmed down after that. It was the time of power cuts; electricity would be cut off for four hours a day and there was a coal shortage. By 9th December the Water Board told Keele that it couldn't guarantee a water supply because there was no power to run the pumps. A crisis meeting was held in the Architects Office in the dark and they decided that as it was three days before the end of term the students should be sent home.

In January the issue was identity cards. These had just been introduced. There was a ceremonial burning. That was the last major incident. Some concessions were made so eventually everything fizzled out. A special committee was set up to meet every Saturday morning - the Exploratory Committee - an exercise in procrastination. There were months and months of weekly meetings which eventually played out the problem.

I went to Union meetings to keep an eye on what was going on. I was an Associate Member of the Students Union and they knew I was there. So sometimes we were forewarned of events. The meetings could go on until the small hours of the morning. It was the case of the campus coming to terms with life in the 1970s. Many of the students didn't know what was going on. There were leaflets and magazines but you didn't have to read them or go to Union meetings. There wasn't an Information Officer at the time. Roy Shaw was given this task until eventually Brian Rawlins took it on. Meg Broome was the first one to be involved with the Development Trust in the 1960s and this turned into the Public Relations/Information post. I don't think her office was involved with the press on this kind of issue.

ABOVE IT ALL
Princess Margaret used to go to balls in the Students Union. They put on a steel band for her as she liked steel bands. In the Union she would dance with the student President and members of the Committee. Balls were also held in Keele Hall on the eve of Degree Day. They went on until three or four in the morning. They were eventually changed to the Saturday before because there were difficulties in getting the Hall cleaned up in time for Degree Day.

A Student Vantage Point

BEGINNINGS

I was a student from 1967 to 1971. I came from a working class background. There were some students who were very wealthy. One was a member of the Rothschild family. Another rode around in a very expensive sports car and obviously had money to burn. There were more people coming into higher education, but the more vociferous students on the left were from a middle-class background.

There were political organisations already on the campus. The main ones were the International Socialists, the SWP and the International Marxist Group, whose members were really behind a lot of what happened. It was a mixed group. I wouldn't say they had a large membership but they were well organised and vociferous. There was a left-wing journal that appeared intermittently and I was editor for a time. By modern standards it was very amateurish. There was one notorious issue which came to the notice of the University Authorities, where we printed on the front cover instructions on how to make a Molatov Cocktail. It wasn't intended to be particularly serious. I worked with a chap who was a bit of an artist and he did the front cover. It was a sketch that he had produced. It wasn't intended that students go out and make one. It was intended to be a bit provocative. The University Authorities were angry. We produced another journal, Penny Red, which came out sporadically.

GETTING STARTED

When I came to the University in 1967, I joined the Labour Club, but that moved quickly to the left and actually changed its name to the Socialist Society because it didn't want to be overtly associated with the Labour Party. Later on the Labour Club was restarted and the two ran side by side.

Student protest began during the first year that I was at Keele, with the setting up of an organisation called Action for a Free University - the AFU. The AFU was an amorphous group which overlapped with the Labour Club, which changed its name to the Socialist Society. There was another group called the Revolutionary Socialist Students' Federation. These overlapped. But the AFU was the umbrella action group. The original name was Action for a Free University at Keele, with the slogan 'AFUK creates'. It was supposed to be an obscene pun, to shock. But the K was dropped. I was made the Treasurer - I must have been because I found a cheque book at home with Keele stamps on it, recently. The AFU wasn't that organised to have a membership list. At the height of things, about 100 would have been involved - that's a wild guess - but meetings in the Students Union Ballroom were very full, and that held a couple of hundred people. There was a lot of debate in the early days of the AFU on curriculum content and the whole nature of a bourgeois university and the alternative way of running a university. I think a lot of the debates were revolutionary hot air and sloganising, looking back on it, but at the time it was taken very seriously.

This was at the time when students had no representation on any of the governing bodies of the University, when students were still not permitted to go into the rooms of the opposite sex after a certain hour; they had only just ended the practice of having formal Dinners, with gowns, on a Friday night, so I think that many students felt that the rules were a bit paternalistic and that they deserved the right to be treated like adults. That was one strand to it. Another was the more overt political activism of people with mostly socialist or, in some cases, anarchist views who had a far wider reaching Marxist critique of a bourgeois education, and thought that the system ought to be challenged. Without the more general student feeling about the paternalistic nature of the rules, I don't think it would have taken off. There was an awareness of what was going on elsewhere but I don't remember links with other institutions abroad. There were links with

Warwick. I went with a group from Keele to Warwick at one point.

I didn't go to many lectures. I found a lot of them boring and irrelevant at the time. I did my own studies and got my degree. I went to tutorials and seminars. Lectures were not compulsory, on the whole. I went to a maths lecture once a week which was a subsidiary subject. The chap in charge of that actually tried passing around a class register to register who was there. He just got stupid answers like Mickey Mouse. It didn't really work. The class register was only tried at this particular one. The University actually wrote letters to students who failed to attend and that became fairly obvious because a lot of fake names were put on the register at the beginning that were not repeated, so those names were taken and letters were sent to the phony names saying 'You have not attended ...'. They didn't even check that these were real names.

The style of many lectures was to stand at the front and read out in a monotone from a previously prepared set of notes, notes which they'd probably been churning out for years. I felt I could learn a lot more by going to a Library and finding the relevant books, which I did. Not much attention was given, at the time, to developing exciting teaching styles and strategies. The old system was just 'talk at them'.

THE SYSTEM

There was some feeling that the University authorities were in *loco parentis* and responsible for the students' welfare. There were fines for contravening certain rules. I was once fined for coming back a bit drunk and noisy one night and someone informed on me. I was dragged in by the Tutor and fined five shillings. Nobody actually paid their fines and no-one chased them up but when you graduated, the University said, 'You owe us this money, you can't graduate until you've paid'.

You had three termly options of subjects. There were also sessionals where you followed one subject throughout the Foundation Year. These involved tutorials. You had to take a science, a social science and an arts option. In the Foundation Year, there were two lectures every morning. When the year started the lectures were full but as time went on the numbers dwindled. I think that people felt that the quality of the lectures was variable, in some cases they were irrelevant and they could fulfil the requirements of the Foundation Year without attending. By writing the requisite number of essays they got the requisite mark. I think there was a multiple choice exam at the end. I don't know if that was experimental and tried for one year. Most of the assessment was based on essays.

The three year course was brought in whilst I was there. There was controversy over that and I spoke in opposition to a three year course at a meeting that was held. The opposition at the time was that what was supposed to make Keele unique was the all-round nature of the education. If that was taken away then Keele would be like any other higher education institution.

By the 1960s Keele was the most old-fashioned of the newer universities, I would have thought. It didn't seem to have the 'pzazz' of Warwick or Sussex or the other newer ones. You had to live one year off campus and I think people looked forward to that as a way of escaping from the place. Some found the hall-of-residence type of living inhibiting, because it gave little personal privacy or protection against noise and problems with other students. The shared facilities, I think, some students found inhibiting. Towards the end of my stay another system of self-contained flats, where four students shared a flat, was introduced. The first of those was Hawthorns.

There were one or two members of staff who habitually drank in the Students Union and who socialised with students but I think most kept themselves apart from the student body. There was only one member of staff I was friendly enough with to visit his house. I didn't study his subject. Not all the student activity on the left was inward looking - just looking at Keele.

THORNS IN THE FLESH

The files issue was a bit after the first wave which was the creation of the AFU. I was one of the people who started the awareness of the files issue at Keele. After the Warwick thing (where the issue was first raised) we called a meeting and it started from that. The meeting in the Ballroom was attended by either the Vice Chancellor or the Registrar. One of the senior Officials of the University actually agreed to come along and be questioned on the issue of 'secret files' and gave evasive answers. They wouldn't say 'No, there are no secret files, or 'Yes there are, you can look at them'. It was quite a stormy meeting and things were thrown at him and so forth.

In early 1968 there was an occupation of the Registry. The University cut off the 'phones. The students set up an extension to the Students Union 'phone which was taken across the car park to the Registry. There was an action on the files which came a bit later involving the occupation of Keele Hall where the files were supposed to be kept. We actually didn't find very much. We just wanted to know if the same situation existed at Keele as in Warwick. This was the point of inviting a senior Official to the meeting - to find out. Rumour had it that a lorry had arrived earlier in the day and had taken filing cabinets away somewhere else. We found one or two odds and ends that we published, but nothing of any great importance.

I wasn't involved in any sabotage, not at all. I wouldn't accept that. There was one instance when an American turned up - I think he was American - and he was quite a wild anarchist and he was always trying to suggest things like destroying property and buildings. At one time we had a sit-in in the Registry and he actually caused quite a bit of damage and had to be restrained by the others who were there. I don't think he was a student, I think he turned up from outside. I wasn't involved in any activity like that. I was of the view that any protest could still be peaceful and not involve any unnecessary damage to property or violence towards people. I think that most people I was associated with held these views. Those that took more extreme action were a very small minority - if they were students at all.

I was involved with the Travellers' Committee. This was in 1968 at the time of the Caravan Sites Act, and Stoke City Council were attempting to evade their responsibility of providing a site by saying, 'We haven't got a problem ...', and expelling Gypsies from land in Stoke-on-Trent. We were involved in Etruria - roughly where the Sentinel Offices are now. We sat down in front of the caravans to stop the eviction. We also attended meetings at Birmingham University and we linked up with other people who were involved in that activity and other areas. A Gypsy site on campus was also suggested. A Union General Meeting passed a motion to have Gypsies on the campus but I think the Gypsies would have had more sense than to come to a university campus.

The University proposed to bring in identity cards with our photographs on. The logic was that this was an open campus and anyone could stroll in, so it was a means of improving security. On the civil rights side, some people thought that it was an infringement of their liberty. We were asked to provide photographs for these cards, but very few people did. So what happened was that the University used photographs that had been submitted with original applications to the University. Thus there were fresh-faced individuals with short hair cuts who really looked nothing like. It was a failure in terms of identification. A vocal minority protested.

One of the more bizarre activities was the attempt to levitate the Vice Chancellor's house. I went along. There was a march to the Clock House along the sunken lane and people linked arms and started chanting. It was somebody's daft idea, I don't think many took it seriously. It was a way of protesting outside the Vice Chancellor's house.

One November the University issued a proclamation banning fireworks and bonfires on campus. The obvious reaction was that people who normally didn't bother with bonfires and fireworks decided to hold one. They chose the amphitheatre in the woods, near to the Clock

House. The bonfire was built and there were fireworks. I was one of the ringleaders for this. The Vice Chancellor was having one of his soirées the same night. The students who were invited, and went, said afterwards that all they could hear were the bangers going off. The Vice Chancellor wasn't very happy about that. It was rather a silly situation because I think he had provoked it by issuing a ban. Had he said nothing it wouldn't have taken place.

I thought the nudist thing was an absurd and pointless activity. Presumably if there was anything political behind it, it was an anarchist point of view that just wanted to shock. Even at the time I couldn't understand it. Something came before that. There was a particular student - an anarchist - who called a meeting in a room at the top of the Students Union. I don't remember the pretext of it but I went to it. He suggested that everyone take their clothes off, which was a very odd thing to happen at a meeting. Some people did and some didn't. He instigated the nude sunbathing a few days later, so he obviously had the idea in his head that people should take their clothes off.

The Vice Chancellor used to have little soirées at his house with drinks and a buffet supper. He would invite a few students each time. I was invited to one of these. I think he made a point of inviting groups of students including one 'lefty'. Bob Stow was President at the time. Presidents of the Union tended to be moderate labourites in their politics. We were protesting about something, I can't remember what, and he suggested that the sit-in be held in the Walter Moberly Hall. Well, we could have sat there until kingdom come and the University wouldn't have minded. We produced an edition of Penny Red with a cartoon of Bob Stow and the Vice Chancellor on the telephone agreeing that the sit-in should be in the Walter Moberly Hall!

There were porters patrolling the University. It was a way of stepping up security. It was regarded as a sport to intimidate them - it was called Porter Freaking. I wasn't involved in this. It got a bit anarchic and wild. A band came in and caused damage inside and outside the Union. I was not supporting this particular wave of protest, it seemed pointless. I went to a meeting of the Socialist Society to discuss this. I was the only one at the meeting to oppose it. I was, more or less, shouted out of the meeting. Another person who agreed with me walked out with me. All this occurred at the time of the nude sunbathing.

I think that if the University authorities had abolished the house rules - there was a great strength of feeling about these - and had put student representatives on Senate, quite a lot of the student protest could have been prevented. There were political activists who wanted to push things a lot further, but they were in the minority.

REMEMBERING THE GOOD TIMES

Some people were expelled from the University for their activity in the Registry. There was a member of the staff on the Senate who was sympathetic to the students, who told me that the original plan was to discipline a far larger number of students and more severely. There was a list of about 20 but it was decided to be too draconian. Some students who failed their exams felt that they had failed because they were involved.

I worked on the bar at Keele. There was a bar strike. The Students Union was paying bar employees 4/9d an hour and it turned out that the official Whitley Rate for bar work was 5/6d an hour. The Students Union would not increase the pay so we held a series of lightening strikes. We would start work as usual on a Saturday night and when the bar was at its busiest at 10.00pm we'd just walk off. We very quickly got an increase in pay. It was quite disgraceful that the Students Union was paying its own bar staff illegally below the national minimum. The only other issue that went on, and was never resolved, was that the Bar Steward and his wife would only employ men to serve behind the bar and would only employ women as glass collectors and glass washers. The Students Union, from time to time, passed resolutions that these positions were open to either gender, but the Bar Steward stuck his heels in and he wouldn't do it. It was odd that the Students Union had all these policies on gender and race issues but wasn't implementing them in its own bar.

The Steward's wife was quite a character. She would sit at the end of the bar and make rude comments about the students. She would drink a mixture of milk and spirits, I don't know if it was gin or whisky, and her comments would get louder and louder as the night wore on.

I worked on the bar for the Royal Ball. It was a bizarre event because we had to dress up in little white jackets that only came out once a year. There was a special bar set aside for Princess Margaret - the Royal Bar. That was the first year I was at Keele. I introduced a motion to the Union General Meeting to abolish the Royal Ball and replace it with a Revolution Ball to celebrate the anniversary of the Russian Revolution. I think it was opposition to Royalty generally - their wealth and privilege. I felt it wasn't our business as students to spend money on entertaining Princess Margaret. I never actually met her. She was there when I was working on the bar so I caught a glimpse of her. There was the main bar on the first floor for the students and the dance/disco went on in the Ballroom. The upstairs rooms of the Union were opened out to form a smaller Ballroom. They put in a traditional jazz band - I think it was because Princess Margaret liked traditional jazz bands. I think that year it was Monty Sunshine - a top band. She had her own private bar in a room off - the Royal Bar. I wasn't serving in that one, I was in the 'Monty Sunshine Bar'. From what I can recall, she spent a lot of time in that bar. She did come out to dance with the student President - it was a tradition that she did this - but most of the time you didn't see her. She was with her own little retinue in her own private bar.

It was discussed at a Union General Meeting that a student had been approached by Special Branch and asked to inform on left-wing students, prior to Princess Margaret coming.

In 1968 there was a Revolution Ball. The first time we held it the University Authorities over-reacted to it. The Vice Chancellor issued a statement saying he was expecting hordes of militants from outside to converge on the University for this event. This was wide of the mark because the ball was exactly the same as the previous year's ball, except that there was no Princess Margaret.

THE WAY WE WERE
The huts were behind the Registry up a long narrow road we called Sunset Boulevard. There were twelve huts used as residences and I stayed in one for my last year because the new flats at Hawthorns weren't ready for the start of term. Lindsay, Horwood and Hawthorns Halls were up. The huts were called Barnes Hall. They were quite primitive, really. The sinks were continually blocked. They were roomier than the newer Halls of residence. The older the Hall, the bigger the rooms. The two women's blocks - Sneyd House and Harrowby House had enormous rooms compared with some of the newer blocks in Horwood. There was a bit of cachet to living in a Second World War Nissen hut!

I was Chair of the Folk club and every Sunday night we got a singer into the Hexagon. The Drama Group was regarded to be the 'in' Society to be involved with. I did take part in one production - I was the cobbler in *Julius Caesar*. I was specifically invited by the producer. It was an outdoor production, in ordinary clothes, on the paved area outside the Chapel. The producer was different in that he cast from outside the Drama Group. The Group even had its own hut!

PS: A PERSONAL POSTSCRIPT

After Keele's promising start, which, in retrospect, was not so much a quantum leap forward as a slow shuffle down an already ploughed furrow, it appeared to fall into a state of self-satisfied, possibly exhausted, torpor. Having lived on the campus for eight years it was not difficult to be lulled into a false sense of security. It was as if the walls served as a useful barricade against the harsher realities of the outside world. I recall a senior academic in the early 1980s telling me, when we were discussing the way that the Conservative Government was currently cutting a swathe through industry, that he thought the professions and higher education were safe. Less than a year later cuts were announced to University education which would serve to place many institutions in jeopardy for the next decade, at least. Small universities such as Keele were immediately fingered. Big was now more beautiful.

The student 'revolutionary' period had repercussions for many universities which were long-lived. It also served to shift the relationship between student and university onto a less 'matey' and a more business-like footing. The term 'professionalism' entered the higher education vocabulary and with it the notion of 'objectivity'. Ownership of the university by staff and students began to be eroded. Universities became public property, and as such they were expected to be more accountable.

The Conservative victory of 1979 turned the tide on government spending. Britain was now entering into the age of the entrepreneur - the everyman-for-himself syndrome - where if one couldn't swim the alternative on offer was to sink. For a brief period it looked as if Keele might take the latter course. Many non-academic posts were sacrificed as a cost-cutting exercise. Early retirement and voluntary redundancies for academic staff were hastily put together, and those that could went elsewhere. The paring of universities had begun at the edges, which only now, in the late 1990s, threatens the bone.

Technology and the 'small screen' - which in the 1950s, people like George Barnes was said to have thought 'would never catch on', was heralded as a saviour for British enterprise. It has, however, also played a part in the revolutionary downsizing of Higher Education and has now come to dominate university life. Indeed, the small screen could eventually replace the live lecture - a scenario depicted in the serial *A Very Peculiar Practice*, parts of which were filmed on the Keele University campus. The computer, however, appears not to have improved efficiency, and the E-Mail and Internet of the late 1990s is as cumbersome and time-consuming as the sheets of paper that went flying around (and still do) when administration doubled in the 1980s.

Keele's salvation came about when it was discovered that a lot of money could be made out of higher education via 'foreign' students, the burgeoning conference trade, the marketing of intellectual property via the Science Park movement and a greater collaboration with industry and the fact that a more educated workforce was needed to take the UK into the future. How could a Conservative Government do this without public spending? Miraculously Polytechnics were transmogrified into Universities almost overnight. Universities with their own landscaped campuses fared well. They became desirable venues for all kinds of activities, not least wedding receptions! And of course, unlike some of the inner city universities, Keele had park land to develop. The decade from the mid-1980s saw much development: a science park was constructed, new halls of residence sprouted, new teaching blocks emerged. The next phase which will take the university into the twenty-first century will see the development of the sports centre and the construction of the long awaited swimming pool. Home Farm is also ear-marked for refurbishment and development. Meanwhile campus accommodation is now in the hands of a housing association and the idea of the Spring Pool Cooperative is to be extended by building

Off the Record

more houses which will be offered to an open market.

In the mid 1980s emphasis moved from universities being somewhat intellectually and physically removed from their localities, and insular, to universities reaching out to their local clientele. The Development Officer was a new phenomenon on the university administrative circuit - a person who rattled the can and who attempted to interest people in their local university just enough to fund its activities, without involving them too much in university politics. In this respect Keele was successful, although the exercise came somewhat late in the day. By now Princess Margaret, along with Royalty, had become a luxury for the financially challenged Keele, and outmoded. It also didn't help that whilst she was prepared to give her presence and some time to the university, she was less inclined to part with her money. Her parting gift to the University was a black and white photograph of herself. She clearly lacked value added! The Duke of Westminster, a more 'local' figure, and someone who was more clued-in to what was really expected of him, was commissioned to replace her in the late 1980s. His largesse enabled the Westminster Theatre to be refurbished - a far more tangible gift.

As change became forced upon universities, attitudes to what had been regarded as 'tradition' also softened. University terms have now been semesterised, whilst top-up fees and parental contributions to student maintenance heralds a new development which could pave the way for a private higher education system. The academic year is now more concentrated into two semesters and higher education in UK seems poised to adopt the American system whereby the summer semester is given over to lucrative 'summer and crammer school' activities. As a residential campus, Keele appears to be well placed to become privatised. Profit-sharing schemes for academic staff have already been mooted by several universities. Rationalisation is the new 'buzz' word. Although this was mooted in the early 1980s and attempts were made to rationalise and reorganise departments, it didn't quite catch on then. However, 'spin doctors' have emerged to work on changing attitudes, and rationalisation is now being carried out in many institutions as a 'matter of course', although not without some acrimony. Disciplines are being replaced by 'studies' and some students could be forgiven for being confused about which subject they are coming to study at university. The old disciplines of history, geography, geology etc are fast disappearing to give way to trendy, thematic approaches. It will probably catch on.

In a letter to the 'Times Higher Education Supplement' (5 June 1998) the Director of Academic Affairs at Keele announced the demise of the Foundation Year at Keele - almost 50 years after its inception. As an obituary, he wrote: 'We all regret the passing of the Foundation Year, but we have to take a realistic view of the current climate in which we all work in higher education and respond to the changing student demand'. It is doubtful that any opposition to this move will be made. Student energies have now been suitably diverted into staying alive whilst at university and getting a job afterwards to pay off student loans and overdrafts. It would appear that students are now more likely to protest over rent rises on campus than course content or structure.

The approach of a new century, sees Keele University in reflective, if not reflexive, mood in the aftermath of its 'boom' period - 1985-1995. As with most 'booms' they have to be paid for and the University, like many others, is now coming to grips with its debt problems. When the philosophically inclined gather to ask 'Whither Higher Education', these days they might be hard-pressed to come up with any useful answers. Whilst the Dearing Report emphasised the need for quality within the university system, in reality quantity was being substituted and tended to be all that mattered - provided it could be fostered on a shoe-string. In some ways this is where Keele came in - on a shoe-string. And as the practical amongst us know, shoe-strings can be utilised in many ways.